Elizabeth Fries Ellet

Domestic History of the American Revolution

Elizabeth Fries Ellet

Domestic History of the American Revolution

ISBN/EAN: 9783743399921

Manufactured in Europe, USA, Canada, Australia, Japa

Cover: Foto ©ninafisch / pixelio.de

Manufactured and distributed by brebook publishing software (www.brebook.com)

Elizabeth Fries Ellet

Domestic History of the American Revolution

DOMESTIC HISTORY

OF THE

AMERICAN REVOLUTION.

BY

MRS. ELLET.

ILLUSTRATED.

PHILADELPHIA:
J. B. LIPPINCOTT & CO.
1876.

Entered according to Act of Congress, in the year 1850, by
BAKER AND SCRIBNER,
In the Clerk's Office of the District Court of the United States for the Southern District of New York.

Copyright, 1876, by J. B. LIPPINCOTT & CO.

PREFACE

THE design and plan of the present work are entirely new. Its object is to exhibit the spirit and character of the Revolutionary period; to portray, as far as possible in so brief a record, the social and domestic condition of the times, and the state of feeling among the people, with something of the services and experience of a class not usually noticed among those whose names live in historical remembrance. With this view, a short and comprehensive narrative of the successive events of the war is interspersed with domestic details and anecdotes illustrative of the state of the country at various intervals.

My researches during some years past in collecting authentic materials for "The Women of the American Revolution," have brought to light many interesting incidents connected with the war, so strikingly characteristic of the times, that they should not be suffered to pass into oblivion. These are sparingly used, because more of them would have swelled the volume to an unsuitable size; and all that possessed merely a personal interest have been excluded. It has also been found necessary to omit the minor details of military movements, which form the bulk of almost every history of the war. This omission, I think, will prove an advantage. The most attentive reader of history seldom retains in his memory more than the prominent incidents, losing sight of minute and complicated particulars as soon as he rises from his studies; it may be questioned, therefore, whether it be not useless to perplex the learner with a multitude of details comparatively unimportant. I cannot help believing, too, that a really better idea of the Revolution may be obtained from anecdotes that exhibit the spirit which was abroad among all classes, and which prompted to action, than from the most accurate transcript of the manœuvres by which different battles were lost and won, and the most precise statement of the number engaged, or of killed and wounded on either side. Accordingly I have given in general merely the date and locality of the principal battles, with the names of the leaders who were most conspicuous.

Wherever account is given of individual experience, it is for the purpose of showing what *many* did or suffered. An inadequate conception of the character of that heroic age of the Republic is afforded by general tradition, and it is only by collating such authentic records of individual action and endurance as have been preserved, that a correct idea may be formed The great Duke of Marlborough once said he had learned English history from the dramas of Shakspeare; and we all know the effect of a historical romance in impressing events on the memory; how much greater should be the advantage derived from domestic pictures drawn from *actual life* over those which are at best but admirable imitations!

To guard against misapprehension, it is proper to say, that in this attempt to present in a new and interesting light the history of our struggle for national existence, there is nothing of fanciful embellishment. I hold in just aversion the romancing trash under which, at the present day, the simple and picturesque—because simple—realities of our American story seem in danger of being buried. Not only has no aid of fiction been employed, but no traditional matter has been introduced, unless sustained by indisputable authority.

It will be observed that I have entered rather closely into the story of the war in the upper districts of South Carolina. One reason for this is—that no history has ever yet done justice to that section of country, or to the actors who there bore their part in the struggle; another—that its partisan warfare was eminently domestic. Not only were neighbors divided and arrayed against each other, but the demon of civil discord invaded dwellings, and scowled beside the sacred hearthstone; in many cases it was literally true that a man's foes were those of his own household. This state of things gave rise to an unusual variety of picturesque and romantic incidents, from a large store of which but few are selected,— those which merely display the patriotism, fortitude, or prowess of individuals, not being suited to my purpose.

In recording incidents of the war at the South, I have not relied on unsupported tradition. The military movements in that region are detailed in some manuscript records prepared by prominent actors in the scenes described. For a sight of these valuable documents I am indebted to Daniel G. Stinson, Esq., of Chester District, South Carolina, whose aid I have had occasion to acknowledge in another work.

I have not thought it best, by enumerating authorities, to embarrass the volume with notes; but it is not proper to pass without acknowledgement the assistance derived from Mr. Willson's and Mr. Henry's general compendiums, among others, and my obligations to Henry Onderdonk, Jr., Esq., for the notices of the British prisons and prison ships at New York, with the account of the Illicit Trade on Long Island Sound, and the Whaleboat Warfare; as well as for other matters of interest gleaned from his work. Collins' History of Kentucky, with other books on the subject, has been consulted in the brief sketch of early settlements at the West.

E. F. E.

CONTENTS.

CHAPTER I.
The British Colonies in North America.................................. 13

CHAPTER II.
Difficulties with Great Britain....................................... 23

CHAPTER III.
Commencement of the War... 29

CHAPTER IV.
State of Society—Female Influence—Evacuation of Boston—Attempt at the South—Battle of Moore's Creek............................. 39

CHAPTER V.
Declaration of Independence—Female Spy—Battle of Long Island........ 49

CHAPTER VI.
Occupation of New York—State of the Country—Retreat through New Jersey—American Successes.. 59

CHAPTER VII.

Sentiment of Europe—Winter Quarters—New Attempt on Philadelphia—Occupation—March of Burgoyne—Murder of Jane McCrea............ 72

CHAPTER VIII.

The Battles of Saratoga—the Prisoners at Cambridge.................. 85

CHAPTER IX.

Female Agency—Valley Forge—State of Philadelphia................. 96

CHAPTER X.

British Prisons in New York..................................106

CHAPTER XI.

British Prison Ships—The Illicit Trade on Long Island Sound—Whaleboat Warfare 116

CHAPTER XII.

The French Alliance—The Mischianza—Battle of Monmouth—Condition of the Country.. 129

CHAPTER XIII.

Indian Depredations—The Massacres at Wyoming and Cherry Valley..... 140

CHAPTER XIV.

Attack on the South—Subjugation of Georgia—Scenes in South Carolina—Siege of Savannah—Close of the Campaign of 1779................ 151

CHAPTER XV.

Campaign of 1780—Surrender of Charleston—Conquest of South Carolina First Outbreak of Renewed Resistance.......................... 166

CHAPTER XVI.

A Scotch-Irish Settlement—Result of Martin's Preaching—Battle at Mobley's Meeting-House... 175

CHAPTER XVII.

Incursions of Huck—Battle at Williamson's—" Bloody Bill Cunningham."...184

CHAPTER XVIII.

Battles of Rocky Mount and Hanging Rock—Surprise at Fishing Creek... 195

CHAPTER XIX.

Surprise of Steel—Condition of the Country........................ 205

CHAPTER XX.

The Warning at Green Spring—Battle of King's Mountain—Blackstocks—State of Charleston and the Country............................. 218

CHAPTER XXI.

State of the Country in other Districts............................ 229

CHAPTER XXII.

Incursion into New Jersey—Indian Ravages in the Valley of the Mohawk..239

CHAPTER XXIII.

Treason of Arnold—Contributions in Philadelphia—Revolt of Pennsylvania Troops—Greene at the South—Battle of the Cowpens................ 249

CHAPTER XXIV.

Retreat of Greene—Return—Battles of Guilford and Hobkirk's Hill—Fort Motte... 263

CHAPTER XXV.

Attack on Ninety-Six—Battle of Eutaw—March of Cornwallis into Virginia—Siege of Yorktown—Burning of New London—Surrender of Cornwallis..278

CHAPTER XXVI.

Early Settlements at the West—Kentucky—Tennessee...................291

CHAPTER XXVII.

Conclusion... 303

DOMESTIC HISTORY OF THE REVOLUTION.

CHAPTER I.

THE BRITISH COLONIES IN NORTH AMERICA.

It is well known that Christopher Columbus discovered the New World in 1492. The first navigators who reached the American continent were John Cabot and his son Sebastian, who sailed from England and arrived at the coast of Labrador in June, 1497. The French employed discoverers and took possession of lands chiefly in the northern part of the country, while the Spaniards claimed Florida, and finally established the first permanent European settlement on our shores.

The several attempts made to plant colonies within the limits of the United States, in the sixteenth century, proved unsuccessful, and no permanent settlement was made before 1607. Sir Walter Raleigh, having received from Queen Elizabeth a transfer of the patent granted to Sir Humphrey Gilbert, in 1584 visited a portion of the coast. The report brought by the navigators to the queen was so flattering that she gave the new country the name of Virginia, in honor of a virgin sovereign. The whole region between the thirty-fourth and forty-fifth degrees of north latitude was thus called. In the reign of James I. it was granted by royal charter to two companies formed to settle it; the southern part, named South Virginia, to a company of merchants called the London Company; and the northern, or North Virginia, to a corporation called the Plymouth Company.

In 1607 the colonization of VIRGINIA was commenced under the auspices of the London Company. The first settlement was made at Jamestown. Captain John Smith was the leader in this enterprise, and had many adventures. Being taken captive by the Indians, he was condemned to death by Powhatan, the chief of the savage confederacy, but saved by Pocahontas, the chief's young daughter. Smith learned much from the Indians, gained their confidence and good will, and supported his companions by his energy and activity. His genius and wise management established the colony. After his return from Virginia, he explored the north-eastern coast of the United States, and Prince Charles, at his suggestion, gave that country the name of New England.

The Dutch began to settle NEW YORK in 1613. They established themselves on the island of Manhattan, now New York. A naval force from Jamestown, under Capt. Argall, in the same year compelled the Dutch to submit to the authority of the British monarch. In 1664 the English finally conquered and took possession of the colony.

Two unsuccessful attempts were made in the beginning of the century, to form settlements in New England, by the Plymouth Company and Capt. Smith; but the first permanent one—the colony of PLYMOUTH—was formed by the Pilgrims in 1620. These were Puritans, dissenters from the Church of England. Being by law required, under the heaviest penalties, to attend the established worship, they quitted their country, and sought in Holland "freedom to worship God" according to their own consciences. The distresses suffered there determined them to remove to the wilds of America. They procured a patent from England, sailed from Plymouth in a small vessel called the May Flower, and landed on Plymouth rock, Dec. 21st, 1620. They suffered much from hardship and sickness, yet trusted in the protection of the God for whose sake they had left home and friends, and who was to make of them a great people.

The settlement of NEW HAMPSHIRE was begun in 1623, at the mouth of the Piscataqua River, and afterwards at Dover, Portsmouth and Exeter. In 1628 the colony of MASSACHUSETTS BAY was established under a grant of lands from the Plymouth Company. Salem was first settled, and afterwards Charlestown, Boston, and other towns in the vicinity. This colony in 1641 received under its government the settlements in New Hampshire; but in 1679 New Hampshire was made a separate province by royal ordinance. In 1692 the Plymouth and Massachusetts colonies were incorporated into one. Maine, settled in 1629, was united to Massachusetts in 1652.

NEW JERSEY was settled by the Danes about 1624. Some Dutch families soon afterwards planted themselves near New York. The country was conquered in 1655 by Peter Stuyvesant, the Dutch governor of New York, and finally came into the possession of the English on their conquest of New York in 1664.

The king of Sweden, Gustavus Adolphus, sent over a colony of his subjects, who settled in DELAWARE in 1627. The Dutch settlers on the other side of the Delaware river disputed the possession of the country with the Swedes. They obtained it in 1655, and in 1664 yielded it to the English. MARYLAND was settled by English Roman Catholics, in 1634. Lord Baltimore, who had explored the country, obtained the territory by royal patent, and it was called Maryland in honor of Queen Henrietta Maria.

Both CONNECTICUT and RHODE ISLAND were first settled by companies from Massachusetts; the settlement of the former province being commenced at Hartford, 1635, and that of the latter at Providence in the following year. Providence was established by Roger Williams, a Baptist, who had been persecuted in Massachusetts on account of his religion. The followers of Mrs. Anne Hutchinson, whose religious opinions were condemned by the Puritans, also sought homes in Rhode Island.

NORTH CAROLINA was occupied by settlers from Virginia about the middle of the century; SOUTH CAROLINA some years later. In 1680 Charleston was founded, and about ten years afterwards came the French Protestants, or Huguenots, driven from their country by religious persecution, after the revocation of the edict of Nantes. They made their home chiefly in South Carolina.

PENNSYLVANIA was settled in 1682, under a grant made by Charles II. to William Penn, the great Quaker, after whom the province was named. He drew the plan of Philadelphia and gave it its name, which signifies " brotherly love." Thus all the colonies composing the original thirteen States, except Georgia, were established before the close of the seventeenth century.

GEORGIA became a colony in 1733. It was settled under a patent granted to twenty-one trustees, for the purpose of giving land gratuitously to the poor of Great Britain. A number of benevolent persons in England sent over the new colonists, and provided them with necessaries to begin the settlement. The province was named Georgia in honor of the British monarch.

The limits of this volume will not permit us to enter into the history of the separate colonies. Each had its peculiar and separate government, subject to the jurisdiction of Great Britain. In 1643 the four colonies of Plymouth, Massachusetts, Connecticut, and New Haven, formed a union by articles of confederation, and adopted the style of " The United Colonies of New England." The object of this union was to protect themselves against the Indians and against the encroachments of the Dutch of " New Netherlands," as New York was then called. New England suffered much in 1675, in a war with the Indian tribes called " King Philip's war," after the great Indian Sachem.

The rebellion of Bacon in Virginia, which broke out about the same time, was caused by oppressive restrictions on commerce, and heavy taxes imposed by the governor. The New England colonies were severely oppressed in the reign of James II., under the tyrannical administration of the governor appointed by him, Sir Edmund Andros. The troubles and discontents in New York arose from the same causes. Jacob Leisler was at the head of the disaffected. All these commotions tended to develope the spirit which in time aspired to national independence.

The English Revolution, which in 1689 placed William and Mary on the throne, delivered the colonies from the oppressions they had suffered. Massachusetts received a new charter in 1692. In this year occurred the trials for witchcraft, in which so many unfortunate persons were accused, imprisoned and executed. These scenes were enacted chiefly in Salem and the neighboring towns.

The colonies were involved in the war between France and England, commonly called King William's War—which lasted from 1690 to the peace of Ryswick, 1697. It was followed in 1702 by "Queen Anne's War," which was ended by the treaty of Utrecht, 1713. By this France ceded Newfoundland and Nova Scotia to England. In 1744 war was again declared by England against France, and the colonies were plunged into hostilities with the French and their savage allies. This war was most disastrous to the colonies, involving them in losses and debt. It was closed in 1748 by the peace of Aix-la-Chapelle. The conflicting claims, however, of France and Great Britain to the possession of territories in America in a short time rendered another war inevitable This brings us to what is called "The French and Indian War."

The French had possession of Canada and Louisiana, and were engaged in connecting these territories by a chain of military

CHAPTER I.

posts along the Lakes and Ohio River, to prevent the encroachments of the English. The Ohio company in 1750 obtained from the English government a grant of a large tract of land on the Ohio, where they designed to open a trade with the Indians. The French governor in Canada, who claimed the whole country between the Ohio and the Alleghanies, interfered with their proceedings. Gov. Dinwiddie, of Virginia, after complaints of acts of violence to the traders, in 1753 determined to send a remonstrance to the French commandant stationed near the Ohio, and require him to withdraw his troops from the territory, which he regarded as belonging to the charter limits of Virginia. The bearer of this despatch was GEORGE WASHINGTON, who, then a youth, thus entered first on his career of public service.

The French commandant refused to comply with the demand; the British government determined to resist the French claim by force, and in 1754 Washington conducted a hostile expedition into the disputed territory. He was obliged by the French to capitulate, and returned with his troops to Virginia. The British government now recommended the colonies to unite for their common defence. At this period their general history may be said to commence. Before this time they had been distinct and separate; bound to each other only by a common origin and language.

A convention of delegates from the northern colonies met at Albany in 1754, a. ¹ a plan of union, drawn up by Benjamin Franklin, was adopted. It was rejected, however, both in England and America; the British conceiving that it gave too much power to the people, and the colonists, too much to the crown. Hostilities went on, and the English forces gained possession of Nova Scotia. An expedition under Gen. Braddock against Fort Du Quesne was less fortunate. His troops were surprised on the banks of the Monongahela, and defeated by an inferior force of French and Indians. Braddock fell, mortally wounded, and Col. Washington, who, though shot at repeatedly by the Indians, had been wonderfully preserved in the battle, conducted the retreat, and saved the army from destruction.

A victory over the French on the borders of Lake George, in which their commander, Baron Dieskau, fell, followed in a few weeks, and revived the spirits of the Americans. In 1756 war was formally declared between Great Britain and France, and what is called "the seven years' war" began in Europe. This year's campaign in America was extremely disastrous to the colonists, and they accomplished little. The French, on the other hand, took Fort Oswego, and thus gained command of Lakes Ontario and Erie. In 1757 Montcalm, the French commander, besieged and took Fort William Henry, on the southern shore of Lake George. This fort was defended by Col. Munroe. The British troops, after the capitulation, were treacherously massacred by the Indians in Montcalm's army.

The campaign of 1758 was more successful. The great statesman, William Pitt, afterwards Earl of Chatham, became prime minister, and took the guidance of public affairs. The colonies answered his call by new supplies of men, and the tide of success turned in favor of Britain. Fort Du Quesne was occupied by the English and named Pittsburgh; Fort Frontenac at the outlet of Lake Ontario was captured, and in the following year the other French strongholds in Canada, with Ticonderoga, Crown Point, and Niagara, fell into the hands of the British. The celebrated Gen. Wolfe led the British and colonial troops against Quebec, defeated the French under Montcalm on the Plains of Abraham, and died on the field in the moment of victory. In less than a year from the fall of Quebec, the French were dispossessed not only of the disputed territories, but of their ancient province of Canada.

By the treaty of peace signed at Paris in 1763, France ceded to Great Britain her northern possessions, and Spain gave Florida in exchange for Havana. England was now almost sole mistress of the northern continent, and had three millions of loyal subjects in the colonies. These colonies had increased in wealth as well as population, had made rapid progress in commerce, and poured agricultural riches into the lap of the mother country. They loved and revered England, but her avarice and desire of power led her to oppress her dutiful children. For more than a century restrictions had been imposed on colonial trade and manufactures discouraged, to compel the Americans to buy and sell exclusively in the British markets.

These enactments of Parliament were regarded as oppressive and unjust, and produced much dissatisfaction. Respectful remonstrance, however, passed unnoticed, and the right of the home government to legislate for and tax the colonies was maintained by the universal sentiment in Britain. Thus grew and ripened the discontent which, with progressive encroachments, led the way to a final rupture. On the other hand, the necessity of uniting for their common defence, and concerted action against the enemy, had created a national spirit, and strengthened the ties of friendship between the colonies.

DESTRUCTION OF THE TEA AT BOSTON.

CHAPTER II.

DIFFICULTIES WITH GREAT BRITAIN.

THE Edinburgh Review says of the Declaration of American Independence, that it is the most important event in the history of mankind Certainly the great Act by which thirteen colonies shook off the British yoke, and sprang into being as independent States, had remarkable consequences on both sides of the Atlantic. The war was one of principle—of principle involving the welfare of all nations; for it decided whether or not men were to be ruled without their own consent; whether or not one privileged class was to trample at will on the rights of another. It declared the common rights of mankind. It proved a warning to oppressors, and an encouragement to the oppressed, throughout the world. We are now to trace, as briefly as possible, the causes which led to this Revolution.

In 1764 it was proposed in England to replenish the exhausted treasury by taxing the colonies. George Grenville gave notice that at the ensuing session he should propose a duty on stamps. Great dissatisfaction prevailed in America at these proceedings. The people urged that as the colonies were not represented in parliament, they should not be taxed Remonstrances were addressed to government, and agents were sent to prevent the passage of the Stamp Act. It passed in March, 1765. By this act, no instruments of writing—deeds, bonds, notes, etc., could be legal unless drawn on stamped paper, for which a duty was to be paid to the crown.

The night after the passage of this bill, Dr. Franklin wrote to Charles Thomson, " The sun of liberty is set ; you must light up the candles of industry and economy." The next day, Dr. Fothergill, on a visit to Miss Graeme, a young American lady in London, said—" Betsy, yesterday you were made a slave of." She imagined he was jesting on the subject of matrimony, and answered—" No, sir, I am slave to no man ; my heart is my own !" The physician replied, "*Heart* has nothing to do with it ! you and all your country-people were yesterday enslaved, for the bill passed the House for the American Stamp Act."

The passage of the Stamp Act was the entering wedge to the dismemberment of the British empire. The news was received in America with a perfect storm of opposition. Patrick Henry, the first to hurl the gauntlet, introduced resolutions against it into the Virginia Assembly ; Massachusetts was moved by a kindred spirit, and a congress of deputies from several of the colonies, forming the first Colonial Congress, was convened in October. The popular feeling became inflamed to the utmost, and all classes were excited. The daughter of Dr. Franklin wrote to her father—" The subject now is Stamp Act, and nothing else is talked of. The Dutch talk of the 'Stamp tack'—the negroes of the 'tamp'—in short everybody has something to say."

The first of November, the day on which the Act was to go into operation, was kept as a day of mourning. The shops were shut, the flags of the vessels were at half mast, and the bells were tolled as if for a funeral. At Portsmouth a coffin inscribed with the name of " Liberty" was buried with a funeral procession. In New York the Act was printed and paraded through the streets, with a death's head and cross-bones substituted for the royal arms, and the title " England's Folly and America's Ruin." Popular detestation of the measure was further manifested by destroying and sending back large quantities of the stamped paper. The merchants of New York, Boston, and Philadelphia entered into engagements not to import goods from Great Britain till the Act should be repealed, and individuals gave up foreign luxuries to support these measures for suspending trade.

In March, 1766, the Stamp Act was repealed, and a temporary calm succeeded the storm. But the flame of discord was soon fanned anew by other encroachments. It seemed, indeed, at this dreary period of British history, that the monarch and his ministry were laboring hard to tear from its socket and cast away forever, the brightest jewel of the imperial crown. At this interval, even Chatham's voice was powerless to arouse the nation, and induce Parliament to pause. By the revival of the scheme of taxation, the varied vexations of obnoxious duties, and the display of military force to compel submission, did penny-wise politicians, in the happy phrase of the day, "tease America into resistance," and hasten the great catastrophe.

There were not wanting some, even in England, who sought by moderate and constitutional means to stay the hand of misgovernment and oppression. Yet onward, step by step, the monarch and his ministers—he, if possible, more infatuated than they, advanced in the career of tyrannical folly. Remonstrance was vain; they could not be persuaded that it would ever become resistance. In 1769 and 1770, after five years of folly, the crisis was almost reached. The duties on *tea* being still imposed, while others were removed, the ports of New York and Philadelphia were closed against the tea ships, and that landed in Charleston was not permitted to be sold, but was stored in damp cellars, and spoiled. Associations in every part of the country were formed against the use of tea, and the women showed themselves ready to give up this much loved luxury, when it could only be procured at the sacrifice of their country's honor and liberties. The Boston Gazette, the leading "rebel newspaper," mentions an agreement signed by the Boston women in February, 1770, not to drink any tea till the revenue acts were repealed. Similar movements were made in New York and Virginia, and few ventured to sell the prohibited article. Mrs. Adams, in a letter to Mrs. Warren, calls the tea "that baneful weed," and hopes opposition will be made to its landing in Boston.

In December, 1773, a party of several men, in the costume of Mohawk Indians, went after dark, followed by a multitude of people, to the wharf where the tea ships were lying, boarded the vessels, broke open the chests of tea, and threw their contents into the sea. Three hundred and forty-two chests of tea were thrown overboard in three hours. After this exploit they marched back quietly. These proceedings excited the anger of the British government, and in March, 1774, a bill was passed prohibiting all commercial intercourse with Boston, and forbidding the landing and shipping of goods at that port. This was called the "Boston Port Bill," and was followed by other violent measures. Well might one of the women of that day write—"Oh, America! you have reason to tremble and arouse, if we on this side the Atlantic are not able to say to this royal vengeance—'hitherto shalt thou come and no further; here shall thy proud waves be stayed!'"

All the colonies sympathized in the common cause. The tyranny of Gov. Tryon of North Carolina had inflamed the love of liberty in that province. The association of Regulators had spread over the western counties of the Carolinas, and kept alive a spirit of resistance to governmental oppression. In the spring of 1771 Gov. Tryon proceeded against them with an armed force, a battle ensued, and the cruelties practised by Tryon towards the vanquished, for the purpose of awing the people, planted more deeply the seeds of discontent.

The general Congress met at Philadelphia, 1774, in the full determination to effect, if possible, a reconciliation with the mother country. It was not their wish to rush madly into an unnatural contest. They declared their rights and grievances, and appealed to the King and people of Great Britain for re dress. These peaceful measures, however, were ineffectual, and the approach of the storm was perceived by the sagacious on both sides of the Atlantic. Ships of the line and troops were ordered by the British government to America to reduce the rebels to obedience, and hostile preparations were made in Massachusetts and other colonies to meet determined oppression by resistance The people practised military tactics; the fife and drum were heard on every side, old and young being engaged in martial exercises, and stores of arms and ammunition were collected. The crisis had arrived, and there was a general waiting for the signal of open war.

One manifestation of the general feeling in Boston, the winter after the arrival of the British troops, was remarkable. Some of the crown officers who thought the public gloom disloyal, got up a series of dancing assemblies, in hopes, by engaging the higher classes in festivity, to contradict the assertions of prevailing distress, and undermine the stern reserve maintained towards the army. But out of their own limited circle they could not induce any ladies to attend. Elegant manners, gay uniforms, animating music—all were resisted by the women, who refused to join in gaieties while their country was in mourning.

BATTLE OF LEXINGTON.

Page 29.

CHAPTER III

COMMENCEMENT OF THE WAR.

AT length the storm burst forth. On the night of April 18th, 1775, Gen. Gage, the royal governor of Massachusetts and commander of the British forces in Boston, sent a detachment of eight hundred soldiers to destroy some military stores at Concord. His design became known to patriots in the city, and early on the following morning the firing and ringing of bells spread the alarm that the royal troops were in motion. A number of provincial militia were found assembled at Lexington, on the road to Concord, when the British appeared on the morning of the 19th. Major Pitcairn rode up and ordered them to throw down their arms and disperse. Not being obeyed, he ordered his men to fire upon them. Eight of the militia were killed, and the detachment proceeded to Concord and destroyed the stores. But the spirit of the people was roused, and on the return of the British troops to Boston they were continually fired at along the way from behind bushes, fences, and buildings, suffering severe loss. The American loss was much less.

The affair is thus described, in a letter written at the time, by a lady of Cambridge:

"Nor will old time ever erase the horrors of that midnight cry, preceding the bloody massacre at Lexington, when we were roused from the benign slumbers of the season, by beat of drum and ringing of bells, with the dire alarm that a thousand of the troops of George the Third had gone forth to murder the peaceful inhabitants of the surrounding villages. A few hours, with the dawning day, convinced us the bloody purpose was executing; the platoon firing assuring us the rising sun must witness the bloody carnage. Not knowing what the event would be at Cambridge, at the return of these bloody ruffians, and seeing another brigade dispatched to the assistance of the former, looking with the ferocity of barbarians, it seemed necessary to retire to some place of safety, till the calamity was passed. After dinner we set out, not knowing whither we went. We were directed to a place called Fresh Pond, about a mile from the town; but what a distressed house did we find it, filled with women whose husbands had gone forth to meet the assailants, seventy or eighty of these (with numberless infant children,) weeping and agonizing for the fate of their husbands! In addition to this scene of distress, we were for some time in sight of the battle; the glittering instruments of death proclaiming by an incessant [fire] that much blood must be shed; that many widowed and orphaned ones [must] be left as monuments of British barbarity. Another uncomfortable night we passed; some nodding in their chairs, some resting their weary limbs on the floor. The welcome harbingers of day gave notice of its dawning light. [It] brings no news It is unsafe to return to Cambridge, as the enemy were advancing up the river, and fixing on the town to stay in.

"Thus with precipitancy we were driven to the town of Anderson, following some of our acquaintance—five of us to be conveyed with one poor tired horse and chaise; thus we began our pilgrimage, alternately walking and riding, the roads filled with frighted women and children; some in carts with their tattered furniture, others on foot fleeing into the woods. But what added greatly to the horrors of the scene, was our passing through the bloody field at Monotong, which was strewed with the mangled bodies. We met one affectionate father with a cart, looking for his murdered son, and picking up his neighbors who had fallen in battle, in order for their burial."

Intelligence of this event spread rapidly through Massachusetts and the adjoining provinces, and everywhere the militia of the country took up arms, and hastened to the scene of action. Col. Prescott, the grandfather of the American historian, heard the news at Pepperell about nine o'clock the same morning, and immediately gave orders to his companies in Pepperell and Hollis, to march to Groton, proceeding thence to Concord and Cambridge. Rumors were flying abroad that the regulars were approaching, and frightful stories of slaughter flew rapidly from place to place, and from house to house. It is said that a number of women, clothed in the apparel of their absent husbands, and armed with muskets, pitchforks, and such other weapons as they could find, collected at the bridge over the Nashau, between Pepperell and Groton, to arrest any "foe to freedom" who might pass.

A Capt. Whiting, bearing despatches from Canada to the British in Boston, was arrested by them, unhorsed and searched, and sent prisoner to Oliver Prescott of Groton.

Matthew Buell, a farmer of Connecticut, was plowing in the field when news came that blood had been shed; he instantly unyoked his cattle, and leaving his plow standing in the furrow, repaired to the house to take leave of his wife and family. Putnam, who was also at work in the field, did the same, starting for Cambridge without waiting to change his apparel. Stark was sawing pine logs without his coat; he shut down the gate of his mill, and commenced the journey to Boston in his shirt sleeves. The same spirit prevailed far and near. In New York, the mechanics of the city had a procession, and having deposited their tools in a large coffin made for the purpose, marched to the solemn music of a funeral dirge, and buried the coffin in Potter's Field, returning to present themselves, each with musket in hand, in readiness for military service.

The volunteers waited not to be supplied with arms, but seizing on whatever rude weapons were at hand, hastened away to fight for home and liberty. The women, lacking not their share of patriotic zeal, were active in preparations to encourage, assist, and sustain them. One, the wife of Capt. Draper, living on a farm at Dedham, Massachusetts, exhorted her husband to lose no time in hastening to the scene of action, and with her own hands bound knapsack and blanket on the shoulders of her only son, a stripling of sixteen, bidding him depart and do his duty. To the entreaties of her daughter that her young brother might remain at home to be their protector, she answered that every arm able to aid the cause belonged to the country. "He is wanted, and must go You and I, Kate, have also service to do. Food must be prepared for the hungry; for before to-morrow night, hundreds, I hope thousands, will be on their way to join the continental forces. Some who have travelled far will need refreshment, and you and I, with Molly, must feed as many as we can."

This undertaking, though of no small labor, was presently commenced. Capt. Draper was a thriving farmer; his granaries were well filled, and his wife's dairy was her special care and pride. Assisted by her daughter and the domestic, she spent the whole day and night, and the succeeding day in baking brown bread. The ovens of that day were not the small ones now in use, but suited for such an occasion, each holding bread sufficient to supply a neighborhood. By good fortune two of these monster ovens appertained to the establishment; these were soon in full blast, and the kneading trough was plied by busy hands. At that time of hurry and confusion none could stop long enough to dine. The people were under the influence of strong excitement, and all were in such haste to join the army, that they stayed only to relieve the cravings of hunger, though from want of food, and fatigue, many were almost exhausted. With the help of a disabled veteran of the French war, who had for years resided in her family, Mrs. Draper had soon her stores in readiness. A long form was erected by the road-side; large pans of bread and cheese were placed upon it, and replenished as often as was necessary; while old John brought cider in pails from the cellar, which, poured into tubs, was served out by two lads who volunteered their services. Thus were the weary patriots refreshed on their way. Mrs. Draper presided at the entertainment, and when her own stock of provisions began to fail, applied to her neighbors for aid. By their contributions her hospitable board was supplied, till in a few days the necessity for extraordinary exertion had in a measure passed. When each soldier carried his rations, the calls on private benevolence were less imperative.

Another anecdote will show the spirit that was abroad. On the morning after the battle of Lexington, a company of nearly a hundred halted before the house of Col. Pond of West Dedham. They had marched all night, and were covered with dust, and faint from fatigue and want of food. Their haste was urgent, and the mistress of the house, whose hospitality they claimed, was unprepared for the entertainment of so large a party. Her husband was absent, and she had only one female assistant and a hired man. But the willing heart can do wonders. In a few minutes she had a large brass kettle, holding ten pails full, over the fire, filled with water and Indian meal for hasty pudding. In the barn-yard were ten cows ready to contribute their share to the morning meal. Near the farm-house was a store well supplied with brown earthen dishes, and pewter spoons tied in dozens for sale. The military guests volunteered their aid. Some milked the cows, others stirred the pudding; while the two domestics collected all the milk in the neighborhood. Thus, in the short space of an hour, by the energetic efforts of one kind-hearted woman, a hundred weary, hungry soldiers were

CHAPTER III. 35

provided with refreshment. They ate, and marched on to the place of their destination.

In a few days a large army was thus collected, and the British forces in Boston were closely environed.

Other portions of the country sympathized in the general movement. Associations were formed to support any measures that should be recommended by the Continental Congress to oppose the execution of the arbitrary acts of Parliament. Arms found in the possession of persons who had not signed the Association were impressed for the use of the Continental troops. In distant colonies the same feeling was exhibited. The Southern women formed themselves into associations renouncing the use of teas and imported luxuries, and engaging to card, spin, and weave their own clothing. In Mecklenburg and Rowan counties, North Carolina, young ladies of the most respectable families, pledged themselves not to receive the addresses of any suitors who would not obey the country's call for military service.

It was in Mecklenburg County that the idea of National Independence was first proclaimed to the world. A large concourse of people was assembled in the frontier settlement of Charlotte, on the 19th of May, 1775, agitated with the excitement which had plunged the whole land into commotion. On that day came the first intelligence of the commencement of hostilities at Lexington, and when the convention and the people were addressed, the universal cry was—" Let us be independent ! Let us declare our independence, and defend it with our lives and fortunes !" Dr. Brevard drew up resolutions, unanimously adopted on the following day by the convention and the approving multitude, by which the citizens of Mecklen burg declared themselves a free and independent people.

The Americans next took the important fortresses of Ticonderoga and Crown Point, which commanded the entrance into Canada. The British troops were reinforced by troops from England under Generals Howe, Clinton and Burgoyne, and Gen. Gage issued his proclamation, declaring those rebels who were in arms, and offering pardon to all who would return to their allegiance, except Samuel Adams and John Hancock. Congress again met in Philadelphia in May, and issued a large amount of bills of credit, to defray the expenses of the war. They again addressed the King and people of Britain, and published to the world the reasons of their appeal to arms. On the 15th of June they elected GEORGE WASHINGTON Commander-in-Chief of the army of the United Colonies. He accepted the appointment, and set out at once, accompanied by the best citizens of the liberal party, to enter on his duties at Cambridge.

The memorable battle of Bunker's Hill was fought on the 17th of June. Col. Prescott took the most conspicuous and efficient part in this action, the moral effect of which was favorable to the American cause, though the Continental troops, their ammunition failing, were obliged to retreat. Among the killed was Gen. Joseph Warren. While the battle was going on, a young lady in Boston, by whose house many of the wounded brought from the field of action were carried, mixed a refreshing beverage, and standing at her door with a female domestic, offered it to the sufferers. Some of the British, supposing her a loyalist, expressed their gra-

CHAPTER III.

titude for the relief by telling her how her countrymen had been beaten. One young officer said: "Never mind, my brave young lady, we have peppered them well!" thus wounding her feelings while she was showing compassion for his. While the British troops advanced to the attack, Gen. Gage had ordered the village of Charlestown to be burned. By the execution of this order multitudes were deprived of their homes, and that, too, after they had given shelter to the wounded British soldiers on their return from Concord.

While Boston was blockaded, several of the inhabitants were obliged to remain in the city. A besieging army without and an insolent soldiery within, while provisions and fuel were scarce—for a long time their sufferings were great. A letter says:—"The desk, the pews, and other incumbrances are taken down in the Old South church to make it convenient for the accommodation of Gen. Burgoyne's light horse; while the infamous Dr. Morrison reads prayers in the church in Brattle street to a set of banditti, who, after the rapines, robberies and devastations of the week, dare, some of them, to lift up their sacrilegious hands, and bow before the altar of mercy."

It should be noticed that there was still a large number of Americans who favored the royal cause, and joined the British against their countrymen. These were called tories, or loyalists, while those of the other party were known by the name of whigs, or patriots.

The summer of this year may be said to have ended the royal authority in the colonies. Congress planned an expedition against Canada, and Generals Montgomery and Schuyler commanded the troops sent. St. Johns and Montreal were successively taken. During the siege of the first, Col. Ethan Allen, a brave officer in the army, was captured and sent in chains to England. Gen. Arnold joined Montgomery, and their forces environed Quebec; but the siege, though prosecuted three weeks, was unsuccessful; and in the attempt made to storm the city on the 31st of December, Gen. Montgomery fell beneath its walls. The Americans, for want of forces, were compelled to retire, and by the ensuing June, 1776, had evacuated Canada.

CHAPTER IV.

STATE OF SOCIETY—FEMALE INFLUENCE—EVACUATION OF BOSTON—ATTEMPT AT THE SOUTH—BATTLE OF MOORE'S CREEK.

BEFORE the Revolution, the state of society was such as might have been expected under a monarchical government The story of the courtship and marriage of Gen. Knox gives some idea of the aristocratic distinctions then prevalent, and the embarrassments growing out of them. He moved in an humble sphere, his energies having been early called into action by the necessity of supporting his mother and young brother; but formed an engagement with the daughter of a gentleman high in office, and prominent among the aristocracy of the land—Thomas Flucker, Secretary of the Province of Massachusetts. It was a grief to this proud family when Miss Flucker was known not only to favor the addresses of young Knox, but to have espoused his republican opinions. Both arguments and entreaties were used to dissuade her from a course which they believed must be destructive to all her worldly prospects. But when the time arrived for her decision, she cast her all upon the die that was to decide the nation's fate, and pledged herself to the fortunes of a soldier's wife. Her father believed she had consigned herself to an unworthy destiny, and predicted that she would suffer in the troubles that were to come, while her sisters were enjoying the luxury and station she had unwisely renounced. How dimly did they discern the future! The proud loyalists who had borne honors conferred by the British government, were compelled to fly from their country, forfeiting the wealth they deemed secure—or inadequately compensated for the sacrifice after long delay—to die in voluntary exile. The poor and self-denying patriots, who gave up affluence and ease for their country's sake, were rewarded by her lasting gratitude.

It was the habit of Washington, at the close of each campaign, to despatch an aid-de-camp to escort Mrs. Washington to head-quarters, where she usually remained till the opening of the succeeding one in the spring. She was accustomed afterwards to say that it had been her fortune to hear the first cannon at the opening, and the last at the closing, of all the campaigns of the Revolutionary war. Her arrival in camp was a noted event; the plain chariot, with the neat postillions in their scarlet and white liveries, was always welcomed with great joy by the army, and brought a cheering influence, which relieved the general gloom in seasons of disaster and despondency.

An incident occurred as she passed through Philadelphia, Nov. 21st, 1775, on her way to Cambridge, which shows the depressed state of popular feeling on the breaking out of the war. A ball was in preparation, to be given on the twenty-fourth, and it was expected that both she and the wife of Col. Hancock would grace the entertainment with their presence.

But from some threats that were thrown out, it was feared that a commotion would be made, which might result in disturbance of the peace of the city. A large and respectable committee was held at the Philosophical Hall, called together for the purpose of considering the propriety of allowing the ball to be given that evening; and after mature consideration it was concluded that no such entertainment should take place, either then, or during the continuance of those melancholy times. A committee was appointed to inform the managers that they must proceed no further in the preparations; and also to wait upon 'Lady Washington,' and request her not to attend at the assembly to which she had been invited. The committee acted agreeably to directions; and reported that Lady Washington had received them with great politeness, thanked the committee for their kind care and regard in giving her timely notice, and assured them that their sentiments on this occasion were perfectly agreeable to her own.

The example of Mrs. Washington was followed by the wives of many of the general officers, who spent the winters with their husbands, passing the active season of the campaign at home. The wife of Gen. Greene, when the army went into winter quarters, always set out to join him, sharing cheerfully the narrow quarters and hard fare of a camp. The cheerful manners of the ladies enlivened dreary scenes, dissipating the gloom that might have weighed down many a bold heart. Mrs. Greene's home was at Coventry, a village of Rhode Island, where her husband had erected a forge, and built himself what then passed for a princely house on the banks of one of those small streams that form so beautiful a feature in Rhode Island scenery. When the army besieging Boston was inoculated for the small pox, she gave up her house for a hospital.

At this period, and throughout the war, the influence and exertions of women in all parts of the country contributed to promote a spirit of patriotism. They animated the courage, and confirmed the self-devotion of those who ventured all in the common cause. They frowned upon instances of coldness or backwardness, and in the period of deepest gloom, cheered and urged onward the desponding. They willingly shared inevitable dangers and privations, relinquished without regret prospects of advantage to themselves, and parted with those they loved better than life, not knowing when they were to meet again. It is almost impossible now to appreciate the vast influence of woman's patriotism upon the destinies of the infant republic. We have no means of showing the important part she bore in maintaining the struggle, and in laying the foundations on which so mighty and majestic a structure has arisen. We can only dwell upon individual instances of magnanimity, fortitude, self-sacrifice and heroism, bearing the impress of the feeling of Revolutionary days, indicative of the spirit which animated all, and to which, in its various and multiform exhibitions, we are not less indebted for national freedom, than to the swords of the patriots who poured out their blood.

A letter written by a lady of Philadelphia to a British officer in Boston, says: " My only brother I have sent to the camp with my prayers and blessings. I hope he will not disgrace me; I am confident he will behave with honor, and emulate the great examples he has before him; and had I twenty sons and brothers they should go. I have retrenched every superfluous expense in my table and family; tea I have not drunk since last Christmas, nor bought a new cap or gown since your defeat at Lexington; and what I never did before, have learned to knit, and am now making stockings of American wool for my servants; and this way do I throw in my mite to the public good. I have the pleasure to assure you that these are the sentiments of all my sister Americans. They have sacrificed assemblies, parties of pleasure, tea-drinking and finery, to that great spirit of patriotism that actuates all degrees of people throughout this extensive continent."

The patriotic sacrifices of the women were made with a deep enthusiasm. Some gave their own property, and went from house to house to solicit contributions for the army. Colors were embroidered by fair hands, and presented with the charge never to desert them, and arms and ammunition were provided with the same liberal zeal. The needy shared the fruit of their industry and economy, and their firmness and intrepidity supplied every persuasive that could animate to perseverance and secure fidelity. A lady in Ulster County, New York, studied medicine that she might be qualified, while the physicians were absent with the army, to attend to the poor families in the country around her.

When, after the battle of Bunker Hill, Gen. Washington called on the inhabitants of the country to send to head-quarters every ounce of pewter or lead at their disposal, few withheld their portion, and the weights of clocks and window-sashes, as well as cups and dishes, were melted down and sent as willing offerings. At this time the more precious metals had not found their way to the tables of New Englanders, and throughout the country services of pewter, scoured to the brightness of silver, covered the board, even in the mansions of the wealthy. Some who had moulds for casting bullets melted all their platters, pans and dishes into balls.

When the approach of winter this year brought fears that the resources of the country would hardly yield supplies for the pressing wants of the army, the women were active in benevolent efforts. The supply of domestic cloth, designed for families, was in a short time converted by the labor of the females into coats for the soldiers; sheets and blankets were fashioned into shirts; and even the flannel already made up was altered into men's habiliments. Such aid was rendered by many whose deeds of disinterested generosity were never known beyond their own immediate neighborhood!

In March, 1776, Washington executed a plan for driving the British from Boston. He built fortifications on Dorchester heights, which commanded the city and harbor. Gen. Howe's troops and shipping being exposed to the fire of the batteries, on the 17th the royal forces evacuated the town and sailed for Halifax. The Americans entered in triumph, with drums beating and colors flying, and were welcomed with joy by the citizens, who for ten months had endured the severest privations. All necessary articles of food had risen to enormous prices. Vegetables were not to be procured; and it was so difficult to obtain wood that the pews and benches were taken out of churches, and houses were pulled down for fuel.

The popularity of the whig cause meanwhile increased throughout the country. Volunteer troops had been raised, and money in large quantities had been sent from Philadelphia for the relief of the sufferers in New England. In Suffolk County, Long Island, at the first outbreak of rebellion the people assembled in almost every town, and voted resolutions of aid and sympathy for their brethren. When the militia was organized, such as were royalists, or from prudential considerations wished to remain neutral, refused to train, and secreted themselves. Many repaired to the recesses of swamps, and several expeditions were set on foot to drive them thence.

General Washington suspected that New York would be the next point of attack, and leaving Boston in a state of defence, moved with the main body of his army towards that city, arriving early in April. Sir Henry Clinton, with the British fleet, sailed south, his plan being to attack Charleston. Having been joined at Cape Fear River by Sir Peter Parker, with a large squadron from Europe, in June he advanced against Fort Moultrie on Sullivan's Island, which commanded the channel leading to Charleston. The British were repulsed in this attack, the enterprise was abandoned, and the fleet shortly after sailed for New York. On the third day after the battle, which took place on the 28th, the wife of Col. Barnard Elliott presented to the second regiment, commanded by Col. Moultrie, a pair of richly embroidered colors, wrought by herself. They were planted, three years afterwards, on the British lines at Savannah, by Sergeant Jasper, who in planting them received his death-wound.

Shortly before these events, North Carolina had been the theatre of tumult. The colonial governor, Martin, in February, 1776, collected the Highland emigrants, under Gen McDonald, with a large number of rough backwoodsmen. He expected to be joined by regular troops from England, under Lord Cornwallis, who were to land at Wilmington. The patriots of Newbern and Wilmington Districts, on their part, were not idle. Col. Richard Caswell called his neighbors hastily together; the county rose in mass, and scarce a man was left in the Neuse region. The united regiments of Colonels Lillington and Caswell encountered Gen. McDonald at Moore's Creek. On the 27th of February the battle—one of the bloodiest of the Revolution—was fought, and proved disastrous to the royal forces. The unhappy Gen. McDonald, who had been prevented by illness from commanding his troops in the engagement, was found, when it was over, sitting alone on a stump near his tent. As the victorious American officers advanced towards him, he waved in the air the parchment scroll of his commission, and surrendered it into their hands.

Flora McDonald, the celebrated Scottish heroine, who saved the life of "the Pretender," Prince Charles Edward, after the battle of Culloden, was living among the Highlanders at Cross Creek—now Fayetteville—at this time, and it is said went among the soldiers, animating their courage, when on the eve of their march. An American heroine certainly figured on the field at Moore's Creek; the wife of Lieut. Slocumb, whose home was more than sixty miles distant. After her husband, with the men of the neighborhood, had gone to the battle, she dreamed of seeing him lying dead on the ground, and was so much alarmed that she rose in the night, saddled her horse and rode at full gallop in the direction the troops had taken. At sunrise she came upon a group of women and children, standing and sitting by the roadside, anxious to obtain intelligence. Riding on through a thinly-settled, poor and swampy country, at about nine in the morning she came near enough to hear the firing. She dashed on in the direction of the noise, drew near the battle ground, and saw the wounded lying under a cluster of trees. There lay a body, indeed, wrapped in her husband's guard-cloak; but it was another person. Mrs. Slocumb dismounted, gave the wounded man water, washed his bloody face, and bound up his wound with leaves; she then dressed the wounds of the others, and was thus employed when Caswell and her husband came up.

They were, of course, much surprised to see her. She would not tell them of her dream, but thought her visit had been a fortunate one for those who needed nursing. She interceded for the prisoners, and Caswell told her none should be hurt but such as had been guilty of murder and house-burning. In the middle of the night she again mounted and started for home, declining the offer to send an escort with her; for she said—"I wanted to see my child, and I told them they could send no party who could keep up with me." This resolute woman thus rode alone, in the night, through a wild, unsettled country, a distance—going and returning—of a hundred and twenty-five miles, and that in less than forty hours, and without any interval of rest! Her husband was among the brave officers of the Revolution to whom history has done no justice. He bore a gallant part in the action at Moore's Creek; it was his company that forded the stream, and penetrating the swamp, made the furious charge on tne British left and rear which decided the fate of the day.

RETREAT FROM LONG ISLAND.

CHAPTER V.

DECLARATION OF INDEPENDENCE—FEMALE SPY—BATTLE OF LONG ISLAND.

The most formidable preparations were made by Great Britain to carry on the war. By a treaty with German princes, seventeen thousand German or Hessian troops were engaged, while additional English troops, with a large fleet, were ordered to America. The colonies seeing that their grievances were not likely to be redressed, now began to abandon the sentiment of loyalty, and desire nothing less than absolute independence. A committee was instructed by Congress to prepare a declaration in accordance with the object of a resolution offered on the 7th of June by Richard Henry Lee, of Virginia. Thomas Jefferson, John Adams, Benjamin Franklin, Roger Sherman, and Robert R. Livingston, formed the committee. The Declaration of Independence was drawn up by Jefferson, and on the 4th of July, 1776, was adopted by the delegates of all the thirteen colonies. They thus declared themselves free and independent, assuming the name of the UNITED STATES OF AMERICA.

The Declaration was received with every demonstration of public rejoicing. It was read in public from the platform of an observatory in the rear of the State House. On the same day a brilliant fête was given in honor of the nation's birth, on board the frigate Washington in the Delaware, the festivities terminating with a ball in the evening. The Declaration was read at the head of each brigade of the Continental army stationed at New York, and received with joyful huzzas. On the same day all the imprisoned debtors were released. In the evening the equestrian statue of George III., raised in the Bowling Green in 1770, was thrown down. It was determined that the lead of which it was composed should be run into bullets. On the 10th of July it was read in the Court House at White Plains by order of the convention, then in session. The King's coat of arms was brought from the hall where his courts were held, and burned amid the acclamations of the multitude.

Meanwhile General Sir William Howe, who had sailed from Halifax, arrived at Sandy Hook, June 25th, and soon after took possession of Staten Island. Joined by his brother, Admiral Lord Howe, and the repulsed forces of Clinton from the south, he was at the head of a large army of the best troops of Europe. His design was to seize New York, keep possession of the Hudson, open a communication with Canada, cut off the Eastern from the Middle States, and have the adjacent country wholly in his power. The American forces, on the other hand, were composed of undisciplined militia—and many were unprovided with arms. Lord Howe made an attempt at negotiation, and sent a letter, with that view, directed to " George Washington, Esq." Washington refused to receive a letter not addressed to him in his public capacity saying that as a private individual he could hold no intercourse with the enemies of his country. A further attempt at accommodation failing—the British generals resolved to lose no time in prosecuting the war.

We have a picture of female occupation in an American officer's family, in a journal of the daughter of Major Moncrieffe, of the British engineers. She was boarding at Elizabethtown, New Jersey, when the appearance of Gen. Howe at Staten Island compelled the inhabitants to seek refuge in the interior. Having been frightened afterwards by a party of riflemen, she appealed to Gen. Putnam. He answered by a kind invitation to his house, and sent one of his aids to conduct her to New York : " When I arrived in the Broadway," she says, " I was received with the greatest tenderness both by Mrs. Putnam and her daughters, and on the following day was introduced by them to General and Mrs. Washington, who likewise made it their study to show me every mark of regard ; but I seldom was allowed to be alone, although sometimes indeed I found an opportunity to escape to the gallery on the top of the house,* where my chief delight was to view with a telescope our fleet and army at Staten Island.

" My amusements were few ; the good Mrs. Putnam employed me and her daughters constantly to spin flax for shirts for the American soldiery ; indolence in America being totally discouraged. One day after dinner, the Congress was the toast. General Washington viewed me very attentively, and said— ' Miss Moncrieffe, you don't drink your wine.' Embarrassed

* Many of the gentlemen's houses in New York had then a gallery, with a summer house, on the top.

by this reproof, I knew not how to act; at last, as if by a secret impulse, I addressed myself to the American commander, and taking the wine, I said—' General Howe is the toast.' The whole company censured me; but my good friend Gen. Putnam, as usual, apologised, and assured them I did not mean to offend. General Washington then said. ' Well, Miss, I will overlook your indiscretion, on condition that you drink my health, or Gen. Putnam's, the first time you dine at Sir William Howe's table, on the other side of the water.' "

Not very long afterwards this young lady played the part of a spy, during her visit at the house of a Mr. Wood, near Peekskill. Among the visitors who came to pay their respects to her were frequently a number of young officers of the American army. Most of these speedily became enslaved to the charms of Miss Moncrieffe, who entered with apparently warm interest into the discussions she heard, expressing unbounded friendship for the whig cause, and a generous indignation against the oppressors of her native country. The young officers were enchanted to hear her professions of patriotism, and felt no restraint in conversing with her upon the state and prospects of the country, the occurrences of the day, and the plans and movements by which they expected to circumvent the enemy.

Like many women of that day, she was a capital equestrian. One morning she took her accustomed ride without any companion. On passing a farm house, the barking of a dog that suddenly sprang into the road frightened her horse. The animal started aside; she was thrown to the ground, and so

CHAPTER V.

severely stunned as to be entirely insensible. There were no men about the house to render assistance; but the women ran out, lifted her in their arms, carried her in and laid her on a bed. While they were using means for her restoration, one of them unbuttoned her vest to allow her to breathe more freely. A letter dropped out, which was picked up and put on the table. It was not long before she began to recover consciousness; meanwhile the man who lived in the farm house happened to come in, and was informed of the accident. In a few minutes Miss Moncrieffe was fully restored to her senses. Suddenly starting and seizing the open flaps of her vest, she sprang up, and asked for the letter, in tones that betrayed the utmost agitation and alarm. One of the women took it up, and was about to hand it to her quietly, when the man, suspecting from her strange behavior that something was wrong, started forward and seized it. Perceiving that the letter was directed to New York, he refused to give it up, feeling convinced that there was more in the affair than she was willing to admit. There was no resource for the young lady but to adjust her dress and ride back to Mr. Wood's house. She immediately commenced preparations for returning to the city. But before she could get ready to start, information of her proceedings had been carried to the proper quarter; a party of soldiers rode up and entered the house; the officer announced to Miss Moncrieffe that she was their prisoner, and she was conveyed under their escort across the river to a public house, where a guard was placed over her.

It was ascertained that the letter in question contained information respecting some intended movement of the Continental forces. It came out upon examination that the young lady had been in the habit of sending her British friends the information she obtained from the young officers, who, not suspecting any sinister motive in the interest she evinced, confided their plans to her. When she wrote a letter, she concealed it beneath her vest, and in her solitary rides contrived to drop the missive in a certain spot by the road-side. A man who waited, hid among the bushes, came out directly, cautiously picked up the letter, and conveyed it to another secret agent some distance down the river, by whom it was safely forwarded to its destination. All this was brought to light by the confession of the man himself. He had a family in the neighborhood, and fearing discovery of his agency, judged it most prudent to throw himself on the mercy of the Americans by a voluntary confession, hoping to be let off as a reward for his evidence against Miss Moncrieffe. He was kept a long time in custody, but there is no reason to believe he ever received any other punishment.

The baggage of Miss Moncrieffe was examined, and several papers relating to military affairs were found in her trunks. While she remained a prisoner, some of the British officers appealed to the Americans in her behalf. Her countrymen were by no means disposed to deal harshly with a youthful female, especially one so beautiful, accomplished and highly connected, and it was finally decided to give her up to her friends. The crime for which a man would have suffered on the gibbet was pardoned to one of her sex and age, and she was escorted to a place agreed upon, adjoining the British lines, where she was delivered into the charge of those who undertook to conduct her in safety to her father.

This curious story, related by a person who lived in Mr. Wood's house at the time, is confirmed by a letter from a British officer, preserved in the London Universal Magazine. The woman who so early showed herself an adept in deception, ended her career in England in poverty and disgrace.

The vicinity of the royal fleet to New York alarmed the inhabitants, and many removed from the city. The British landed on the south-western shore of Long Island, August 22d, divided their army into three divisions, and commenced a circuitous march to the American camp at Brooklyn. The battle took place on the 27th of August. The Americans were defeated with severe loss, and their strength was still further impaired by the discouragement that ensued. The day following, Gen. Woodhull, President of the Convention of the State of New York, was captured at Jamaica, and barbarously treated by a British scouting party, under Capt. Oliver Delancey. When he was brought, wounded and bleeding, to Mrs. Hinchman's inn, and laid on her best bed, he begged her not to leave him alone with his enemies. "Don't be alarmed, General," said the patriotic hostess, "I shall not leave you; I don't expect to go to bed to-night." The next morning Woodhull, with his head and arm bandaged, was taken westward and left under the horse-shed, with a guard, at Howard's inn. The landlady went out, and invited the weak and fainting General to partake of some refreshment. She then gave him some bread and butter, smoked beef, and wine sangaree. When the guard asked if she had nothing for them, she replied, "I *give* to prisoners, you can *buy*." The General was next conducted to a prison-ship, and as his neglected wounds grew worse, he was removed to a hospital at New Utrecht, whither his wife hastened, but reached hi bedside only in time to receive his parting sigh. She distributed the wagon-load of provisions she had brought, among the suffering, starving American prisoners, and had the melancholy consolation of conveying his remains to a private cemetery on his farm, at Mastic.

On the night of the 29th, Washington secretly withdrew his troops from Brooklyn to New York. This retreat of the defeated Americans had well nigh been frustrated by the vigilance of a female tory—Mrs. Rapalje—who lived at Brooklyn ferry. She suspected what was going on, and sent her negro slave to inform the British General of the intended movement. The negro fell in with a Hessian guard, who could not understand the importance of his errand, and detained him until the next morning. He arrived, in consequence, at headquarters just in time to be too late; the American army, with nearly all their baggage, was safely across the river. This lady had been irritated against the whigs, by the conduct of some of the lawless militia, who had lodged a cannon ball in her wall, a few feet over her tea-table, to show their disapprobation of her drinking the prohibited tea.

After the battle of Long Island, the Americans, finding the British slowly enclosing New York on all sides, withdrew from the city, and removed their stores far up on the shore of the Hudson. Gen. Putnam, with his troops, was the last to leave

New York. To avoid any parties of the enemy that might be advancing towards it, he made choice of a road along the river, from which, at a certain point, another road would conduct him in a direction to join the main army. It happened that a force of British and Hessians more than twice as large as his own, was advancing on the road at the same time, and but for a fortunate occurrence, would have encountered his before he could have reached the turn into the other road. In ignorance that the enemy was before them, the British officers halted their troops, and stopped at a small country seat belonging to Robert Murray, a Quaker. Mrs. Murray, by means of refreshments, and her agreeable conversation, beguiled them to stay a couple of hours—Gov. Tryon jesting with her occasionally about her American friends. She might have turned the laugh upon him; for one half hour, it is said, would have enabled the British to secure the road at the turn, and cut off Putnam's retreat. The opportunity was lost; and it became a common saying among the officers, that Mrs. Murray had saved this part of the American army.

CHAPTER VI.

OCCUPATION OF NEW YORK—STATE OF THE COUNTRY—
RETREAT THROUGH NEW JERSEY—AMERICAN SUCCESSES.

THE British took possession of New York without opposition. Gen. Howe left troops in the city, and advanced northward with his main force, endeavoring to gain the rear of the American army, and cut off their communication with the Eastern States. The movement of the two armies was marked by devastation of the country through which they passed. The Hessians were the peculiar terror of the defenceless people. The wife of Capt. Whetten, who had removed his family from New York to New Rochelle, one day observed that black colors were hoisted in a field near her house, and asked a British officer what it meant. "Heaven help you, madam," was the reply; " a Hessian camp is to be set up there." It turned out better, however, than was anticipated. A good feeling was speedily established between her and the Hessians, who came almost daily to the house; for her acquaintance with the low Dutch dialect, then familiarly spoken in many families in New York, enabled her to converse readily with them. In consequence of this partiality, her house was exempted from depredations to which many of

CHAPTER VI.

her neighbors were subjected, and she was sometimes enabled to save their property from destruction.

At one time, when the village was laid waste, the house of Capt. Whetten escaped destruction, being protected by a guard set by a Hessian officer, at that time quartered in it. Mrs. Whetten, however, not trusting entirely to the enemy's favor, had sent away several articles of value for concealment. A family near them, compelled to fly and leave a dying father in their house, entreated her to take care of the helpless invalid, and, if possible, save their property from the rapacious soldiers. The sacred trust was accepted and fulfilled, but she was not able to protect all the articles left by the fugitives. An iron chest that stood in the piazza, was plundered while the old man was expiring, and while her cares and those of her daughters were in requisition for him. The following evening, Mrs. Whetten requested her daughters to go some distance, to the place were her store had been deposited, for clean sheets to furnish a bed for the Hessian officer. The young girls objected, expressing their opinion—for they supposed that the officer, who was present, could not understand English—that what they had was good enough for their unwelcome guest. The discussion, after being continued some time, was ended by the officer's saying—to the no small consternation of the ladies—" Do not trouble yourself, madam ; straw is a good enough bed for a soldier." It may be conjectured that there was no further delay in procuring the sheets.

But the family was not always so much favored as to be exempted from aggression. On one occasion, after having plundered the house of her mother, heaped her china together and broken it in one crash, the Hessians came to Mrs. Whetten's to finish their work. They snatched a handkerchief from the neck of her daughter, for the purpose of tying up various articles they had found about the house. An officer soon entered, however, and called them off. At another time, when soldiers were robbing the house, a British officer interposed, beating off his men with his own sword.

One night, after the family had retired, Mrs. Whetten was awakened by a noise, and called her husband, supposing some of the Americans had come to the village for provisions. The captain rose, and going to open the door, was assailed by oaths and cries from soldiers demanding entrance. The intruders spread themselves through the house to seize whatever plunder they might find. Several came into the chamber of Mrs. Whetten, who was keeping guard over her infant lying asleep on a pillow. They rudely snatched the pillow, throwing off the child on the floor, and demanded money. The mother had put her purse in one of her pockets, and hid it under the bolster. One of the robbers snatched a pocket from under the pillow, which she strove to get away from him. Presently, perceiving the man had not taken the pocket containing her purse, and, that the one in his possession held only her snuff-box, she relinquished it after some further show of resistance. The soldier bore away his prize, while she took care to secrete her treasure.

The scarcity of provisions caused great suffering among the inhabitants of the village, supplies that might reach the continental troops being intercepted by the enemy. The little the people had was often taken from them. At one time a resident sent word to his neighbors that they could have some milk, as he had been lucky enough to procure a cow. By the next morning nothing was left of the cow but the head and skin—the Hessians having landed and left the usual tokens of their presence. The cattle taken were often slaughtered in the most wasteful manner—butchered, perhaps, on the road, the best parts being cut out, while the rest was left, a fire kindled with rails from the fence, and the meat cooked in a row of camp-kettles by the roadside.

Such things were common; but they did not crush the spirit of patriotism. One mother in New Rochelle, after melting all the pewter she had into bullets for her two sons, sent them forth to join the continental army. As she stood in the door to bid them farewell, one turned back, saying he had no gun; but she bade him go on, for he would find a gun to spare in the army. When she had lost sight of both, she went back, weeping, into the house, to pray for their safety. At this time some thirty of the most respectable ladies in East Haddam, Connecticut, met and husked, in a few hours, about two hundred and forty bushels of corn. The harvests of Connecticut and New Jersey had been got in by the women and old men, while the militia of those States were waiting at New York and on Long Island, for the landing of the enemy. Their noble example was followed by others whose fathers and brothers were fighting the battles of the nation.

While portions of the British army were ranging through Westchester, the peaceful inhabitants were exposed to much annoyance. One family who left their home for safety, and returned after a day's absence, found it a scene of desolation.

Not an article of furniture was left, except a bedstead ; a single glass bottle was the only drinking utensil, and one ham was all that remained of the provisions ; having, by good fortune, been hung in an obscure part of the cellar. At another time, in broad day, and in sight of the family, a horse was brought up with baskets fastened on either side, and a deliberate ransacking of the poultry-yard commenced. The baskets were presently filled with the fowls, and the turkey-gobbler, a noisy patriarch, was placed astride the horse, the bridle being thrown over his head. His uneasiness when the whip was used, testified by clamorous complaints, made the whole scene so amusing, that the depredators were allowed to depart without a word of remonstrance. One day, when the British were in the neighborhood, a soldier entered the house, and walked unceremoniously towards the closet. The lady asked what he wanted. " Some brandy," was his reply. When she reproved him for the intrusion, he presented his bayonet at her breast, and calling her a rebel, swore he would kill her, but left the house on her threat of sending information to his officer.

One morning a British captain rode up to a house, and asked for the mistress. When she appeared, he told her he was much in want of something to eat. She left the room, and soon returning, brought a loaf of bread and a knife. This, she assured him, was all she had, the soldiers of his army having taken away everything else. " But I will divide this," she said : " you shall have one half, and I will keep the other for my family." This magnanimity so struck the officer, that he thanked her cordially, and requested her to let him know

CHAPTER VI.

if in future any of his men ventured to annoy her, promising that the offence should not be repeated.

The action at White Plains took place on the 28th of October. The British general, discontinuing his pursuit, then directed his attention to the American posts on the Hudson, with the apparent design of penetrating into New Jersey. Fort Washington and Fort Lee were successively taken, and other reverses befel the Americans. The army of General Washington then retreated across New Jersey before the pursuing enemy for nearly three weeks, and finally across the Delaware into Pennsylvania. This retreat was, indeed, "the darkest hour of the Revolution." The American forces, crippled and disheartened by misfortune, diminished daily, till but a bare remnant remained. They were exposed during the inclement November weather in an open country, without tools or camp equipage, and almost destitute of clothes, blankets, shoes, or provisions. So close was the pursuit, that the rear of the army was often in sight of the van of the British, who, in their triumphant march, took possession successively of Newark, New Brunswick, Princeton and Trenton, and early in December found the Delaware the only barrier between them and Philadelphia.

On this march through New Jersey, the beautiful residence of Richard Stockton, at Princeton, was directly in the route of the British army. Warned of the approach of the victorious invaders, he had barely time to remove his wife and family to a place of safety. His eldest son, Richard, then a boy twelve years of age, with an old family servant, remained in the house, while everything was left to the mercy of the enemy. The house was pillaged, the horses and stock were driven away, and the estate was laid waste. The furniture was converted into firewood ; the old wine, stored in the cellar, was drunk up, and the valuable library, with all the papers of Mr. Stockton, committed to the flames. The plate, and other valuable articles belonging to the family, had been packed in three boxes and buried in the woods, at some distance from the mansion. Through treachery, the place of concealment was discovered by the soldiers, and two of the boxes were disinterred and rifled of their rich contents. As there were no banks for keeping money, every one at that time took care of his own. It was usual to bury money as well as plate ; to conceal it under stones, or in the sand at the bottom of springs of water ; to thrust it behind joists, or between the roof and rafters; lay it under the hearth, put it in teakettles, or secrete it in any way ingenuity could devise. Sometimes these treasures were forgotten or left by the owners, and it was not unusual, years afterwards, to find money on tearing down old houses, removing fences, or digging in cellars.

On the same day that Washington was driven across the Delaware, the British took possession of Rhode Island. They now held in their power New York and New Jersey, and it was the general expectation that they would cross the Delaware as soon as the ice was firm, and take possession of the capital. Congress adjourned to Baltimore, and many of the inhabitants of Philadelphia sought refuge in the country, at no great distance from the edge of the Pines.

We, contented citizens of a peaceful land, can form but a faint conception of the horrors and desolation of those ancient times of trial. The terrors of invasion are things which nowadays imagination can scarcely compass; but then, it was rugged reality. The unbridled passions of a mercenary soldiery, compounded not only of the brutal element that forms the vigor of every army, but of the ferocity of Hessians, hired and instigated to violence and cruelty, were let loose on the land. The German troops, as if to inspire especial terror, had been sent in advance, occupying, in December, a chain of posts extending from Trenton to Mount Holly—Rhal commanding at the first, and Donop at the other—while Gen. Howe and his main army were rapidly advancing by the great route to the Delaware. On the other hand, the river was filled with American gondolas, whose crews, landing from time to time on the Jersey shore, by their lawlessness and threats of retaliation, kept the peaceful inhabitants in constant alarm. The continental army, meanwhile, if it deserved the name, was literally scattered along the right bank of the Delaware.

Family tradition has described the anxious hours passed by one sorrowing group of women and children at a little farm-house near Evesham—the family of Gen. Reed. Their only male attendant was a boy of fourteen, and the wagon was kept ready to be driven by him. In case of a sudden advance of the British, which would cut them off from the ordinary avenues of escape, their plan was formed to cross the river near Salem, and push on to the westward settlements. The wives and children of American patriot soldiers thought themselves safer on the perilous edge of an Indian wilderness, than in the neighborhood of the soldiers who, commanded by noblemen—by " men of honor and cavaliers," for such, according to all heraldry, were the Howes and Cornwallises, the Percies and Rawdons of that day—were sent by a " gracious monarch" to lay waste this land. The British campaigning of our Revolution—and no part of it more so than this—is the darkest among the dark stains that disfigure the history of the eighteenth century. There was, in the one colony of New Jersey, and in this single year, blood enough shed, and misery enough produced, to give a sanguinary character to the whole war.

The following extract from the private journal of a lady who lived at Burlington, New Jersey, shows something of the condition of that part of the country:

Dec. 16th, 1776.

" About noon this day, a terrible account of thousands coming into town. My incautious son caught up the spyglass, and was running towards the mill to look at them. He returned much dissatisfied, for no troops could he see. As he came back, poor Dick took the glass, and resting it against a tree, took a view of the fleet. The people on board suspected it was an enemy who was watching their motions. They manned a boat and sent her on shore. A loud knocking at my door brought me to it. I was a little fluttered, and kept locking and unlocking that I might get my ruffled face a little composed. At last I opened it, and half a dozen men, all armed, demanded the key of the empty house. I asked what they wanted there; they replied—' to search for a tory who had been spying at them from the mill.'

" The name of a *tory*, so near my own door, seriously alarmed me; for a poor refugee, dignified by that name, had claimed the shelter of my roof, and was at that very time concealed. I rang the bell violently—the signal agreed upon if they came to search; and when I thought he had crept into the hole, I put on a very simple look and exclaimed—'Bless me! I hope you are not Hessians!' 'Do we look like Hessians?' asked one, rudely. 'Indeed, I don't know.' 'Did you never see a Hessian? 'No—never in my life; but they are *men*; and you are men; and may be Hessians for aught I know! But I'll go with you into Col. Cox's house; though indeed it was my son at the mill; he is but a boy, and meant no harm; he wanted to see the troops.'

"So I marched at the head of them, opened the door and searched every place; but we could not find the tory. We returned—they greatly disappointed; I pleased to think my house was not suspected. They left us and searched James Verree's and the two next houses; but no tory could they find. In the evening I went to town with my refugee, and placed him in other lodgings. I was told to-day of a design to seize upon a young man in town, as he was esteemed a tory. I thought a hint would be kindly received; and as I came back, called upon a friend of his, and told him. Next day he was out of reach of the gondolas."

The journal continues, at a later period:

"By a person from Bordentown, we hear that twelve expresses came in there to-day from the camp. Some of the gondola-men and their wives being sick, and no doctor in town to apply to, they were told Mrs. Morris was a skillful woman, and kept medicines to give to the poor; and notwithstanding their late attempts to shoot my poor boy, they ventured to come to me, and in a very humble manner begged me to come and do something for them. At first I thought they might design to put a trick on me, get me aboard their gondola and then pillage my house, as they had done some others; but on asking where the sick folks were, I was told they were lodged in the Governor's house. So I went to see them; there were several, both men and women, very ill with a fever; I treated them according to art, and they all got well. I thought I had received all my pay when they thankfully acknowledged my kindness; but lo! in a short time afterwards a very ill-looking man came to the door and asked for me. When I went to him he drew me aside, and asked me if I had any friends in Philadelphia. The question alarmed me, supposing there was some mischief meditated against that poor city; however, I calmly said—' I have an ancient father, some sisters, and other near friends there.'

"' Well,' said the man, ' do you wish to hear from them, or send anything by way of refreshment to them? If you do, I will take charge of it, and bring you back anything you may send for.' I was very much surprised, and thought, to be sure, he only wanted to get provisions to take to the gondolas; but when he told me his wife was one of those I had given medicine to, and this was the only thing he could do to pay me for my kindness, my heart leaped with joy, and I set about preparing something for my dear absent friends. A quarter of beef, some veal, fowls and flour, were soon put up, and about midnight the man called and put them aboard his

CHAPTER VI. 69

boat. He left them at the Point—whence my beloved friends took them to town.

"Two nights afterwards, a loud knocking at our front door greatly alarmed us, and opening the chamber window, we heard a man's voice, saying, 'Come down softly and open the door, but bring no light.' There was something mysterious in such a call; but we concluded to go down and set the candle in the kitchen. When we got to the front door we asked, 'Who are you?' The man replied, 'A friend; open quickly.' So the door was opened: and who should it be but our honest gondola-man, with a letter, a bushel of salt, a jug of molasses, a bag of rice, some tea, coffee and sugar, and some cloth for coats for my poor boys; all sent by my kind sisters!

"How did our hearts and eyes overflow with love to them, and thanks to our Heavenly Father, for such seasonable supplies! May we never forget it! Being now so rich, we thought it our duty to hand out a little to the poor around us, who were mourning for want of salt; so we divided the bushel, and gave a pint to every poor person who came for it—having abundance left for our own use."

In the midst of the universal gloom, when the hopes of the country were on the verge of utter extinction, a sudden and unexpected turn was given to affairs. Washington conceived and executed the daring plan of crossing the Delaware, and making an attack on the advanced posts of the enemy. He crossed, accordingly, on the night of December 25th, surprised the Hessians at Trenton by an attack, and took a thousand prisoners, their commander, Col. Rhal, being killed

This brilliant success was inspiriting. The battle of Princeton, fought on the 3d of January, 1777, was also fortunate for the Americans, and Philadelphia was relieved from further alarm.

When news of the passage of the Delaware was brought to the mother of Washington, she expressed pleasure at the intelligence, but disclaimed praise for her son, and listened calmly to the congratulations of her visitors. She was then residing in the village of Fredericksburg, whither she had been removed by Washington before he took the command of the American army at Cambridge. She remained there during nearly the whole period of the Revolution.

One little incident illustrates the spirit of the women at this time. A lady of New Jersey, at whose house several American officers were quartered, occupied herself before the battle, with other women, in preparing bandages and wrappings for the use of the soldiers—every article of linen in the house having been torn up for that purpose. Her husband was absent, but returned just in time to join the troops, only stopping at home to change his wearied horse for another. As he galloped down the lane leading from the house, he heard his wife's voice calling after him, and saw her leaning from a window. He turned and rode back to hear her parting words—which were—" Remember to do your duty! I would rather hear that you were left a corpse on the field, than that you had played the part of a coward !"

Gen. Mercer was mortally wounded at the battle of Princeton His death-bed was attended by two females of the Society of Friends, who inhabited the house to which he was carried, and refusing to fly during the action, were there when he was brought wounded and dying to the threshold. The effect of these American successes was decisive. In a short time Washington had overrun the northern part of New Jersey, and the people rose in every direction to drive out the invaders from whose cruelty they had suffered so much. The British army was soon restricted to two posts—New Brunswick and Amboy. Congress returned to Philadelphia, and agents were sent to France and other courts to negotiate for the acknowledgment of American Independence, and for aid in the struggle.

CHAPTER VII.

SENTIMENT OF EUROPE—WINTER QUARTERS—NEW ATTEMPT ON PHILADELPHIA—OCCUPATION—MARCH OF BURGOYNE —MURDER OF JANE M^CCREA.

THE powers of Europe had regarded the struggle, so far, with wonder and sympathy. The novelty of the spectacle of a new nation suddenly rising up to dispute the possession of America with proud and powerful Britain—the grandeur of the idea of an independent empire in the New World—had awakened universal attention; and jealousy of England, as well as respect for the common interests of mankind, caused a general wish to prevail for the success of the American cause France was deeply interested in its favor; and the high repu tation and popularity of Dr. Franklin, who was at the court, increased the general enthusiasm. Several gentlemen of rank and fortune proffered their services. The young Marquis de La Fayette, having fitted out a vessel at his own expense, arrived in the spring of 1777, and received from Congress the appointment of Major-General.

There was a suspension of important operations in both armies till the latter part of May, varied only by a British expedition up the Hudson to Peekskill, for the purpose of destroying stores; a similar one under Tryon against Danbury, Connecticut, in which the town was burned; and one by some Connecticut militia against Sag Harbor, on Long Island. Washington took the opportunity of having his army inoculated for the small-pox, and went into winter quarters in Morristown. It was probably while he was at Pluckemin, that Mrs. Washington arrived. When the carriage stopped, and a female in a plain russet gown, with white handkerchief neatly folded over her neck, was seen, the lady whose house was the chief's headquarters, imagined her to be a domestic. But she was undeceived when the General went forward to receive her, assisted her from the carriage, and, after the first greeting, began to inquire after his pet horses. A ball was given in honor of the arrival of "Lady Washington," at which her brave husband himself condescended to lead a minuet; it being the first occasion, in a long time, on which he had been known to dance.

The life in camp, with all its privations and trials, was sometimes pleasant enough, even to the ladies. Mrs. Knox often remarked that she *lived* more in one year at this period of excitement, than in a dozen of ordinary life. Trying as were some scenes through which patriotic wives were called to pass, there were times when care was cast aside, and a brief repose was granted from the fears of war. Yet they knew not what an hour might bring forth. At one time, when the ladies remained later than usual in camp on the Hudson, an alarm was given that the enemy was approaching from New York The aids-de-camp proposed sending them away under an escort. But Washington would not consent, saying that their presence would inspire courage for a brave defence. The night was dark, and the words of command from the officers, the marching of the troops, the dragging of artillery into the yard, and the noise of removing the windows, the house itself being filled with soldiers, gave "dreadful note of preparation." The enemy, however, probably finding there was no hope of a surprise, withdrew without coming to blows.

The description given by Chastellux of head-quarters at Newburgh, may show how plainly the great American chief was often lodged. "They consist of a single house, built in the Dutch fashion, and neither large nor commodious. The largest room, converted by Gen. Washington into his dining-room, is tolerably spacious; but it has seven doors and only one window. The chimney is against the wall, so that there is but one vent for the smoke, and the fire is in the room itself. I found the company assembled in a small room, which served as a parlor. At nine, supper was served; and when bed-time came, I found that the chamber to which the General conducted me was the very parlor spoken of, wherein he had made them place a camp-bed. We assembled at breakfast the next morning at ten, during which interval my bed was folded up, and my chamber became the sitting-room for the whole afternoon. The smallness of the house, and the inconvenience to which I saw that General and Mrs. Washington had put themselves to receive me, made me apprehensive lest M. Rochambeau might arrive on the same day."

Another incident, remembered by an aged veteran, exhibits the kindness of Mrs. Washington towards those in the humblest sphere. It occurred when she came to spend the cold season with her husband in winter-quarters. There were but two frame-houses in the settlement, and neither had a finished upper story. The General was contented with his rough dwelling, but wished to prepare for his wife a more retired and comfortable apartment. He sent for the young mechanic, and desired him and one of his fellow-apprentices to fit up a room in the upper story for the accommodation of Lady Washington through the winter. She herself arrived before the work was commenced. " She came," says the narrator, " into the place —a portly-looking, agreeable woman of forty-five—and said to us: 'Now, young men, I care for nothing but comfort here; and should like you to fit me up a beauffet on one side of the room, and some shelves and places for hanging clothes on the other.' We went to work with all our might. Every morning about eleven Mrs. Washington came up stairs with a glass of spirits for each of us; and after she and the General had dined, we were called down to eat at their table. We worked very hard, nailing smooth boards over the rough and worm-eaten planks, and stopping the crevices in the walls made by time and hard usage. Then we consulted together how we could smooth the uneven floor, and take out, or cover over some of the huge black knots. We studied to do everything to please so pleasant a lady, and to make some return, in our humble way, for the kindness of the General. On the fourth day, when Mrs. Washington came up to see how we were getting along, we had finished the work, made shelves, put up the pegs on the wall, built the beauffet, and converted the rough garret into a comfortable apartment. As she stood looking round, I said, ' Madam, we have endeavored to do the best we could; I hope we have suited you.' She replied. smiling, ' I am not only satisfied, but highly gratified with what you have done for my comfort.'"

The English Generals, deeply mortified at their discomfiture in New Jersey, resolved on a new and more elaborate attempt on Philadelphia, and in July, 1777, set sail, with the most complete equipment they had yet been able to prepare, for the capes of the Chesapeake. The army landed near the head of the Elk, in Maryland, August 28th, and marched to encounter the continental forces, which were withdrawn across the Brandywine to make a stand for the defence of the capital.

A little incident that occurred while the Americans were encamped here, shows the part taken by the ladies. A Mrs. Biddle chanced to hear that a large British foraging party was within the distance of a few miles; that orders had been issued for a party to start before day for the purpose of cutting off their retreat, and that, as an engagement might be expected, the women were directed to leave the camp. Not willing to consider herself included in the order, she sent word to General Washington that as the officers would return hungry and fatigued from the expedition, she would, if allowed to stay, make provision for their refreshment. He assured her she might remain in safety, but recommended that she should hold herself in readiness to remove at a moment's warning. She immediately despatched her servant through the neighborhood to collect provisions. At a late hour the American troops returned, after a fatiguing march. Mrs. Biddle had the pleasure of giving the dinner she had provided to at least a hundred officers; each remarking, as he entered, "Madam, we hear that you feed the army to-day," which she really did, till not a crust remained.

The disastrous battle of Brandywine, September 11th, was followed by the retreat of the American army to Philadelphia, and the adjournment of Congress to Lancaster. The massacre of three hundred American soldiers under Gen. Wayne, surprised at night near Paoli, took place at this time. The efforts of the American Commander-in-chief failed to arrest the advance of the British, and he was obliged to withdraw with his army. The British entered Philadelphia on the 26th of September, and the main body of their army encamped at Germantown. The battle of Germantown, so disastrous to the patriots, was fought October 4th, and after that Gen. Howe removed into the city. His army, on its first entrance, was received with a welcome apparently cordial, by some timid or interested citizens. A private letter from a lady to her friend, gives an account of the taking possession.

"We had for a neighbor, and an intimate acquaintance, a very amiable English gentleman, who had been in the British army, and had left the service on marrying a rich and excellent lady of Philadelphia some years before. He endeavored to give my mother confidence that the inhabitants would not be ill-treated. He advised that we should be all well dressed and that we should keep our houses closed. The army marched in, and took possession of the town in the morning. We were up stairs, and saw them pass to the State House. They looked well—clean and well-clad; and the contrast between them and our poor barefooted and ragged troops was very great, and caused a feeling of despair. It was a solemn and impressive day; but I saw no exultation in the enemy, nor indeed in those who were reckoned favorable to their success.

"Early in the afternoon Lord Cornwallis's suite arrived, and took possession of my mother's dwelling. But my mother was appalled by the numerous train in her house, and shrank from having such inmates; for a guard was mounted at the door, and the yard filled with soldiers and baggage of every description; and I well remember what we thought of the haughty looks of Lord Rawdon and the other aid-de-camp, as they traversed the apartments. My mother desired to speak with Lord Cornwallis, and he attended her in the front parlor.

"She told him of her situation, and how impossible it would be for her to stay in her own house with such a train as composed his lordship's establishment. He behaved with great politeness to her; said he should be sorry to give trouble, and would have other quarters looked out for him. They withdrew that very afternoon. But it did not last long; for directly the quartermasters were employed in billeting the troops, and we had to find room for two officers of artillery, and afterwards for two gentlemen, secretaries of Lord Howe. Gen. Howe, during the time he stayed in Philadelphia, seized and kept for his own use, Mary Pemberton's coach and horses, in which he used to ride about the town."

The neighborhood of the city was infested by gangs of armed loyalists, who threatened the safety of every patriot they met. Tempted by the hard money which the British promised, they dared any danger, and were willing to commit any enormity.

Howe's first care was to reduce the fortifications on the

Delaware, and remove the obstructions prepared by the Americans to prevent the British fleet from ascending the river. While Fort Mifflin, at Mud Island, and Fort Mercer, at Red Bank, were occupied by their garrisons, he could have no communication with his fleet, and was in danger of being soon compelled to evacuate the city. Count Donop, detached with Hessian troops to take possession of the fort at Red Bank, was repulsed and mortally wounded. The invader's fortune, however, triumphed; the Americans were finally driven from their posts, and the British gained free communication between their army and the shipping.

While these reverses cast a gloom over the whole country, events of importance were transpiring at the North. In the spring of this year Gen. Burgoyne arrived at Quebec, having been commissioned to invade the States by the way of Lake Champlain and the Hudson, with a view to form a communication between Canada and New York, and cut off New England from the more southern States. He had secured for the British service several tribes of Indians in the country between the Mohawk and Lake Ontario. His army of British and Germans, Canadians and savages, advanced triumphantly southward, spreading dismay and terror as they came, and driving the pacific inhabitants from their homes. The inhabitants of the village of Tomhanick, terrified by the news that the enemy were at hand, burning and murdering all before them, fled to a place called Stony Arabia. The roads were crowded with carriages loaded with women and children; distress and weeping were everywhere; no one spoke to another, and the tramping of horses and the dismal creaking of burdened wheels, alone interrupted the mournful silence. One matron obtained a place for her children in one of the wagons, and herself performed the journey on foot. But when she reached the place where she hoped to find friends, no door was open to her. She wandered from house to house, and at length obtained an asylum in the garret of a rich acquaintance, where a couple of blankets, spread on boards, were given her as a bed. The night was passed in tears; but the next day her husband came and brought them to Albany, whence they set off with several other families by water.

Gen. Schuyler, who occupied Fort Edward on the Hudson, was forced to retreat, but embarrassed the enemy's march by destroying bridges and felling trees. During this retreat, Mrs. Schuyler went herself in her chariot from Albany to Saratoga, to see to the removal of her furniture. While there, she received directions from the General to set fire, with her own hand, to his extensive fields of wheat, and to require his tenants and others to do the same, rather than suffer them to be reaped by the enemy.

Burgoyne reached Fort Edward, July 30th, and despatched Col. Baum, a German officer, to sieze some stores at Bennington, where he was defeated by Gen. Stark at the head of the New Hampshire militia. Immediately before this battle, Stark, with several of his officers, stopped to obtain a draught of milk and water at the house of Mr. Munro, a loyalist, who chanced to be absent. One of the officers walked up to Mrs. Munro, and asked where her husband was She replied that she did not know; whereupon he drew his sword, and endeavored to intimidate her into a more satisfactory answer. The General, hearing the commotion, severely reproved the officer for his uncivil behavior to a woman; and the offender went out, apparently much abashed. Mrs. Munro always remembered Stark's words—"Come on, my boys,"—as they marched to battle. The firing continued till late; and after a sleepless night, Mrs. Munro and her sister repaired with the earliest dawn to the battle-field, carrying pails of milk and water—and wandering among the heaps of slain and wounded, relieved the thirst of sufferers, of whom some—the Hessians—were unable to express their thankfulness, save by the mute eloquence of grateful looks. Towards noon wagons were sent to convey them to hospitals, and to bring away the dead for burial.

The consequence of this battle was the delay of the British at Fort Edward for nearly a month. The tragedy of the murder of Miss McCrea, which caused so deep a sensation both in Europe and America, occurred while Burgoyne's army was approaching the fort. The young lady was on a visit to a widow, Mrs. McNiel. Her house stood near the foot of the hill, a little northward from the fort, which was surrounded by a cleared and cultivated plain. The hill-side was covered with bushes, while a quarter of a mile above, on the summit of the hill, a huge pine tree shadowed a clear spring.

Jane McCrea was friendly to the English, having formed a matrimonial engagement with a young man, David Jones, who had taken part with them. It is supposed she had been counselled by her lover not to leave Mrs. McNiel's house till the advance of the British troops should enable both to join him. This may account for her remaining unprotected in so exposed a situation, although alarmed by rumors of the approach of the Indians, and reminded of her danger by the Americans at the fort. The woods being filled with American scouting parties, it would have been dangerous for her lover to attempt a visit to her.

The timid but confiding girl expected, from hour to hour, intelligence from her betrothed, and awaited the long desired moment when they should meet to part no more. She and her friend were at last alarmed by seeing a party of Indians advancing towards the house. The savages had been a terror to all that part of the country, and the tales told of their unsparing cruelty were fresh in remembrance. Their first impulse was to endeavor to escape; but the Indians made signs of a pacific intent, and one of them held up a letter, intimating that it would explain their business.* This removed all apprehensions, and the letter was taken from the messenger. It proved to be from Capt. Jones. He entreated Jane and her friend to put themselves under the protection of the Indians, whom he had sent for the purpose of taking charge of them, and who would escort them in safety to the British camp.

The two women, notwithstanding some misgivings, lost no time in preparation, and set off under the guidance of the savages. It happened that two separate parties of Indians, commanded by two independent chiefs, had come forth on this enterprise. They had another object in view—an attack

* Mr. Lossing says they were taken forcibly from the house by the Indians. The particulars of the murder were told Mr. Sparks by Standish.

CHAPTER VII.

upon a picket guard stationed in the woods on the hill. This arrangement, it is probable, was not known to Jones, or he would hardly have trusted the safety of Miss McCrea to the contingencies of such an expedition.

The party attacking the guard rushed upon it through the woods from different points, making the forest resound with their horrible yelling; killing the lieutenant and five others, and wounding four more. One of the guard was Samuel Standish, whose post was near the pine tree. He discharged his musket at an Indian, and ran down the hill towards the fort; but being intercepted on the plain by three Indians, who rushed from the thicket, fired at and wounded him slightly, and then secured him, he was forced to re-ascend the hill, where he saw several Indians at the spring beneath the pine tree.

Here he was left alone, bound, and expecting death every moment, to witness, at a short distance, the appalling scene that ensued. Another party of Indians came in a few minutes up the hill, bringing with them Miss McCrea and her companion. The two parties of savages here met; and it was presently apparent that a violent altercation had arisen between them. The dispute was about the division of the reward they were to receive for the service rendered. The savages to whom the mission had been entrusted, it appears, were not aware of the relation in which the girl stood to their employer, and looked upon her rather as a prisoner, decoyed by a stratagem into their power. This supposition accounts for their conduct, consistently with the usages of the Indians in the case of captives whom they feared to lose. The quarrel became furious; violent words and blows ensued, and in the midst of the fray, one of the chiefs fired at Miss McCrea. The shot entered her breast; she sank to the ground and instantly expired. The Indian grasped her long, flowing locks, drew his knife and took off the scalp; then, leaping from the ground with a yell of savage exultation, he brandished it in the air, and tossed it in the face of a young warrior who stood near him.

This murder terminated the quarrel, and the Indians, fearful of being pursued by men from the fort, where the alarm had already been given, hurried away with their two prisoners, Standish and Mrs. McNiel, towards Gen. Frazer's encampment on the road to Fort Anne. The body of the murdered girl was left under the tree, gashed in several places by a tomahawk or scalping knife, and was found, with the others who had been slain, by the party in pursuit. A messenger was immediately despatched with the dreadful tidings to her brother, who soon after arrived and took charge of his sister's corpse. It was buried on the east side of the river, about three miles below the fort.

CHAPTER VIII.

THE BATTLES OF SARATOGA—THE PRISONERS AT CAMBRIDGE.

GENERAL BURGOYNE, in the midst of a wilderness, and surrounded by enemies, had little reliance on his savage allies. Before the middle of September he broke up his encampment, crossed the Hudson and took his position on the heights and plains of Saratoga. Gen. Gates, who had recently been appointed to the command of the northern American army, had removed from the mouth of the Mohawk, and occupied Behmus' Heights, near Stillwater. By the 18th of September Burgoyne had advanced within two miles of the American camp, and on the 19th was fought the bloody battle of Stillwater. Burgoyne then determined to await the co-operation of Gen. Clinton from New York; but his Canadian and Indian forces began to desert him on the prospect of a reverse.

After frequent skirmishes, another general battle was fought on the 7th of October. This, though a fierce and desperate conflict, proved decisive in favor of the Americans. The journal of the Baroness Riedesel, the wife of one of the German officers in the royal army, who, with her three children, had followed its march, describes these memorable scenes. On that day the English generals, Burgoyne, Phillips, and Frazer, were invited to dine with her and the Baron. She had observed in the morning an unusual movement in the camp; and had seen a number of armed Indians in their war dresses, who answered " War! war !" to her inquiries whither they were going. As the dinner hour approached, an increased tumult, the firing, and the yelling of the savages, announced the approaching battle. The roar of artillery became louder and more incessant. At four o'clock, instead of the guests invited, Gen. Frazer was brought in mortally wounded. The table already prepared for dinner, was removed to make room for his bed.

The Baroness, terrified by the noise of the conflict raging without, expected every moment to see her husband also led in pale and helpless. Towards night he came to the house, dined in haste, and desired his wife to pack up her camp furniture, and be ready for removal at an instant's warning. His dejected countenance told the disastrous result. Lady Ackland, whose tent was adjoining, was presently informed that her husband was wounded and a prisoner ! Thus through the long hours till day, the kind ministries of the Baroness were demanded by many sufferers. " I divided the night," she says, " between her I wished to comfort, and my children, who were asleep, but who I feared might disturb the poor dying General. Several times he begged my pardon for the trouble he thought he gave me. About three o'clock I was informed he could not live much longer; and as I did not wish to be present at his last struggle, I wrapped my children in blankets, and retired into the room below. At eight in the morning he expired."

All day the cannonade continued, and the women attended the wounded soldiers who were brought in. Frazer's last request had been that he should be buried at six in the evening in the great redoubt on the hill, and the retreat of the British was delayed for this purpose. The generals, with their retinues, followed the corpse to the spot in the midst of a heavy fire from the Americans; for Gen. Gates knew not that it was a funeral procession. The women stood in full view of the scene, while the deepening shadows of evening closed around the group thus rendering the last service to one of their number, while each might anticipate his own death in the next report of artillery. "Many cannon balls, said the Baroness, "flew close by me; but I had my eyes directed towards the mountain where my husband was standing amidst the fire of the enemy, and I did not think of my own danger."

The story of female heroism and fidelity with which the name of Lady Harriet Ackland is associated, belongs to this time. She was the wife of Maj. Ackland, one of Burgoyne's officers, and like Madame de Riedesel, had accompanied the army from Canada to Saratoga, her vehicle of conveyance a small two-wheeled tumbril, drawn by one horse, over almost impassable roads and through extensive forests. The women generally followed in the rear of the artillery and baggage, but heard all the uproar in encounters with the enemy.

When the fate of Ackland was announced, his unhappy wife, sustained by the counsels of her friend the Baroness, determined to join him in the American camp. She sent a message to Gen. Burgoyne, to ask permission to depart. The British commander was astonished at this application; he could hardly understand the courage of a woman, who after suffering so long the agitation of suspense, exhausted by want of rest and want of food, was ready to brave the darkness of night and the drenching rain for many hours, and to deliver herself to the enemy, uncertain into what hands she might fall! "The assistance I was able to give," he says, "was small indeed. I had not even a cup of wine to offer her All I could furnish was an open boat, and a few lines written on dirty and wet paper to Gen. Gates, recommending her to his protection."

She set out in an open boat, accompanied by the British chaplain Brudenell, her own maid, and her husband's valet, who had been severely wounded in the search for his master when first missing from the field of battle. They went down the river during a violent storm of rain and wind, and arrived at the American outposts in the night, having suffered much from wet and cold. The sentinel of the advance-guard heard the sound of oars, and hailed the boat. What must have been his surprise to hear that a woman had braved the storm on such an errand! He sent for Maj. Dearborn, the officer of the guard, who invited Lady Ackland to his guard house, offered her a cup of tea and every accommodation in his power, and gave her the welcome intelligence of her husband's safety. In the morning she experienced the kindness of Gen. Gates, receiving every attention which her circumstances required. She was conveyed, under a suitable escort, to the quarters of Gen. Poor on the heights, to her wounded husband; and there remained till he was taken to Albany. Her resolution and devotion to him touched the feelings of the

Americans, and won the admiration of all who heard her story.

That night the British army commenced its retreat, leaving the sick and wounded; a flag of truce waving over the hospital thus abandoned to the mercy of the foe. The rain fell in torrents all day of the 9th, and it was dark when they reached Saratoga. Madame de Riedesel suffered cruel suspense as to the fate of her husband. She had taken charge of some valuables belonging to the officers, and having no place to change her drenched apparel, lay down with her children upon some straw by the fire. Her provisions were shared the next day with the officers; and being insufficient to satisfy their hunger, she made an appeal to the Adjutant-General in their behalf.

Again the alarm of battle, and reports of muskets and cannons, drove them to seek shelter in a house, which was fired at under the impression that the generals were there. It was occupied by women and crippled soldiers. They were obliged at last to descend into the cellar, where the Baroness laid herself in a corner, supporting her children's heads on her knees. The night was passed in the utmost terror and anguish; and with the morning the terrible cannonade commenced anew. So it continued for several days. But in the midst of the dreadful scenes, when the Baron spoke of sending his family to the American camp, the heroic wife declared that nothing would be so painful to her as to owe safety to those with whom he was fighting. He then consented that she should continue to follow the army. "However," she says, "the apprehension that he might have marched away, repeatedly entered my mind; and I crept up the staircase more than once to dispel my fears. When I saw our soldiers near the watch-fires, I became more calm, and could even have slept."

"The want of water continuing to distress us, we were extremely glad to find a soldier's wife so spirited as to fetch some from the river, an occupation from which the boldest might have shrunk, as the Americans shot every one who approached it. They told us afterwards that they spared her on account of her sex. I endeavored to dispel my melancholy by continually attending to the wounded. I made them tea and coffee, and often shared my dinner with them. One day a Canadian officer came creeping into our cellar, and was hardly able to say that he was dying with hunger. I felt happy to offer him my dinner, by eating which he recovered his strength."

At length Burgoyne and his officers decided on surrender. On the 17th the capitulation was carried into effect. The generals waited upon Gates, and the troops yielded themselves prisoners of war. "At last," writes Madame de Riedesel, "my husband's groom brought me a message to join him with the children. I once more seated myself in my dear calash; and while driving through the American camp, was gratified to observe that no one looked at us with disrespect, but on the contrary, greeted us, and seemed touched at the sight of a captive mother with three children When I drew near the tents, a fine-looking man advanced towards me, helped the children from the calash, and kissed and caressed them. He then offered me his arm, and tears stood in his eyes. ' You

CHAPTER VIII. 91

tremble, madam,' said he; "do not be alarmed.' He then ushered me into the tent of Gen. Gates, whom I found engaged in friendly conversation with Burgoyne and Phillips. Gen. Burgoyne said to me—' You can now be quiet and free from all apprehension of danger.'

" All the generals remained to dine with the American commander. The gentleman who had received me with so much kindness, came and said to me : ' You may find it embarrassing to be the only lady in so large a company of gentleman. Will you come with your children to my tent, and partake of a frugal dinner ?' ' You show me so much kindness,' replied I, ' I cannot but believe that you are a husband and a father.' He informed me that he was Gen. Schuyler. The dinner was of excellent smoked tongues, beefsteaks, potatoes, fresh butter, and bread. After our dinner, Gen. Schuyler begged me to pay him a visit at his house near Albany, where he expected that Gen. Burgoyne would also be his guest. I sent to ask my husband's directions, and he advised me to accept the invitation.

" Our reception at Albany, from Gen. Schuyler and his wife and daughters, was not like the reception of enemies, but of the most intimate friends. They loaded us with kindness; and they behaved in the same manner towards Gen. Burgoyne, though he had without any necessity ordered their splendid country-seat near Saratoga to be burnt. All their actions proved that at the sight of the misfortunes of others, they quickly forgot their own. Burgoyne was so much affected by this generous deportment, that he said to Schuyler : ' You are too kind to me, who have done you so much injury.'

'Such is the fate of war,' Schuyler replied; 'let us not dwell on this subject.' We remained three days with that excellent family, and they seemed to regret our departure."

It was one of the most picturesque incidents of the war, that the captive British general with his suite, should be entertained by those whose property he had wantonly laid waste. Gen. Schuyler had written from Saratoga to his wife, to make every preparation for giving the prisoners the best reception. This narrative teaches us one of the great lessons belonging to the story of battle and victory. In the midst of admiration for the brilliant achievement of Saratoga, we should not lose pity for the disasters that accompanied the triumph. We may see humanity and courtesy prevailing in the midst of the strife. "If the figures of the picture are fierce and repulsive—the figures of brethren armed against brethren—of mercenary Germans and frantic savages—Canadian rangers and American ploughmen—all bristling together with the horrid front of war, what a charm of contrast is presented, when among these stern and forbidding groups is beheld the forms of Christian women moving to and fro, softening the misfortunes of defeat, and checking the elation of victory."

The prisoners were conveyed to Boston, and, after a stay of three weeks, were removed to Cambridge. A letter written by a Cambridge lady, dated Nov. 11, 1777, thus describes their entrance: "Last Thursday, which was a very stormy day, a large number of British troops came softly through the town by Watertown to Prospect Hill. On Friday we heard the Hessians were to make a procession in the same route. To be sure the sight was truly astonishing. I never had the least idea that the creation produced such a sordid set of creatures in human form—poor, dirty, emaciated men, and great numbers of women, who seemed to be the beasts of burden, having bushel baskets on their backs, by which they were bent double. The contents seemed to be pots and kettles, various sorts of furniture, children peeping through gridirons and other utensils—some very young infants, who were born on the road—the women barefoot, clothed in dirty rags. Such effluvia filled the air while they were passing, that had they not been smoking all the time, I should have been apprehensive of being contaminated. After a noble-looking advanced guard, Gen. Burgoyne headed this terrible group on horseback. The other generals, also clothed in blue cloaks—Hessians, Waldeckers, Anspackers, Brunswickers, etc.—followed. The Hessian generals gave us a polite bow as they passed. Not so the British. Their baggage-wagons were drawn by poor, half-starved horses. But to bring up the rear, another fine, noble-looking guard of American brawny victorious yeomanry—some of our wagons drawn by fat oxen, driven by joyous-looking Yankees—closed the cavalcade. The generals and other officers went to Bradish's, where they quarter at present. The privates trudged through thick and thin to the hills, where we thought they were to be confined. But what was our surprise when, in the morning, we beheld an inundation of those disagreeable objects filling our streets, in a manner demanding our houses and colleges for their accommodation! Did the brave General Gates ever mean this? Is there not a degree of unkindness in loading poor Cambridge, almost ruined before this great army seemed to be let loose upon us?"

"Gen. Burgoyne dined on Saturday in Boston with Gen. —. He rode through the town properly attended, down Court street and through the main street; and on his return walked on foot to Charlestown Ferry, followed by a great number of spectators as ever attended a Pope; and generously observed to an officer with him, the decent and modest behavior of the inhabitants as he passed; saying, if he had been conducting prisoners through the city of London, not all the guards of Majesty could have prevented insults. He likewise acknowledges Lincoln and Arnold to be great generals. It is said we shall have not less than seven thousand persons to feed in Cambridge and its environs, more than its inhabitants. Two hundred and fifty cords of wood will not serve them a week. Think, then, how we must be distressed! Wood has risen to five pounds ten shillings a cord, and but a little to be purchased. I never thought I could lie down to sleep surrounded by these enemies; but we strangely become inured to those things which appear difficult when distant."

The ladies belonging to Burgoyne's army received many courtesies from Mrs. Hancock and others in Cambridge. Gen. Riedesel and his family were lodged in one of the best houses, and the Baroness occasionally visited whig ladies in the village and Boston. A ball given by her was so brilliant and so numerously attended, that the house was surrounded with people, who began to suspect a conspiracy. She noticed the American method of telegraphing by lighting torches on surrounding heights, when they wished to call troops together, and called to mind that when Gen. Howe attempted to rescue the troops detained in Boston, the inhabitants planted their torches, and a crowd of people, without shoes or stockings, their rifles on their shoulders, flocked together.

The British general, Sir Henry Clinton, had proceeded up the Hudson early in October, in hopes of making a diversion, by his devastations, in favor of Burgoyne. Two important forts (Forts Clinton and Montgomery) were captured, and Esopus, now Kingston—one of the earliest Dutch settlements in New York, and a populous and wealthy town—was laid in ashes.

A spy, sent after the capture of Fort Montgomery, carried a letter from Clinton to Burgoyne, enclosed in a silver bullet, which, when taken prisoner, he swallowed. The action was observed, and an emetic administered to the messenger, who was afterwards executed. On the news of Burgoyne's surrender, Gen. Clinton withdrew to New York.

The intelligence of the brilliant victories of Saratoga raised the hopes of the country, which had been deeply depressed by the reverses of Washington's army. The necessity for some bond of union between the States had begun to be felt, and, in November, the articles of confederation proposed by Franklin more than a year before, were adopted by Congress. "This confederation amounted to little more than a league of friendship between the States;" but its deficiencies were hardly noticed while a common sense of danger bound all together. After the close of the war it was found necessary to revise the system for a permanent government.

CHAPTER IX.

FEMALE AGENCY—VALLEY FORGE—STATE OF PHILADELPHIA.

WHILE the American army remained encamped at White Marsh, the British being in possession of Philadelphia, Gen. Howe made some vain attempts to draw Washington into an engagement. An incident of female agency is well remembered by many aged persons. The house opposite the headquarters of Gen. Howe, in the city, tenanted by William and Lydia Darrah, members of the Society of Friends, was the place selected by the superior officers of the army for private conference, whenever it was necessary to hold consultations. On the afternoon of the 2d of December, the British Adjutant-General called and informed the mistress that he and some friends were to meet there that evening, and desired that the back room upstairs might be prepared for their reception. "And be sure, Lydia," he concluded, "that your family are all in bed at an early hour. When our guests are ready to leave the house, I will myself give you notice, that you may let us out, and extinguish the fire and candles."

Having delivered this order, the Adjutant-General departed. Lydia betook herself to getting all things in readiness. But the words she had heard, especially the injunction to retire early, rang in her ears; and she could not divest herself of the feeling that something of importance was in agitation. The evening closed in, and the officers came to the place of meeting. Lydia had ordered all her family to bed, and herself admitted the guests, after which she retired to her own apartment.

But sleep refused to visit her eyelids. She became more and more uneasy, and at last slid from the bed, and taking off her shoes, passed noiselessly from her chamber and along the entry. Approaching cautiously the apartment in which the officers were assembled, she applied her ear to the key-hole. For a few moments she could distinguish but a word or two amid the murmur of voices. At length there was profound silence, and a voice was heard reading a paper aloud. It was an order for the troops to quit the city on the night of the 4th, and march out to a secret attack upon the American army at White Marsh.

Lydia retreated softly to her own room, and laid herself quietly on the bed. It seemed to her that but a few moments had elapsed, when there was a knocking at her door. She knew well what the signal meant, but took no heed. It was repeated again and again; and then she rose quickly, and opened the door. It was the Adjutant General, who came to inform her they were ready to depart. Lydia let them out, fastened the house, and extinguished the lights and fire. Again she returned to her chamber; but her mind was more disquieted than ever, for she thought of the danger that threatened the lives of thousands of her countrymen.

Her resolution at length was formed, and at dawn of day she waked her husband, and informed him flour was wanted for the use of the household, and that it was necessary she should go to Frankford to procure it. Taking the bag with her, she walked through the snow, having first obtained a written permission to pass the British lines. She reached Frankford, distant four or five miles, and deposited her bag at the mill. Now commenced the dangers of her undertaking, for she pressed forward with all haste towards the outposts of the American army. Her determination was to apprise General Washington of the danger.

She was met on her way by an American officer, who had been selected by General Washington to gain information respecting the movements of the enemy. He inquired whither she was going, and she disclosed the secret, after having obtained from him a solemn promise not to betray her, since the British might take vengeance on her and her family. He thanked her for her timely warning, and directed her to go to a house near at hand, where she might get something to eat. But Lydia preferred returning at once; and did so, carrying her bag of flour, while the officer made all haste to the Commander-in-chief. Preparations were immediately made to give the enemy a fitting reception.

None suspected the grave, demure Quakeress of having snatched from the English their anticipated victory; but after the return of the British troops, a loud knocking was heard at Lydia's door. The visitor was the Adjutant General, who summoned her to his apartment, locked the door with an air of mystery, and motioned her to a seat. After a moment of silence, he said—" Were any of your family up, Lydia, on the night when I received company in this house?"

"No," was the reply. "They all retired at eight o'clock."

"It is very strange," said the officer, and mused a few minutes. "You, I know, Lydia, were asleep, for I knocked at your door three times before you heard me—yet it is certain that we were betrayed. I am altogether at a loss to conceive who could have given the information of our intended attack to General Washington! On arriving near his encampment we found his cannon mounted, his troops under arms, and so prepared at every point to receive us, that we have been compelled to march back without injuring our enemy, like a parcel of fools."

The American army now went into winter quarters at Valley Forge. This was a dreary, rugged valley, about twenty miles north-west of Philadelphia. The army encamped on its mountainous borders. The condition of the troops was deplorable enough to change hope into despair, and presented a spectacle unparalleled in history. During one of the most rigorous winters ever experienced in the country, the soldiers were without shoes, blankets, clothing, or provisions; and their rude log-huts, built to accommodate twelve men each, scarcely covered them from the falling snow, or sheltered them from the cutting blasts. Their feet, cut by the ice, left their tracks in blood, and their only bed was straw, on the damp ground. Marshall's MS. journal, after describing their destitution and suffering, says: "Our enemies revelling in balls, attended with every degree of luxury and excess in the city; rioting and wantonly using our houses, utensils, and furniture."

The farmers of the country refused to exchange their produce for the depreciated paper currency, and hard money was extremely scarce. Even the officers were so destitute of decent clothing, it was afterwards jocosely remarked that a single suit of dress uniform served them all for dining in, when invited by turns to head-quarters.

The ladies did not shrink from their share in these privations, or from labors of kindness. Mrs. Knight was one of many who aided to relieve the horrible sufferings of the army —cooking and carrying provisions to them through the snow, alone; even passing through the outposts of the British army in the disguise of a market woman. Mrs. Washington, with others, by her cheerful endurance of hardship, strengthened the fortitude of many who would have complained, and gave hope and confidence to the desponding. She soothed the distresses of many sufferers, seeking out the poor and afflicted with benevolent kindness, extending relief wherever it was in her power, and with graceful deportment presiding in the Chief's humble dwelling. In a letter to a friend she says, " The General's apartment is very small; he has had a log cabin built to dine in, which has made our quarters much more tolerable than they were at first." Their table was scantily furnished; but the soldiers fared still worse, sitting down at a board of rough planks, set with horn spoons and a few cups, the food being often salt herrings and potatoes, without other vegetables, or tea, coffee, or sugar. The stone jug passed round was filled with water from the nearest spring; and rare was the privilege of toddy, in which to drink the health of the nation. Yet here, forgetful of herself, the patriot wife anxiously watched the aspect of affairs, and was happy when the political horizon brightened. She writes to Mrs. Warren —" It has given me unspeakable pleasure to hear that Gen. Burgoyne and his army are in safe quarters in your State. Would bountiful Providence aim a like stroke at Gen. Howe, the measure of my happiness would be complete."

Some of the whig families who remained in Philadelphia were plundered by the soldiers, and often wanted the comforts of life. Many ladies here visited the American prisoners, carrying them provisions from their own tables. They also took food and medicines to the soldiers who were brought to the city ill with the camp-fever and placed in empty houses, often ministering themselves to their wants. An anecdote of an American farmer, Israel Israel, who came from Wilmington to bring provisions and money to his mother, entering Philadelphia at night, may give some idea of the state of the times A tory neighbor at Wilmington having given him the countersign for the night, he was permitted to pass by the sentinel at the ferry, and went to his mother's house There he found his younger brother, who served in the army, and had also ventured on a secret visit to his relatives. At eleven o'clock, while the family was seated at supper, the tramp of horses was heard without, and the rough voices of soldiers at the door. These, with a Hessian officer, had been quartered upon the family, and of course entered the house at what hours they pleased. The terrified mother and sisters entreated the brothers to fly, and followed the younger upstairs, where he made his escape from the roof. The knocking and shouting continued below ; Israel descended, accompanied by the females, and opened the door. The soldiers rushed in, at their head the Hessian sergeant, who seized the young man, exclaiming, " We have caught the rebel!" A black slave belonging to the household had given information, under threats, of his young master's visit.

Israel, with great presence of mind, explained that his brother was the person meant, produced his uniform, and showed that it did not fit him. The sergeant then shook hands with him, assuring him that he was convinced of his being a loyal subject, and seated himself at the supper-table. The ladies were obliged to take their places, and listen in silence to the coarse remarks of their unwelcome guest, and his boastful details of his exploits in slaughtering " the rebels," especially in the affair at Paoli. At length he bade the family good-night, saying he was on duty, and quitted the house. Israel then set out on his journey homeward, but arrived only to be made a prisoner. The loyalist who had given him the countersign, had betrayed the secret of his expedition. He and his wife's brother were seized and carried on board the royal frigate Roebuck, lying in the Delaware, a few miles from the then borough of Wilmington—and directly opposite his farm—in order to be tried as *spies*.

Being one of the " Committee of Safety," his position under such an accusation, was extremely critical. On board the ship he was treated with the utmost severity. His watch, silver shoe-buckles, and various articles of clothing were taken from him ; his bed was a coil of ropes on deck, without covering from the bitter cold of the night air ; and to all appearance his fate was already decided. The testimony of his tory neighbors was strong against him. Several were ready to swear to the fact, that while the loyal population of the country had willingly furnished their share of the provisions needed by the ships of war, he had been heard to say repeatedly, that he " would sooner drive his cattle as a present to General Washington, than receive thousands of dollars in British gold for them."

On being informed of this speech, the commander gave orders that a detachment of soldiers should proceed to drive the rebel's cattle, then grazing in a meadow in full view, down to the river, and slaughter them in the face of the prisoners. The farm was a mile or more from the river; but there was nothing to intercept the view—the ground from the meadow sloping down to the water.

Mrs. Israel saw the soldiers land from the ships, shoulder arms, and advance towards the meadow. In an instant she guessed their purpose; and her resolution was taken. With a boy eight years old, whom she bade follow her, she started from the house, determined to save the cattle at the peril of her life. Throwing down the bars, and followed by the boy, she ran to drive the herd to the opening. The soldiers called out repeatedly to her to stop, and threatened, if she did not, to fire upon her. She heeded not, and they fired. The frightened cattle ran in every direction over the field, but not one escaped! The little boy fell; Mrs. Israel seized him by the arm, lifted him over the fence, and herself drove the cattle into the barn-yard. The assailants, probably not daring, for fear of the neighbors, to invade the farm-houses, retraced their steps and returned disappointed to the ship. All this scene passed in sight of the officers of the "Roebuck" and the two prisoners.

A kind-hearted sailor sought an opportunity of speaking with Israel in private, and asked him if he were a free-mason. The answer was in the affirmative. The sailor then informed him that a lodge was held on ship-board, and the officers, who belonged to it, were to meet that night. The trial was held the same day on board; the tory witnesses were examined in due form; the prisoners were called up before their judges, and permitted to answer to the accusations against them. Israel, in bold but respectful language, related his story, and acknowledged his secret visit to Philadelphia, not in the character of a spy, but to carry relief to his suffering parent and her family. Afterwards, watching his opportunity, he made to the commanding officer the secret sign of masonic brotherhood. The effect was instantly observable. The officer's stern countenance softened; his change of opinion, and that of the other judges, became evident; and after some further examination, the court was broken up. The acquitted prisoners were dismissed, loaded with presents of pins, handkerchiefs, and other articles not to be purchased at that time, for the intrepid wife, and were sent on shore in a splendid barge, as a mark of special honor from the officer in command.

An anecdote of a female spy is related in the journal of Maj. Tallmadge. While the Americans were at Valley Forge, he was stationed in the vicinity of Philadelphia with a detachment of cavalry, to observe the movements of the enemy, and limit the range of British foraging parties. His duties required the utmost vigilance; his squad seldom remained all night in the same position, and their horses were rarely unsaddled. Hearing that a country girl had gone into the city with eggs—having been sent by one of the American officers to gain information—Tallmadge advanced towards the British lines, and dismounted at a small tavern within view of their outposts. The girl came to the tavern, but while she was communicating her intelligence to the Major, the alarm was given that the British light-horse were approaching. Tallmadge instantly mounted, and as she entreated protection, bade her get up behind him. They rode three miles at full speed to Germantown, the damsel showing no fear during the ride, though there was much firing of pistols, and some wheeling and charging.

Tradition relates that some of the women in Philadelphia, whose husbands were in the American army, used to procure intelligence through a market boy, who came into the city to bring provisions, and carried the dispatches sent by his friends in the back of his coat. One morning, when there was some reason to fear he was suspected, and his movements watched, a young girl undertook to get the papers. She went to market, and in a pretended game of romps, threw her shawl over the boy's head, thus securing the prize. She hastened with the papers to her friends, who read them with deep interest, after the windows had been carefully closed. When news came of Burgoyne's surrender, the sprightly girl, not daring to give vent openly to her exultation, put her head up the chimney and gave a shout for Gates.

CHAPTER X.

BRITISH PRISONS IN NEW YORK.

SOME notice of the British prisons in New York will be here appropriate; the more so, as no account of them is given in any general history.

At the battle of Long Island twelve hundred Americans fell into the hands of the enemy. These prisoners were distributed into the churches of Brooklyn, Flatbush, Flatlands, and New Utrecht, while some were put on board the British shipping in Gravesend Bay. Here the sick and wounded suffered much from neglect of cleanliness, breathing an infected air, and want of medical attendance. Ten days after the battle, Dr. Richard Bailey, of New York, a loyalist, was appointed to the charge of them. He was assisted by Dr. Silas Holmes, of Norwich, a prisoner. Dr. Bailey procured a sack-bed, sheet and blanket for each patient, put them into the adjacent barns, and permitted them to visit the neighboring houses to buy milk and other refreshments. When the British occupied New York, the prisoners were removed thither, and placed in the city prisons. The tide of war was now turned in favor of the royalists. The action at White Plains, and the capture of Fort Washington, combined with the defeat at

Brooklyn, placed in their power upwards of four thousand men. If to these we add the private citizens who were arrested for political considerations in the vicinity of New York and on Long Island, we may safely conclude that the British commander had at least five thousand souls to provide for.

The sudden influx of so many prisoners, the recent capture of the city, and the unforeseen conflagration of a fourth part of it, threw the commandant's affairs into such confusion, that the captives must of necessity have suffered much from want of food and other comforts. To these privations were superadded the wanton cruelty of Capt. Cunningham, the Provost-marshal, and his deputies, and the criminal negligence of Sir William Howe. The ordinary places of confinement were totally inadequate to contain so vast a number of prisoners. Accordingly the Sugar House, the North and Middle Dutch Churches, the Brick Church, King's (now Columbia) College, the New Bridewell, the Old City Hall, and the New Jail, were appropriated to their use.

Till within a few years the Sugar House stood in Liberty street, south of the Middle Dutch Church; a dark, stone building, with small, deep, port-hole looking windows, rising tier above tier, exhibiting a dungeon-like aspect. It was five stories high, and each story was divided into two dreary apartments. On the stones and bricks in the walls were to be seen initials and dates, as if done with a prisoner's penknife or nail. There was a strong, jail-like door opening on Liberty street, and another on the south-east, descending into a dismal cellar, also used as a prison. There was a walk nearly broad enough for a cart to travel around it, where, night and day, two British or Hessian guards walked their weary rounds. The yard was surrounded by a close board fence, nine feet high. " In the suffocating heat of summer," says Dunlap, " I saw every narrow aperture of those stone walls filled with human heads, face above face, seeking a portion of the external air." While the jail-fever was raging, in the summer of 1777, the prisoners were let out, in companies of twenty, for half an hour at a time, to breathe fresh air; and inside they were so crowded, that they divided their numbers into squads of six each. Number one stood for ten minutes as close to the window as they could crowd, and then number two took their places; and so on. Seats there were none; and their beds were but straw infested with vermin. For many weeks the dead-cart visited the prison every morning, into which eight to twelve corpses were flung and piled up, like sticks of wood, and thrown into ditches in the outskirts of the city.

The North Dutch Church, corner of William and Fulton streets, was made to hold eight hundred prisoners; its pews were ripped out, and used probably for fuel; its mahogany pulpit was sent to London, and put in a chapel there, and a floor was laid across from one gallery to the other. Bayonet marks are yet discernible on the pillars; and those walls that had reverberated with the praises of the Most High, then resounded with curses and blasphemy. In the Middle Dutch Church, says Pintard, " the prisoners taken on Long Island, and at Fort Washington, sick, wounded and well, were all indiscriminately huddled together, by hundreds and thousands. Large numbers of them died by disease—and some were undoubtedly poisoned by inhuman attendants, for the sake of their watches or silver buckles. Soon afterwards it was turned into a riding-school to train dragoon horses. The floor was taken up and the ground covered with tan bark. A pole ran across the middle for the horses to leap over. The glass was taken from the windows, and the shutters unhung."

A prisoner taken at Fort Washington, who was confined in the New Bridewell, says—"On Thursday morning they brought us a little provision, which was the first morsel we got to eat or drink after eating our breakfast on Saturday morning. We never drew as much provision for three days' allowance as a man would eat at a common meal. I was there three months during that inclement season, and never saw any fire except what was in the lamps of the city. There was not a pane of glass in the windows, and nothing to keep out the cold except the iron grates." The old City Hall stood on the site of the present Custom House, and was converted into a guard-house, for the main guard of the city. It had dungeons and prisons below; and a court room on the second floor, where the refugee clergy preached during the latter part of the war. At first, civil offenders were confined here; but subsequently whaleboatmen and robbers.

The New Jail, or " the Provost, now the Hall of Records, was destined for the more notorious rebels, civil, naval and military. An admission into this modern bastile was enough to appal the stoutest-heart. On the right hand of the main door was Capt. Cunningham's quarters; opposite to which was the guard-room. At the entrance door two sentinels were always posted, by day and night. Two more on the first and second barricades, which were grated, barred and chained also at the rear door, and on the platform at the grated door; at the foot of the second flight of steps leading to the rooms and cells in the second and third stories. When a prisoner, escorted by soldiers, was led into the hall, the whole guard was paraded, and he was delivered over with all formality to Capt. Cunningham or his deputy, and questioned as to his name, rank, age, &c., all of which were entered in a record book. What with the bristling of arms, unbolting of bars and locks, clanking of enormous iron chains, and a vestibule dark as Erebus, the unfortunate captive might well shrink as he crossed the threshold of that door which possibly closed on him for life. The northeast chamber, turning to the left, on the second floor, was appropriated to officers, and characters of superior rank, and was called Congress Hall. In the day time the packs and blankets of the prisoners were suspended around the walls—every precaution being used to keep the rooms ventilated, and the walls and floors clean, to prevent jail fever; and as the Provost was generally crowded with American prisoners or British culprits of every description, it is really wonderful that infection never broke out within its walls. In this gloomy abode were incarcerated at different periods, many American officers and citizens of distinction, awaiting, with sickening hope, the protracted period of their liberation. Could these dumb walls speak, what scenes might they not disclose! The Captain and his deputies were enabled to fare sumptuously, by dint of curtailing the prisoners' rations, exchanging good for bad provisions, and other embezzlements."

CHAPTER X.

Many of the American officers who were prisoners in New York, were paroled in January, 1777, and billeted on the inhabitants of Flatbush, New Lots, Flatlands and Gravesend on Long Island, Congress agreeing to pay two dollars a week for their board. The British soldiers also, who in summer encamped in tents, when the army retired, on the approach of winter, from active service in the field, were usually distributed in the dwellings of the inhabitants within the British lines. An officer first visited each house, and in proportion to its size, chalked on the door the number of soldiers it must receive. The first notice the hostess received of this intrusion was the address: " Madam, I have come to take a billet on your house." Their hammocks, made of boards stripped from some fence or outbuilding, were ranged around the room, one tier above another. The best houses were reserved as quarters for the officers. In this way American women were forced into the society of British officers, and in order to conciliate their good will and protection, would invite them to tea, and show them other civilities. Some of them thus obtained influence which they used to alleviate the hardships suffered by their countrymen.

Col. Graydon, a prisoner taken at Fort Washington, thus describes the living at Flatbush, where he was billeted on a Dutch family : " Though we were in general civilly enough received, it cannot be supposed we were very welcome to our Low Dutch hosts, whose habits were extremely parsimonious and whose winter provision was barely sufficient for themselves Had they been sure of receiving the two dollars a week, it might have reconciled them. They were, however, a people who seemed thoroughly disposed to submit to any power that might impose upon them: and whatever might have been their propensities at an earlier stage of the contest, they were now the loyal subjects of His Majesty George III. Their houses and beds we found clean; but their living extremely poor. A sorry wash made of a sprinkling of bohea, and the darkest sugar on the verge of fluidity, with half-baked bread, (fuel being among the scarcest articles at Flatbush,) and a little stale butter, constituted our breakfast. At our first coming, a small piece of pickled beef was occasionally boiled for dinner, but to the beef, which was soon consumed, there succeeded *clippers* or clams; and our unvaried supper was *supon* or mush, sometimes with skimmed milk, but more generally with buttermilk blended with molasses, which was kept for weeks in a churn, as swill is saved for hogs. I found it, however, after a little use, very eatable; and supper soon became my best meal."

The mother of Col. Graydon came from Pennsylvania and waited on Sir William Howe, to solicit permission for her son to go home on his parole. The General, influenced by sympathy for her feelings, after some hesitation gave the desired permission. The captives who remained having been kept in the dark as to the state of public affairs, one of them furnished Graydon with a kind of cypher by which intelligence could be conveyed to him. For instance, a lady named was to signify the American army; if that was prosperous, the fact was to be indicated by announcing her health and charming looks; and there was a scale in the key by which intelligence might be graduated. Others of the prisoners owed their release to female influence. Dr. Z. Platt, imprisoned in New York in 1777, was restored to liberty through the application of his daughter to Sir Henry Clinton; and in many instances clothing and provisions were brought to the captives by their anxious female relatives.

The women of New York did their part bravely in relieving the wants and sufferings of the prisoners. The case of the Quakeress, Deborah Franklin, who was banished from the city by the British commandant for her liberality in thus doing, was but one among many. The services of Mrs. Whetten are noticed in some of the public journals, and were acknowledged after the war with gratitude by Washington himself. The British were sometimes quartered upon her, and she was required to board many of the prisoners, who had reason to remember her generous kindness. She made it her daily business to prepare food for the American soldiers, and sent it regularly to the prisons, as well as mush to the hospitals, using thus all the Indian meal she could obtain. She went sometimes with her daughters to see the prisoners, and encouraged them by cheerful conversation. Occasionally they visited the Provost, where the marshal, Cunningham, would now and then show his displeasure by kicking over the baskets of food or vessels of soup they brought, and beating the unfortunate prisoners with his keys. Sometimes he received them with a surly courtesy, making himself amends, however, by indulging in boastful language. He told a gentleman that these ladies were the " worst rebels in New York." They continually provided not only provisions but clothes for the use of the captive soldiers, not heeding the

surliness of their jailors, or the risk of indignity to themselves
Sometimes they went to a guard-house close to the old Sugar-
house, and the sergeant permitted them to sit at the window
while the prisoners came into the yard below and talked with
them. Not satisfied with such daily ministrations, Mrs.
Whetten often had provisions conveyed to the unfortunate
inmates of the prison ships. A boat was usually sent to receive the supplies.

The wife of a prisoner thrown into the Provost in 1777,
came alone from Nyack to the city to visit him and bring provisions, leaving six children at home. She was detained four
months, and every day took her husband his meals, which he
shared with other prisoners. Such and other acts of kindness were continually performed by women, not only in New
York, but wherever their good offices were needed. They
visited hospitals daily, and provisions were carried from their
stores to the captive whose only means of recompense was
the blessing of those who were ready to perish. Many in the
country raised grain, gathered it, made bread, and carried it
to their relatives in prison or in the army, accompanying the
supply with exhortations never to abandon the cause of their
country.

The prisoners who had been taken, at the battle of Saratoga fared comparatively well. They were ordered to set out
for Virginia at the approach of the winter of 1778-9.
Madame de Riedesel mentions in her letters several instances
in which the republicanism of the inhabitants of the country
through which they passed put her to much inconvenience.
At one place the hostess refused to sell the royalists fresh

meat, but was softened by the offer of a paper of tea. A day or two before they reached their place of destination, their stock of provisions gave out. Coming to a house, they begged for some dinner; but all assistance was denied them, with many imprecations upon the royalists. "Seeing some maize, I begged our hostess to give me some of it to make a little bread. She replied that she needed it for her black people. 'They work for us,' she added, 'and you come to kill us.' Capt. Edmonstone offered to pay her one or two guineas for a little wheat, but she refused."

The captive army was quartered in the neighborhood of Charlottesville, Virginia—a few miles from the town. Barracks were built for them on the summit and brow of a ridge, and the surrounding land was laid out in several hundred gardens—each enclosed with a paling, and cultivated. The officers rented houses and settled their families, most of them purchasing cows and sheep, and occupying themselves in farming. Their society was sought by gentlemen residing in that portion of country; they cultivated the arts and amused themselves with literature, and the time passed not without enjoyment. The region was remarkably healthy, and the soldiers were generally quiet and contented. The Baroness was much visited, and remembered long afterwards the hospitality and kindness received on a subsequent journey northward. "The loyalists," she says, "received us with frank hospitality from political sympathy, and those of opposite principles gave us a friendly welcome, merely from habit; for in that country it would be considered a crime to behave otherwise towards strangers."

CHAPTER XI

BRITISH PRISON SHIPS—THE ILLICIT TRADE ON LONG
ISLAND SOUND—WHALEBOAT WARFARE.

THE Prison ships were intended for sailors taken on the high seas, while the landsmen were generally confined in churches and jails. The transports that brought the soldiers of Britain to Staten Island in 1776 were the first prison-ships. On board these, as they lay in Gravesend Bay, the American prisoners taken at the battle of Long Island were kept for a few weeks, till the British were in possession of New York. They were then removed thither, and the vessels were anchored in the North and East Rivers. In a year or two the prison ships were mostly moored a few rods from the Long Island shore, in a retired nook called the Wallebocht. Here, sheltered from wind and wave, lay in succession a dozen old hulks, usually two or three at a time—such as the Whitby, Good Hope, Falmouth, &c. Two were burned by the prisoners themselves, either in the extremity of despair, or the vain hope of liberty. In 1780 the Jersey was stationed in the Wallebocht. The large numbers confined in her, the great mortality among them, and the length of time she was used as a prison ship, have given such notoriety to her inglorious name, that in popular story she seems to have been the only prison ship during the whole war; while the accumulated horrors and miseries of all the others have been laid on the ill-fated Jersey alone. The number that perished was doubtless fearfully great, and needed no exaggeration.

It would be impossible to convey an idea of the sufferings of the prisoners, whether occasioned by sickness, neglect of cleanliness, or the want of wholesome food and comfortable clothing. Although hospital ships were provided to which the sick were removed, yet from the malignity of disease, despondency, or the want of good nursing and proper medical attendance, they perished by scores. It does not appear that there was any systematic plan of charity formed by the people of New York for their relief. No female ever visited those pestilential hulks to administer aid, or bestow encouragement or sympathy. All was solitary, sullen gloom, varied only by the taunts and imprecations of their unfeeling guards.

During the whole war there was more or less difficulty in exchanging prisoners, each party fearing the other would get some advantage. The captives, meanwhile, suffered, languished and died. The long detention of prisoners must be in part attributed to Congress, who were unwilling to release healthy British soldiers for emaciated Americans, mostly, too, privateersmen, and not engaged in the Continental service; for this would give the enemy permanent strength without an equivalent. Often, too, the balance was against the Americans; they had no prisoners to give in exchange; for although their privateers captured numbers of British vessels, yet their crews often enlisted in the American vessels, or were suffered to go at large.

The Jersey was originally a sixty-gun ship; but becoming unfit for sea service, she was dismantled in 1776, and lay as a store ship at New York. In 1780, when the Good Hope was burned, she was removed to the Wallebocht and used as a prison ship till the close of the war. She was then suffered to go to decay; worms destroyed her bottom, and she sank. Her ribs lay exposed at low water for more than twenty years, and are now covered by the United States Navy Yard.

The crew of this vessel consisted of a captain, two mates, a steward, cook, and a dozen sailors. There was also a guard of about twelve old invalid marines, and about thirty soldiers. Near her lay three hospital ships—the Scorpion, Strombolo and Hunter. When a prisoner was first brought on deck, his name and rank were registered, and he was searched for money and weapons, but allowed to retain his clothes and bedding. He was then ordered down into the hold, where he found perhaps a thousand human beings, generally covered with rags and filth, their faces pale with disease and emaciated with hunger and anxiety. He joined a "mess" of six persons, who every morning, at the ringing of the steward's bell, received their allowance of biscuit, peas, and beef, or pork, which was cooked in a large copper boiler. Oatmeal, flour, butter, and suet were occasionally added, but no vegetables. The food was usually deficient in quantity and quality; the biscuit mouldy and crawling with worms; the peas damaged, the butter rancid, the meal and flour often sour, the pork and beef unsavory; yet the highest prices were charged to the

King by the rapacious commissaries, who exchanged good for bad provisions, and by curtailing the rations, and other embezzlements, amassed large fortunes, at the expense of the health and life of the helpless captives.

Those who contrived to conceal a little money were enabled to procure, at exorbitant prices, such small articles as bread, sugar, tobacco, thread, needles, combs, &c., sold by an old woman, who daily approached the ship in her little boat. Every morning the prisoners brought up their bedding to be aired, washed the floors, and spent the day on deck. At sunset the cry was, " Down, rebels, down !" the hatches were fastened, and the prisoners lay down in rows to sleep, if sleep they could, amid the mingled horror of sighs and groans, of putrid air and stifling heat.

When a prisoner died, his companions sewed up the body in a blanket, (if he had one,) lowered it into a boat, and were allowed to go on shore under a guard. There they made a slight excavation in the bank, or on the shore, in which the body was hastily buried. Many of these bodies were afterwards uncovered by the action of wind or wave, and the bones lay for years whitening in the sun. In 1808, nearly twenty hogsheads were collected and deposited in one common sepulchre.

The prisoners were at first allowed the free use of the deck, till a successful attempt at escape, after which they were generally kept below, only a few being allowed to come up at a time for fresh air and exercise. They were under the watch of a guard who constantly paced the deck, yet escapes were not unfrequent. One evening, in 1777, a boat happened to be fastened to the vessel's side. Three or four prisoners quietly let themselves down into her, cast her off, and let her drift astern of the ship. They were lucky enough to get clear unperceived, and to reach the Jersey shore in safety. Their flight was soon discovered, but the darkness rendered pursuit unavailing.

There were several other instances of the kind. In 1779, at midnight, nine sea captains and two privates escaped from the Good Hope in the North River. They confined the mate, disarmed the sentinels, and hoisted out the boat, which was on deck. They had scarcely got clear when the alarm was given, and they were fired on by three ships, but not hurt. In the cold winter of 1780 fifteen prisoners escaped on the ice in the East River. Others made the attempt, but being unable to endure the cold were retaken and carried back. One was frozen to death before he reached the shore. A prisoner on board the Falmouth, having as if by accident thrown his hat overboard, begged leave to go after it in a small boat which lay alongside. A sentinel with only his side-arms on got into the boat with four of the prisoners. Having reached the hat, they secured the sentinel, and made for the Jersey shore, which they gained, though pursued by several armed boats, and fired at from the shipping.

The prisoners in the Jersey, it is said, had obtained a crowbar, which was kept concealed in the berth of a trusty officer, and used to break off port gratings in stormy nights. A number who were good swimmers thus escaped. The Rev. Thomas Andros, of Berkley, Mass., when a young man, enlisted on board an American privateer, but was soon after captured and incarcerated in the Jersey. Hence he made his escape by obtaining leave to go on shore for water, and straying away from his guard. In his wanderings to the east end of Long Island, he gratefully acknowledges the protection he received. "I came," he says in his Journal, "to a respectable dwelling-house and entered it. Among the inmates were a decent woman and a tailor. To the woman I expressed my want of something to nourish my feeble frame, telling her if she would give me a morsel, it would be a mere act of charity. She made no objection, asked no questions, but promptly furnished me with the dish of light food I desired Expressing my obligations to her, I rose to depart. But going round through another room, she met me in the front entry, placed a hat on my head, put an apple pie in my hand, and said, 'You will want this before you get through the woods.' She would not stay to hear my thanks, and I supposed she was satisfied that I had escaped from prison, and if she granted me any succor, knowing this, it might cost her family the confiscation of their estate. She did not therefore wish to ask any questions, or hear me explain who I was, in the hearing of the tailor, who might turn informer.

"Some time after, in Suffolk County, being repulsed from one dwelling, I entered another, and informed the mistress of the house of my wants. By the cheerfulness and good nature depicted in her countenance and first movements, I knew my suit was granted, and I had nothing more to say than to apprise her I was penniless. In a few moments she placed on the table a bowl of bread and milk, a dried blue fish roasted, and a mug of cider—and bade me sit down and eat. It was now growing dark, so I went but a short distance further, entered a house and begged the privilege of lodging by the fire. There was no one in the house but the man and his wife. Before it became late in the evening the man took his Bible and read a chapter. He then arose and offered up his grateful acknowledgments and supplications to God through the Mediator. I now began to think I had got into a safe and hospitable retreat. They had before made many inquiries such as indicated that they felt tenderly and took an interest in my welfare. I confessed my situation to them. All was silence. It took some time to recover themselves from a flood of tears. At last the kind woman said, 'Let us go and bake his clothes.' No sooner said than the man seized a brand of fire and threw it into the oven. The woman provided a clean suit of clothes to supply the place of mine till they had purified them by fire. The work done, a clean bed was laid down on which I was to rest, and rest I did as in a new world, for I had got rid of a swarm of cannibals that were eating me up alive! In the morning I took my leave of this dear family, with a gratitude that for fifty years has suffered no abatement. In a week after I reached Sag Harbor, where I found others of my fellow prisoners who had also escaped, and were waiting for an opportunity to cross the Sound undiscovered by British guard-boats. We happily succeeded, and reached home in October, 1781."*

* For a detailed account of the sufferings of American prisoners, the reader is referred to the History of the British prisons and prison-ships at New York, in "Revolutionary Incidents of Long Island," by Henry

CHAPTER XI.

The escape of seven prisoners in March, 1781, from a prison-ship at Charleston, furnishes another illustration. The boat was sent some distance up Cooper River for fresh water, two British soldiers acting as a guard. The prisoners rose on the guard, disarmed them, and effected their escape. After encountering many difficulties, they reached a plantation belonging to Col. Pinckney, and were received with the most cordial hospitality by Mrs. Pinckney, who, though alone—her husband not daring to venture home—and plundered of everything by the royalists, so that she depended on her negroes for daily supplies, was ready to share what she had with them. From this place they made their way to the residence of Mrs. Motte, who gave them lodging in an outhouse, where they were hid during the day, for it was thought unsafe to let the blacks on the premises know of their presence. She sent them provisions every day, and often paid them visits, accompanied by a young lady whose residence was on the north side of the Congaree River, and who was on a visit to her house. "These ladies," said one of the prisoners, "were elegant and polished in their manners; we were ragged, dirty, rough-looking fellows; yet, notwithstanding our forlorn condition, they treated us as equals, spoke to us kindly, and made us feel that we had not served our country in vain."

The young lady at length proposed to assist the men in getting across the river. She told them she and Mrs. Motte had decided that she was to go home the next day, and make

Onderdonk, Jr., Esq. The same work gives a full account of the adventures of the whaleboatmen.

arrangements to send some of her negroes to the river side on the following night with canoes to convey them across. Accordingly, on the appointed night Mrs. Motte's trusty house servant came and conducted them to the landing. Several blacks were there with canoes; they were taken over the river, and led up to the overseer's house, where a table was set out, covered with abundance of provisions. Bedclothing was also furnished, so clean and fresh, that the hardy travellers would not soil the snow-white sheets and quilts by sleeping in them, but stretched themselves before the fire. In the morning, before they had all risen, breakfast was on the table, and they were invited to take for the journey as much as they could conveniently carry. In two days more they were safely sheltered in the upper country.

The associations that had existed for many years against the use of foreign goods, and in favor of wearing homespun, instead of foreign silks and calicoes, had so discouraged their importation that the Revolution found the country almost destitute of all articles of dress and luxury. But after the line of separation had been drawn between Britain and her colonies, there existed no longer the same reasons of patriotism for abstaining, and people felt disposed to indulge their taste and vanity in the use of articles so long prohibited. Tea from China was found to be more fragrant than that prepared from sage and sassafras. Silks, calicoes, gauzes, and ribbons resumed their former place in woman's estimation, and the portraits and satires of the day show that her affections were as much set on dress as before or since.

Those within the British lines had no difficulty in procuring imported articles in exchange for the products of the soil, which were in unprecedented demand for the armies quartered by the King in our country. With those outside the lines the case was different. An occasional prize taken by some New England privateer might enliven some seaport for a day or two by the display of foreign tinsel and finery, but the supply was totally inadequate. Although it was the policy of the contending parties to prohibit any and all intercourse with their enemies, yet the calculating avarice of the trader overcame the dictates of patriotism. Accordingly, a new line of business sprung up, called the Illicit Trade, which prevailed extensively on Long Island Sound during the whole war.

Every device which the cunning of smugglers could conceive, was resorted to. Goods were bought in the city of New York, ostensibly for the purpose of retailing to the King's subjects on Long Island. These were carted to some solitary harbor on the Sound, and secretly put on board small vessels that lay there concealed. With the same secresy these goods were "run" into Connecticut, and being quietly disposed of to petty dealers, found a ready sale at large profits. The vigilance of keen-eyed smugglers was too active for the drowsy watch of government officials, who also too often connived at what they could not prevent, and shared in the profits. In 1783 a patriotic Connecticut mob seized a boat belonging to an American officer, who had engaged in the illicit trade, dragged it to the public market place, and burnt it in sight of a large concourse of spectators, who closed the bonfire with three hearty cheers.

In the Revolutionary war the American navy was merely

nominal. Its place was partially supplied by privateers and whaleboats. New York city, and Staten and Long Islands being in the enemy's possession, the partisan warfare carried on by American whaleboats against the King's subjects residing there, forms an episode in our history.

These boats were a sharp-built craft, twenty or thirty feet long, and without decks, impelled by from four to thirty-two oars. Being light, they could be borne on the shoulders and concealed in bushes along the shore. In a calm they would shoot out from their lurking places on the Jersey or Connecticut shore, intercept a coasting vessel, and by the velocity of their oars elude the pursuit of British guard-ships. They were commissioned by the States to cruize against British vessels, and were limited to high water mark; but this line on various pretexts was overpassed.

A party of "rebels" was often accustomed to cross by night from the main to Long Island, transport their light boats to some neighboring thicket, march inland, plunder a store, surprise a British outpost, or seize some distinguished loyalist; then hasten back to their boats ere the day dawned, or the alarm could be spread. Sometimes the British retaliated; as when they surprised and burned all the whaleboats in the Raritan, or carried off Gen. Silliman and other prominent whigs. One Sunday they made prisoners of a whole congregation of worshippers at Darien, leading forty men, with the pastor, into captivity. Those national and very important expeditions from Connecticut to Setauket, Lloyd's Neck, Sag Harbor, Fort St. George and Slongo—all on Long Island, were accomplished by means of whaleboats. But in time

CHAPTER XI.

their crews became freebooters, who plundered public and private property, without distinction of friend or foe, till whig and tory made common cause against them. Several bloody encounters thus ensued. After this, the system was abandoned by the States, though pursued by a few daring outlaws till the close of the war. After the war it was ascertained that some of these illicit traders had been spies in the secret service of General Washington, who often boasted that he had better intelligence of the enemy's movements on Long Island than at any other place.

The frauds and robberies growing out of this system were numerous, as might be expected. Sometimes the owner of a well-filled store on the Island would arrange with some friendly whaleboatman from the main to cross the Sound by night, march inland, and carry off his goods, which were then transported and sold in Connecticut for their mutual benefit To save appearances, reports were spread next day of an extensive robbery by rebel whaleboats, the goods were described and rewards offered! Even the State of New York, in want of clothing for her soldiers, was forced to stoop from her dignity so far as to purchase British cloth procured in a clandestine way by means of her secret agents. The State of Connecticut, too, connived for a time at this illicit traffic, till the abuses that grew out of it became too wide-spread for longer toleration, and the permission was revoked in November, 1781.

The British, also, allowed this trade when it suited their interest. In 1778, when they were in want of provisions for carrying on the war, Gov..Tryon proposed through the Rev. Mr. Buell, to give rum, sugar, tea, and whatever might please the ladies, in exchange for American beef. It is certain that the constant want of cattle and farming produce for the British army, and of silks and India goods for the people of New England, kept up a very active illicit trade during the whole war.

Ever and anon the British commandant at New York, the great entrepôt for foreign goods, issued his proclamations, and did all in his power to restrict this trade. No countryman was allowed to buy and carry out of the city any articles, unless he was known to be a loyal subject. Even then, the quantity of every article purchased must be distinctly specified in his permit, which was examined by a guard as he left the city. Stories are told of country girls who went shopping in New York, and being tempted to buy some finery not previously enumerated in their permit, were forced to leave it at the ferry, a prize to the wife or sweetheart of the ungallant guard.

All prohibited goods, when seized, were confiscated, and part given to the informer as an encouragement to watchfulness. But here, too, there was collusion. The owner of a boat laden with European and India goods would set out from the Long Island shore and allow himself to be captured by some seemingly vigilant American cruiser. The goods were then taken to New England, condemned in a court of Admiralty, sold at exorbitant prices, and the profits divided between the partners in this nefarious traffic. In this way British merchandise became so abundant, that in 1783 there were auction sales at Norwich, Connecticut, "twice a week, of a variety of European and other goods by piece or pattern."

SPECIMENS OF CONTINENTAL BILLS.

CHAPTER XII.

THE FRENCH ALLIANCE—THE MISCHIANZA—BATTLE OF
MONMOUTH—CONDITION OF THE COUNTRY.

The British ministry had expected that the war would soon be terminated by the conquest of the rebellious colonies. But the news of Burgoyne's defeat lowered their hopes, and disposed them to more conciliatory measures. Commissioners were sent to America to propose an amicable adjustment of difficulties. It was too late, however, to offer full redress of the grievances formerly complained of. Congress refused even to negotiate till the national independence should be acknowledged. The gloom that had brooded over the country was now turned into joy by the news that a treaty of alliance had been concluded with France, that power recognizing the independence of the United States. The daughter of Lord Stirling writes from Valley Forge to a friend—" We have nothing here but rejoicings ; every one looks happy, and seems proud of the share he has had in establishing the name of America as a nation." The event was publicly celebrated in various parts of the country.

This treaty, which was ratified by Congress May 4th, 1778, secured the aid of France to the United States, and was of course equivalent to a declaration of war on her part against Great Britain. Preparations were made by those two nations for the impending contest. It was determined in England immediately to evacuate Philadelphia, and concentrate the royal forces in the city and harbor of New York.

The officers of Sir William Howe, in Philadelphia, gave him a splendid entertainment as a parting compliment, just before his relinquishment of the command to Sir Henry Clinton, and his departure for England. This singular fête was called the Mischianza—an Italian word signifying a medley or mixture, applied to a series of entertainments. It was given on the 18th of May. The following description of it is abridged from one said to have been written by Maj. André:

It commenced with a grand regatta in three divisions. In the first was the Ferret galley, on board of which there were several general officers and ladies. In the centre, the Hussar galley bore Sir William and Lord Howe, Sir Henry Clinton, their suite, and many ladies. The Cornwallis galley brought up the rear—Gen. Knyphausen and suite, three British generals, and ladies being on board. On each quarter of these galleys, and forming their division, were five flat boats lined with green cloth, and filled with ladies and gentlemen. In front were three flat boats, with bands of music. Six barges rowed about each flank, to keep off the swarm of boats in the river. The galleys were dressed in colors and streamers; the ships lying at anchor were magnificently decorated; and the transport ships with colors flying, which extended in a line the whole length of the city, were crowded, as well as the wharves, with spectators. The rendezvous was at Knight's

CHAPTER XI. 131

wharf, at the northern extremity of the city. The company embarked at half-past four, the three divisions moving slowly down to the music. Arrived opposite Market wharf, at a signal all rested on their oars, and the music played " God save the King," answered by three cheers from the vessels.

The landing was at the Old Fort, a little south of the town, and in front of the building prepared for the company, a few hundred yards from the water. The regatta was gazed at from the wharves and warehouses by the uninvited population of the city. When the general's barge pushed for shore, a salute of seventeen guns was fired from his Majesty's ship Roebuck; and after an interval, seventeen from the Vigilant. The procession advanced through an avenue formed by two files of grenadiers, each supported by a line of light horse. The avenue led to a spacious lawn, lined with troops, and prepared for the exhibition of a tilt and tournament. The music, and managers with favors of white and blue ribbons in their breasts, led the way, followed by the generals and the rest of the company.

In front, the building bounded the view through a vista formed by two triumphal arches in a line with the landing place. Two pavilions, with rows of benches rising one above another, received the ladies, while the gentlemen ranged themselves on each side. On the front seat of each pavilion were seven young ladies as princesses, with Turkish habits, and wearing in their turbans the favors meant for the knights who contended. The sound of trumpets was heard in the distance; and a band of knights in ancient habits of white and red silk, mounted on gray horses caparisoned in the same colors, attended by squires on foot, herald and trumpeters, entered the lists. Lord Cathcart was chief of these knights, and appeared in honor of Miss Auchmuty. One of his esquires bore his lance, and another his shield; and two black slaves in blue and white silk, with silver clasps on their bare necks and arms, held his stirrups. The band made the circuit of the square, saluting the ladies, and then ranged themselves in a line with the pavilion in which were the ladies of their device. Their herald, after a flourish of trumpets, proclaimed a challenge; asserting the superiority of the ladies of the Blended Rose, in wit, beauty and accomplishment, and offering to prove it by deeds, according to the ancient laws of chivalry.

At the third repetition of the challenge, another herald and trumpeters advanced from the other side of the square, dressed in black and orange, and proclaimed defiance to the challengers, in the name of the knights of the Burning Mountain. Capt. Watson, the chief, appeared in honor of Miss Franks; his device—a heart with a wreath of flowers; his motto—Love and Glory. This band also rode round the lists, and drew up in front of the White Knights. The gauntlet was thrown down and lifted; the encounter took place. After the fourth encounter, the two chiefs, spurring to the centre, fought singly, till the marshal of the field rushed between, and declared that the ladies of the Blended Rose and the Burning Mountain were satisfied with the proofs of love and valor already given, and commanded their knights to desist. The bands then filed off in different directions, saluting the ladies as they approached the pavilions.

The company then passed in procession through triumphal arches built in the Tuscan order, to a garden in front of the building; and thence ascended to a spacious hall, painted in imitation of Sienna marble. In this hall and apartment adjoining, were tea and refreshments; and the knights, kneeling, received their favors from the ladies. On entering the room appropriated for the faro table, a cornucopia was seen filled with fruit and flowers; another appeared in going out, shrunk, reversed and empty. The next advance was to a ball-room painted in pale blue, pannelled with gold, with dropping festoons of flowers; the surbase pink, with drapery festooned in blue. Eighty-five mirrors, decked with flowers and ribbons, reflected the light from thirty four branches of wax lights. On the same floor were four drawing rooms with sideboards of refreshments, also decorated and lighted up. The dancing continued till ten; the windows were then thrown open, and the fireworks commenced with a magnificent bouquet of rockets.

At twelve, large folding doors, which had hitherto been concealed, were suddenly thrown open, discovering a splendid and spacious saloon, richly painted and brilliantly illuminated; the mirrors and branches decorated, as also the supper table, which was set out, according to Major André's account, with four hundred and thirty covers, and twelve hundred dishes. When supper was ended, the herald and trumpeters of the Blended Rose entered the saloon, and proclaimed the health of the king and royal family—followed by that of the knights and ladies; each toast being accompanied by a flourish of music. The company then returned to the ball-room, and the dancing continued till four o'clock.

This was the most splendid entertainment ever given by officers to their general. The next day the mirrors and lustres borrowed from the citizens were sent home, with their ornaments. The pageant of a night was over; Sir William Howe departed. The folly and extravagance displayed were apparent not only to the foes of Britain; it did not escape satire in England as well as America. It is interesting to contrast the situation of the two hostile armies at this time, and to follow the destiny of the revellers. In one month knights and army marched from the city they had occupied. Gen. Wayne writes, on the 12th of July: "Tell those Philadelphia ladies who attended Howe's assemblies and levees, that the heavenly, sweet, pretty redcoats—the accomplished gentlemen of the guards and grenadiers, have been humbled on the plains of Monmouth. The knights of the Blended Roses, and of the Burning Mount, have resigned their laurels to rebel officers, who will lay them at the feet of *those* virtuous daughters of America who cheerfully gave up ease and affluence in a city, for liberty and peace of mind in a cottage."

But the empire of beauty was not to be overthrown by political changes. The belles who had graced the fête found the reproach cast on them by indignant patriots speedily forgotten. When the Americans, on their return to the capital, gave a ball to their own and the French officers, and it was debated whether the ladies of the Mischianza should be honored with invitations, the question was soon decided by the reflection that it would be impossible to make up an agreeable company without them.

One of the commissioners sent under parliamentary authority to settle the differences between Great Britain and America—Gov. Johnstone,—employed Mrs. Ferguson, a most accomplished lady, whose husband was in the British service, to confer with Gen. Reed on the subject. He requested her to inform Gen. Reed, that if he would exert his influence to settle the dispute, "he might command ten thousand guineas and the best post in the government." Mrs. Ferguson was desirous of seeing an end put to the horrors of civil war, and when the British left the city, sent for Gen. Reed, and repeated the proposition to him. His reply has become celebrated: "I am not worth purchasing; but such as I am, the King of Great Britain is not rich enough to do it." Congress was indignant at this attempt at private bribery, and declared it incompatible with their honor to hold any communication with Johnstone.

The troops of General Washington followed the British army as it retreated towards New York, and the battle of Monmouth took place on the 28th of June. The Americans had the advantage. Gen. Clinton drew off his troops at night and proceeded rapidly. In this action Gen Lee's inadvertence endangered the American army; he was rebuked by Washington, and replied with disrespect. A court-martial suspended him from his command, which he never resumed.

At this time, and throughout the war, the country, even at a distance from the seat of actual warfare, was continually disturbed by bands of lawless marauders, who made plundering their vocation, and greatly distressed the defenceless inhabitants. During the two years following, the Cowboys infested the country between the hostile armies, their robberies abounding chiefly between Peekskill and Kingsbridge. These lurking miscreants were called Cowboys, from their stealing cattle near the lines, which they drove to the British in New York. They were mostly refugees, friendly to the royal cause, and were encouraged by the British, who found their advantage in doing so, since the whigs near the lines often retaliated on the tories, and thus strife was kept up between neighbors and acquaintances.

The Skinners were another order of banditti, and, living within the American lines, pretended affection for the whig cause, though they often proved as perfidious as cruel. It was a common remark that those who professed allegiance to the State of New York were plundered by the Cowboys, while those who avowed loyalism were sure to have their property pillaged by the Skinners. It is said, too, that they often leagued for the exchange of their goods—the Skinners pretending to capture the other robbers, and selling for their mutual benefit the articles brought from New York.

During the time that the British kept possession of New York, the adjacent country, with the whole of Staten and Long Island, was held under military rule. The leading whigs were driven away, or thrown into prison, their property in many cases being seized, and the defenceless families who remained were obliged to submit to depredation and insult. Sometimes female spirit rose successfully in opposition. The house of Mrs. Jackson, who lived on Staten Island, while her husband was a prisoner in the Provost, was for a long time the abode of British officers and soldiers. On one occasion a soldier, carrying through the house a tin pail, used for milking, was asked by her what he meant to do with it. "My master wants to bathe his feet," was the insolent reply. "Carry it instantly back," said she, authoritatively; "not for your master's master shall you touch what you have no business with!" By the exhibition of such spirit she saved herself much inconvenience. When the Americans were on the opposite shore, she was in the habit of sending them provisions from time to time. This she was obliged to do with the utmost secrecy; and many a time would she set going the mill which belonged to her husband—to allow the black man she employed to cross the water unsuspected by the watchful enemy. At one time, having a calf which she was anxious to send, she kept it concealed all day under her bed, having muzzled it to prevent its cries. She sometimes came to New York, with friends, to visit prisoners in the Provost. They were received on such occasions at Whitehall by a gentleman who accompanied them to the prison, and directed them, when they wished to give money to the captives, to drop it silently as they went past, while he would walk just behind, so as to screen them from the observation of the Provost-marshal.

Some British officers quartered themselves at the house of Mrs. Dissosway, at the west end of Staten Island. Her husband was a prisoner; but her brother, Capt. Randolph, who was in the American army, gave much annoyance to the loyalists by his frequent incursions. A tory colonel once promised her to procure the release of her husband, on condition of her prevailing upon her brother to stay quietly at home. "And if I could," she replied, with a look of scorn, and drawing up her tall figure, "think you that General Washington has but one Capt. Randolph in his army?"

When the house of Hendrick Onderdonk, at Roslyn, was robbed by British soldiers, his wife resolutely went after them about the house, telling them not to enter such a room, as her daughter slept there. They picked up some rolls of fine goods and hurried away—Mrs. Onderdonk following and pulling away now and then a piece, till they were out of the house.—When a robber grasped the throat of Martin Schenck at Manhasset, to make him say where his treasures were hid, his wife caught up a bellows, and so belabored the soldier that he let go his hold and her husband escaped. When a foraging officer at Cedar Swamp demanded of the wife of Jotham Townsend the keys of her corn-crib, and on her refusal drew his sword, she flourished an oven-peel—for she was preparing to bake bread —at the representative of the Crown, and asked, scornfully, "if he drew his sword upon women?" The disconcerted officer smiled, and was soon out of sight.

When the house of John Burtis, in Manhasset Valley, was attacked by a gang of whaleboatmen, his wife measured out and handed the charges of powder to those that fired, and the party was driven off.—Sarah Amberman, daughter of a miller at Foster's meadow, when her father was brutally attacked by two drunken British officers, in 1780, endeavored to defend him at the risk of her life, while men who witnessed the cruelty dared offer no assistance.

These few instances are but fragments of a vast store of experience; but from them we may form some idea of the condition of the whole country in those days of bloody peril, when households were broken up by war in its worst form—the conflict of brothers in arms against each other.

CHAPTER XIII.

INDIAN DEPREDATIONS—THE MASSACRES AT WYOMING AND
CHERRY VALLEY.

For a long time before the Revolution, the people in various parts of the country had been harassed by Indian depredations. During the war many of the savage tribes were incited and employed against the Americans by the policy of Great Britain. The history of this warfare, and of the sufferings of the inhabitants in these hostile incursions, by far too extensive for a single volume, may be found in different works devoted exclusively to the subject. It forms but a repetition of the same story of barbarities and massacres, of burning and devastation, of captivity and torture. In some sections, the men at work in the field were obliged to have riflemen stationed near to guard them. Some romantic incidents are related of the attacks on the Schoharie forts. The commander of one ordered the women and children who had taken refuge there, to go into the cellar. One woman refused to go; but took a spear, and stood at the pickets to assist in the defence. At another fort, a number of women stood ready at the pickets, armed with spears, pitchforks, poles, &c., to await the attack.

CHAPTER XIII.

Leaving such scenes and incidents, we will direct our attention to a tragedy, the record of which forms one of the darkest pages in history. In the summer of 1778, a considerable force of tories and Indians, under the command of Col. John Butler and an Indian chief, appeared in the beautiful valley of Wyoming on the Susquehannah. The valley had been drained of its strength to supply the continental army. The band of four hundred fighting men, who marched out to meet the enemy on the 3d of July, were totally defeated, but a few surviving the battle. The forts were then taken, the inhabitants massacred, and the settlements ravaged with fire and sword. A nearer view of the picture may be given by the mention of one or two sufferers.

On the night of the 3d of July, a Mrs. Gould, with the women who still remained in Wyoming, sought refuge in the fort. Her brother-in-law, one of the brave men who survived the massacre, was with her family, but many of the terrified inhabitants had already fled. It was quite dark when they entered the fort, and so great were the terror and confusion, that it was not perceived till they went in that a boy four years old, one of Mrs. Gould's children, was missing! The effect on the mother of this fearful discovery may be more readily imagined than described. Disregarding all remonstrances and entreaties not to expose herself to deadly peril, she set out immediately, alone and in the darkness, to search for the missing child. For more than an hour she wandered, seeking him in every spot where it was likely he could have strayed; taking her way across the plain strewed with the dead and dying of the recent battle—where the savages, eager for blood, were still lurking—fearing only for her child, lest he might be lost in the river, or might have fallen into the hands of the merciless red-men! At last the little truant was found playing with some other children on the banks of the river The young mother clasped to her bosom her recovered treasure, and hurried back with him to the place of partial safety. The night, measured through its hours by so many mourners, at length passed. In the morning all within the fort was a scene of confusion. Not a moment was to be lost, for all knew too well the mercy they must expect from their foes when they should fall into their power, and that their only hope lay in immediate flight. Preparations for this were going forward on all sides. Mrs. Gould's brother-in-law assisted her in the few and hurried arrangements she made for departure. A fine horse belonging to her husband was laden with a bed, on which she was placed with her four children, the youngest an infant.

The writer of "The Hazleton Travellers" says, describing the flight after the massacre—" What a picture for the pencil! Every pathway through the wilderness thronged with women and children, old men and boys. The able men of middle life and activity were either away in the general service, or had fallen; and in one drove of fugitives, consisting of a hundred persons, there was only one man. Let the painter stand on some eminence, commanding a view at once of the valley and the mountain. Let him paint the throng climbing the heights; hurrying on, filled with terror, despair, and sorrow. Take a single group; the affrighted mother, whose husband has fallen, an infant on her bosom, a child by

CHAPTER XIII.

the hand; an aged parent slowly climbing the rugged way behind her; hunger presses them sorely; in the rustling of every leaf they hear the approaching savage; the valley, all in flames, behind them; their cottages, their barns, their harvests, all swept in the flood of ruin."

In this pilgrimage over the rugged wilderness of the mountains, where the sick and wounded, the young and the aged, took their weary way, Mrs. Gould was moved beyond endurance by the sights of weakness and misery every where surrounding her. With the prospect of a long and perilous journey before her, she dismounted, took down the children, and with the youngest in her arms, pursued her way on foot, leaving the horse she had rode for the use of those fugitives who, from sickness or old age, were unable to accomplish a journey of any length on foot, or even to make good their escape. With a heart filled with forebodings of evil, she turned her face towards the rising sun, and with her young children resumed the toilsome march seventy miles in length; sleeping at night under the canopy of heaven, subsisting on fruits of the forest and the handful of spoiled meal which was all she had been able to secure in the way of provision for the journey. But her unfaltering trust was fixed on Him who feedeth the young ravens when they cry. Sustained and guided by His protecting care, they at length reached the Delaware in safety.

One young man who escaped after the battle, plunged into the water for safety, and swam to a small island. Here, immersed in water, protected by the bushes at the water's edge, and screened by the darkness of night, he happily cluded the search of the pursuing foe, thirsting for blood, while about twenty of his companions, who had retreated to the same spot, were all massacred within a few yards of him. He heard the dismal strokes of the tomahawk, and the groans of the dying, expecting every moment himself to become the next victim. One savage foot trod upon the very bush to which he clung. A solitary individual besides himself was left, at the departure of the savages, to weep with him over the mangled bodies of their friends.

One among the company of women who fled amid the horrors of the conflagration, with her six children, the youngest but five years of age, hastened to the water-side, where boats were prepared for their conveyance down the river. The little ones, half destitute of clothing, were ready to cry with the anguish of their bruised and lacerated feet; but the chidings of the mother, and the dread of being heard by the lurking savage, repressed their weeping. The widow's thoughts were turned towards the land of her birth, formidable as the journey was on foot, without money, clothes, or provisions Her way lay in part through Dutch settlements, where she could only by signs tell the story of her sufferings, or make known her wants. The tale of woe, however, swifter in its flight, had spread far and wide, and she received many kindnesses from the people of a strange language. Sometimes, indeed, she was refused admission into their houses; "but," she would add in her narration, "they had nice barns, with clean straw, where my children lodged very comfortably." After travelling one hundred miles by water, and nearly three

CHAPTER XII.

hundred by land, she arrived in safety at the place of her former residence in Connecticut.

Another, who had lost five brothers in the battle, made her escape with six others in a canoe, on hearing of the issue of the conflict and of the enemy's approach—and pushed off into the river, without provisions, to seek safety from the murderous tomahawk. Meeting a boat coming up with stores for Capt. Spalding's company, the sufferings of hunger were relieved; and the distressed fugitives, not knowing the fate of their friends, after a dangerous navigation of one hundred and twenty miles, landed near Harrisburg, where being hospitably received and kindly treated, they remained till Gen. Sullivan's army came to Wyoming and rendered it safe to return.

The sufferings of numberless families in the frontier settlements were hardly exceeded even by those of Wyoming. In Wawasink the women bore their share in the efforts made for defence—loading guns for their defenders, and carrying water to extinguish the flames of their dwellings. In an attack upon the house of the widow Bevier, after it was fired, the two women sought refuge in the cellar, the daughter taking with her the Dutch family Bible. When the flames approached them, they decided to deliver themselves up to the savages, and made their way through the cellar window— the mother in advance. The daughter threw her apron over her head, fearing to see her parent killed. As she feared, the widow fell a prey to the cruel tomahawk, while the Bible was wrested from Magdalen's hands and stamped in the mud, she herself being retained a prisoner. In another house— Bevier's—defended by its inmates, the powder was laid in basins on the table, and the women helped to load the pieces. till at length the old log house was fired at a point where they could not bring their guns to bear. Their situation now became most alarming, and they applied every drop of liquid in the house to check the progress of the flames; taking milk, and even swill, in their mouths, and spirting it through the cracks of the logs, in hopes thus to protract existence till relief might come. At this crisis, when death appeared inevitable, the prayers of the pious mother seemed to be answered by direct interposition from Heaven. The brother of Bevier, warned of danger by the mute appeal of the dog belonging to the house, came with another to his assistance, and the Indians and tories, not knowing, when they heard the firing of their sentry, how large a force was coming, withdrew from the house just as the flames had extended to the curtains of the bed.

In October an American expedition was undertaken against the Indians on the upper branches of the Susquehanna. In November there was a repetition of savage barbarities at Cherry Valley in New York. A part of the same force that had desolated Wyoming, invaded and utterly destroyed the settlement. The tragedy here enacted stands next in atrocity to the destruction of Wyoming. Some instances of individual suffering are recorded. One young girl was barbarously murdered by an Indian near a pile of wood, behind which she had endeavored to screen herself. Another woman fled with her children into the woods, where she lay concealed under a large log during a cold rainy day and night, hearing the yells of the savages as they triumphed in the work of death, and seeing them pass so near that one of them trailed his gun on the log that covered her. The father of Mrs. Campbell, who was in her house, attempted almost single-handed to oppose the enemy, and refused to yield till he was wounded and overpowered. The mother and her children were dragged away as prisoners, and the house was presently in flames.

Leaving the settlement a scene of desolation, the enemy took their departure the same night, with their prisoners, of whom there were between thirty and forty. That night was passed in a valley about two miles south of the fort. "A large fire was kindled, around which they were collected, with no shelter to protect them from the storm. Around them at a short distance on every side, gleamed the watchfires of the savages, who were engaged in examining and distributing the plunder. Along up the valley they caught occasional glimpses of the ruins of their dwellings, as some sudden gust of wind, or falling timber, awoke into new life the decaying flame."

Mrs. Campbell and her children were considered important captives, and while most of the other women and little ones were released, after the detention of a day or two, and permitted to return to their homes, she was informed that she and her children must accompany their captors to the land of the Senecas. On the second day after the captivity her mother was killed by her side. The aged and infirm matron was unable to keep pace with the rest; her daughter was supporting her faltering steps, and encouraging her to exert her utmost strength, when the savage struck her down with his tomahawk. Not a moment was the daughter suffered to linger, to close the dying eyes, or receive the last sigh of her murdered parent; the same Indian drove her on with his uplifted and bloody weapon, threatening her with a similar fate should her speed slacken. She carried in her arms an infant eighteen months old; and for the sake of her helpless little ones, dragged on her weary steps in spite of failing strength, at the bidding of her inhuman tormentors.

This long and melancholy journey was commenced on the 11th of November. Mrs. Campbell was taken down the valley of the Susquehanna to its junction with the Tioga, and thence into the western part of New York, to the Indian Castle, the capital of the Seneca nation, near the site of the present beautiful village of Geneva. The whole region was then an unbroken wilderness, with here and there an Indian settlement, and the journey was performed by Mrs. Campbell partly on foot, with her babe in her arms. Her other children were separated from her on the way, being given to Indians of different tribes; and on her arrival at the village, her infant also was taken from her. The helpless babe clung to her when torn away by savage hands, and she could hear its piercing cries till they were lost in the distance.

Long and dreary was the winter that followed. In one respect Mrs. Campbell was fortunate. She was placed in an Indian family, composed chiefly of females and began at once to make herself useful; thus early securing the confidence and even the admiration of these daughters of the forest. She taught them some of the arts of civilized life, and made garments not only for the family to which she belonged, but for those in the neighborhood, who sent corn and venison in return. In acknowledgment of these services, she was allowed the command of her own time, and freedom from restraint, and was permitted to abstain from her usual labors on the sacred day of rest.

The proposed exchange of Mrs. Campbell and her children for the wife and sons of Col. John Butler—the noted partisan leader—being agreed upon by Gov. Clinton and Gen. Schuyler, early in the spring Col. Campbell despatched an Indian messenger to Col. Butler at Fort Niagara. Butler came soon after to the village of Canadascago, to confer with the Indian council on the subject of giving up their prisoners. The families who adopted captives in the place of deceased relatives were always unwilling to part with them; and Butler had some difficulty in obtaining their assent. It was necessary also to procure the consent of a family in the Genesee village, with whom Mrs. Campbell was to have been placed in the spring. They were kinsfolk of the king of the Senecas; and it is no small proof of the esteem Mrs. Campbell had won from the Indians, that he volunteered to go himself, and persuade them to yield their claim. Though aged, the kindhearted savage performed the journey on foot; and returning informed Mrs. Campbell that she was free, bade her farewell, and promised to come and visit her when the war was over. In June, 1779, she was sent to Fort Niagara, but was not finally released till more than a year afterwards.

The story of Frances Slocum, captured in Wyoming, has a wide celebrity. Her father was a member of the Society of Friends, and having always been kind to the Indians, was at

N*

first left unmolested ; but when they learned that one of his sons had been in the battle, the family was marked out for vengeance. Soon after, the savages entered the house, seized Frances, then about five years old, and carried her off to the mountains. The alarm was instantly given, but the Indians eluded pursuit, and no trace of their retreat could be discovered. Nothing was heard of the captive till fifty-nine years afterwards, when an aged white woman, living with the Miami tribe of Indians in Indiana, was discovered to be the same person. She had become attached to Indian life, having been adopted as a daughter of their people, and living as a queen among them.

The atrocities committed by hostile Indians form so prominent a feature in a history of Revolutionary times, that they should not pass entirely unnoticed. The few incidents described will give some idea of what occurred in various portions of the country—north, south and west—in a thousand similar instances.

The events above noticed were the only prominent ones that took place in the northern section of the country during the latter part of 1778. Washington had proceeded with the army as far as White Plains, and late in the autumn went into winter quarters at Middlebrook, New Jersey.

CHAPTER XIV.

ATTACK ON THE SOUTH—SUBJUGATION OF GEORGIA—
SCENES IN SOUTH CAROLINA—SIEGE OF SAVANNAH—
CLOSE OF THE CAMPAIGN. OF 1779.

SHORTLY after the conclusion of the alliance with France, the French fleet, under the command of Count D'Estaing, had been sent to America. The commander was prevented from an attack on the British fleet at New York, by the difficulty of crossing the bar at the entrance of the bay. He then sailed for Newport, designing an attack on the British force stationed there, co-operating with an attempt by land, to be made at the same time by troops under the command of Generals La Fayette, Greene and Sullivan. On the 10th of August, 1778, Lord Howe's fleet appeared, and D'Estaing sailed out to engage him ; but the battle was prevented by a sudden and violent storm. The French commandant then sailed to Boston to repair the damages his vessels had sustained, and the British fleet returned to New York.

From this time the South was to be the principal field of military operations. In November, Count D'Estaing sailed with his fleet for the West Indies, designing there to attack the possessions of Great Britain. Sir Henry Clinton, on his part, despatched Col. Campbell from New York on an expedition against Georgia, the feeblest of the Southern provinces His troops landed late in December near Savannah, defeated the American commander, and obtained possession of that capital. This was the first step in the British plan of conquering Georgia and South Carolina. But little, however, had been accomplished in the last two years, towards the completion of the great enterprise of reducing the colonies to subjection.

The military operations of 1779 were not of great importance. The British were bent on vigorously prosecuting their scheme of conquest at the South. Shortly after the fall of Savannah, Gen. Prevost, with troops from East Florida, took possession of Sunbury, the only military post in the State held by Americans, and joining his forces to those of Col. Campbell, assumed the chief command of the royal army at the South. The loyalists who came along the western frontier of Carolina to join his standard, committed great devastations on their way. Gen. Lincoln, who commanded the continental forces in the southern department, sent a detachment under Gen. Ashe across the Savannah, to repress the incursions of the enemy. The surprise and defeat of this detachment by Prevost, completed the subjugation of Georgia.

The war swept with violence over this State, the country being overrun with irregular marauders after Col. Campbell took possession of Savannah. As many of the inhabitants as could retire from the storm did so, awaiting a happier time to renew the struggle. One of those who sought refuge in Florida, was Mr. Spalding, whose establishments were on the river St. John's. He had the whole Indian trade from the

Altamaha to the Apalachicola. His property, with his pursuits, was destroyed by the war, yet his heart was ever with his countrymen, and the home he prepared was the refuge of every American prisoner in Florida. Mrs. Spalding twice during the war traversed the two hundred miles between St. John's River and Savannah in an open boat, with only black servants, when the whole country was a desert, without a house to shelter her and her infant son. The first of these occasions was when she visited her father and brothers while prisoners in Savannah.

By great exertions on the part of the whigs, the American General Lincoln was enabled to recommence operations by the middle of April. Leaving Gen. Moultrie to watch the movements of Prevost, he began his march up the Savannah, intending to cross into Georgia near Augusta. Gen. Prevost on his part, attacked Moultrie and Pulaski, compelling them to retreat, and then hurried, early in May, to place himself before Charleston. His approach caused great terror and disturbance among the inhabitants. Mrs. Wilkinson, who lived at Yonge's Island, thirty miles south of Charleston, describes, in her letters, some of the scenes that occurred. She was in Charleston when news came that a large party of the enemy had landed near Beaufort. With a few friends, she went over to her father's plantation, but did not remain long; for upon receiving information that a body of British horse was within five or six miles, they crossed the river to Wadmalaw, and went for refuge to the house of her sister. A large boat-load of women and children hurrying for safety to Charleston, stayed with them a day or two, and presented a sad spectacle of the miseries brought in the train of war.

The surrounding country was waiting in a distressed condition for the coming of Gen. Lincoln, to whom the people looked for deliverance. Many painful days of suspense passed before tidings were received. All trifling discourse was laid aside—the ladies who gathered in knots talking only of political affairs. At last the joyful news was brought of the approach of Lincoln. Mrs. Wilkinson was then with her sister at an inland country-seat. They were called on by parties of the Americans, whom they always received with friendly hospitality. "The poorest soldier," says she, "who called at any time for a drink of water, I would take a pleasure in giving it to him myself; and many a dirty, ragged fellow have I attended with a bowl of water, or milk and water; they really merit everything, who will fight from principle alone; for from what I could learn, these poor creatures had nothing to protect, and seldom got their pay; yet with what alacrity will they encounter danger and hardships of every kind!"

Gen. Prevost was compelled to retire from his position on the approach of Lincoln. He proceeded to the island of St. John's, separated from the mainland by an inlet called Stono River; and leaving a division at Stono Ferry, retired with a part of his force towards Savannah. On the 2d of June, two men belonging to his army, rode up to the house occupied by the lady already mentioned, and asked many questions, saying that Col. M'Girth and his soldiers might be presently looked for, and that the inmates could expect no mercy. The family remained in a state of cruel suspense for many hours.

CHAPTER XIV.

The following morning a party of the whigs called at the gate, but did not alight. One of them in leaping a ditch, was hurt, and taken into the house for assistance; and while they were dressing his wound, a negro girl gave the alarm that the "king's people" were coming. The two men mounted their horses and escaped; the women awaited the enemy's approach. Mrs. Wilkinson wrote to a friend:

"I heard the horses of the inhuman Britons coming—the riders bellowing out the most horrid oaths and imprecations. I had no time for thought—they were up to the house—entered with drawn swords and pistols in their hands, crying "Where are those women rebels?" The moment they espied us, off went our caps, to get a paltry stone and wax pin, which kept them on our heads; at the same time uttering abusive language, and making as if they would hew us to pieces with their swords. They had several armed negroes with them, who also threatened us. They then began to plunder the house of everything they thought worth taking; our trunks were split to pieces, and each mean wretch crammed his bosom with the contents. I ventured to speak to the monster who had my clothes. I represented to him the times were such we could not replace what they had taken from us, and begged him to spare me only a suit or two: but so far was his callous heart from relenting, that casting his eyes towards my shoes, "I want them buckles," said he, and immediately knelt at my feet to take them out. While he was doing this, a brother villain bawled out, "Shares there, I say! shares!" So they divided my buckles between them. The others were employed in the same manner; they took my sister's earrings from her ears, her and Miss Samuells' buckles; demanded her ring from her finger, and, after bundling up all their booty, mounted their horses; each wretch's bosom stuffed so full, they appeared to be all afflicted with some dropsical disorder."

This outrage was followed by a visit from M'Girth's men, who treated the ladies with more civility; one of them promising to make a report at camp of the usage they had received. Yet they were not content without their share of plunder, though more polite in the manner of taking it. " While the British soldiers were talking to us, some of the silent ones withdrew, and presently laid siege to a beehive, which they soon brought to terms. The others perceiving it, cried out, 'Hand the ladies a plate of honey.' This was immediately done with officious haste, no doubt thinking they were very generous in treating us with our own. There were a few horses feeding in the pasture. They had them driven up. 'Ladies, do either of you own these horses?' 'No; they partly belong to father and Mr. Smilie!' 'Well, ladies, as they are not *your* property, we will take them.'" The aged father was visited the same day by another body of troops, who plundered the house. "After drinking all the wine, rum, &c. they could find, and inviting the negroes they had with them, who were very insolent, to do the same—they went to their horses, and would shake hands with father and mother before their departure!"

After such unwelcome visitors, it is not surprising that the unprotected women could not eat or sleep in peace. They lay in their clothes every night, alarmed by the least noise; while the days were spent in anxiety and melancholy. One morning, when Mrs. Wilkinson was coming out of her chamber, her eyes fixed on the window—for she was always on the watch—she saw something glitter through a thin part of the wood bordering the road. It proved to be the weapons of a large body of soldiers. She concluded they were British troops; and every one in the house took the alarm. "Never was there such a scene of confusion.. Sighs, complaints, wringing of hands, one running here, another there, spreading the dreadful tidings; and in a little time the negroes in the field came running up to the house with a hundred stories. Table, tea-cups—all the breakfast apparatus—were immediately huddled together and borne off; and we watched sharply to see which way the enemy took. In a minute or two we saw our avenue crowded with horsemen in uniform. Said I, 'That looks like our uniform—blue and red'—but I immediately recollected to have heard that the Hessian uniform was much like ours; so out of the house we went, into an out-house." Their excessive fright prevented the explanation attempted from being understood. While the officer was endeavoring to reassure the terrified ladies, a negro woman came up, and tapping Mrs. Wilkinson on the shoulder, whispered, "I don't like these men; one of them gave me this piece of silver for some milk; and I know our people don't have so much silver these times."

The horsemen were a party of Americans, under the command of Maj. Moore. The mistake had been mutual—the listress shown at sight of them having caused the officer in ommand to conclude himself and his men unwelcome visitors to some tory family. The discovery that they were friends changed fear into delight. Word was presently brought that a number of the enemy were carrying provisions from a plantation about two miles distant. The whigs marched to the place, and returned with seven prisoners. Two of these were of M'Girth's party, who had treated the ladies so cruelly; yet notwithstanding the injuries received, the kind heart of Mrs. Wilkinson relented at the sight of them. She expressed pity for their distress, and inquiring if they would like anything to drink, supplied them with water, holding the glass to their lips, as their hands were tied behind them. "An officer had a ball through his arm; we could find no rag to dress his wounds, everything in the house being thrown into such confusion by the plunderers; but Miss Samuells took from her neck the only remaining handkerchief the Britons had left her, and with it bound up his arm."

Their friends having left them, Mr. Yonge sent for his daughter to his own plantation. The ladies were obliged to walk three miles in the overpowering heat, the horses having been taken away; but umbrellas were sent for them, and they were attended by two of Mr. Yonge's negro men armed with clubs. While crossing a place called the Sands, the blacks captured and wounded a negro belonging to the loyalists, who came out of the woods. Mrs. Wilkinson interfered to save his life. They arrived safe at their father's, whence they were driven ere long by another alarm. This time their flight was in darkness, through bogs and woods, stumbling against the stumps or each other. In their new abode they had more security. Parties of friends were out continually, keeping the enemy quiet; and sometimes in the night soldiers would ride up, and bid the negroes tell the ladies they might sleep soundly, for they were to maintain a patrol during the night.

At length the arrival of Gen. Lincoln was announced; and he was joyfully welcomed by the inmates of the house That night two or three hundred men were quartered on the plantation—some of the officers sleeping in the hall. They refused to have their beds made. "Beds were not for soldiers; the floor or the earth served them as well as anywhere else." At daybreak they moved to camp.

Gen. Lincoln, with Col. Pickens, attacked the division at Stono Ferry on the 20th June, but was repulsed with loss. The British shortly after established a post at Beaufort, and the main body of the army retired to Savannah; the hot and sickly season preventing further action on either side for some months.

An incident that occurred at this time illustrates the character of some of the American women, as well as the condition of the country. The residence of Robert Gibbes on Stono River, upon John's Island, was known as the seat of hospitality and elegant taste. The rumor of its luxurious living probably attracted attention, and a battalion of British and Hessians, determined to quarter themselves in so desirable a spot, arrived at the landing at the dead of night, and marching up in silence, surrounded the house. The day had not dawned, when an aged and faithful servant tapped softly at the door of Mrs. Gibbes' apartment. The whisper—"Mistress, the redcoats are all around the house," was the first intimation given of their danger. Her preparations were instantly commenced to receive the intruders

Having dressed herself quickly, she went up stairs, waked several ladies who were guests in the house, and requested them to rise and dress with all possible haste. In the mean time the domestics were directed to prepare the children, of whom, with her own eight, and those under her care, there were sixteen. These were speedily dressed and seated in the spacious hall. Mrs. Gibbes then assisted her husband, who was a cripple, to rise and dress, and had him placed in his rolling chair. All these arrangements were made so silently that the enemy had no idea any one was awake within the house. The object of Mrs. Gibbes was to prevent violence by showing them that the mansion was inhabited only by those who were unable to defend themselves. When the door was thrown open, and the stately form of the invalid was seen, surrounded by women and children, they drew back, startled into an involuntary expression of respect. The officers took immediate possession of the house, leaving the premises to their men, and extending no protection against pillage. The soldiers roved at their pleasure about the plantation, helping themselves to whatever they chose; breaking into the wine-room, drinking to intoxication, and seizing and carrying off the negroes. A large portion of the plate was saved by the prudent care of a faithful servant, who secretly buried it. Within the house the energy and self-possession of Mrs. Gibbes still protected her family. Maintaining her place as mistress of her household, and presiding at her table, she treated her uninvited guests with a dignified courtesy that ensured civility while it prevented presumptuous familiarity.

When the news reached Charleston that the British had

encamped on this plantation, the authorities in that city despatched two galleys to dislodge them. These vessels ascended the river in the night, and arriving opposite, opened a heavy fire upon the invaders' encampment. As soon as the firing began, Mr. Gibbes proposed to his wife that they should take the children and seek a place of greater safety. Their horses being in the enemy's hands, they had no means of conveyance; but Mrs. Gibbes set off to walk with the children to an adjoining plantation in the interior. A drizzling rain was falling, and the weather was extremely chilly; the fire was incessant from the American guns, and sent, in order to avoid the house, in a direction which was in a range with the course of the fugitives. The shot, falling around them, cut the bushes, and struck the trees on every side. Exposed each moment to this imminent danger, they continued their flight with as much haste as possible for about a mile, till beyond reach of the shot.

Having reached the houses occupied by the negro laborers on the plantation, they stopped for a few moments to rest. Mrs. Gibbes, wet, chilled, and exhausted by fatigue and mental anxiety, felt her strength fail, and was obliged to wrap herself in a blanket and lie down upon one of the beds. It was then that, on reviewing the group to ascertain if all had escaped uninjured, it was found that a little boy, in the hurry and terror of their flight, had been forgotten and left behind! What was to be done? The servants refused to risk their lives by returning for him. The roar of the distant guns was still heard; the chilly rain was falling, and the darkness was profound. In this extremity Mary Anna, the eldest daughter, only thirteen years of age, determined to venture back alone Hastening along the path, she reached the house, still in the possession of the enemy; entreated permission from the sentinel to enter, and searching anxiously, found the child in a room in the third story. Lifting him joyfully in her arms she carried him down, and fled with him to the spot where her anxious parents were awaiting her return. The shot flew thickly around her, frequently throwing up the earth in her way; but protected by the Providence that watches over innocence, she joined the rest of the family in safety.

The anniversary of the alliance with France was celebrated by an entertainment given in the camp near Middlebrook, New Jersey. On this festive occasion Mrs. Washington, Mrs. Greene and Mrs. Knox, with the wives of several officers, were present; and ladies and gentlemen from a large circuit around the camp, attended the celebration. It was opened by a discharge of cannon, and dinner was prepared in a building used for an academy. There was dancing in the evening, and a grand display of fire-works. The ball was opened by General Washington. As this was a festival given by men who had not enriched themselves by the war, the illuminations were on a cheap scale, being entirely of their own manufacture; the seats were adorned with no armorial blazonry, but were the work of native, and rather unskilful artizans. " Instead of knights of different orders, such as pageants like the Mischianza could boast, there were but hardy soldiers; happy, however, in the consciousness that they had contributed to bring about the auspicious event they had met to celebrate "

Among the lively sallies of the belles of this entertainment, one is recorded, that caused no inconsiderable amusement A young lady, when asked if the roaring of the British lion in his late speech had not somewhat depressed the spirit of the dance—replied: " No, it should rather enliven it; for I have heard that such animals always increase their howlings when frightened."

During this year the forces of Sir Henry Clinton were employed at the north in various incursions from New York, for the purpose of ravaging the coasts and laying waste the country. The object was to impoverish and distress it. An expedition was sent to Virginia; Gov. Tryon plundered New Haven, Connecticut, and wantonly burned other towns in that State. Their inhabitants were treated with great cruelty. The Americans on their part accomplished little, with the exception of Gen. Wayne's brilliant exploit—the recapture of Stony Point, and an expedition under Gen. Sullivan against the Six Nations of Indians. Sullivan chastised their depredations upon the border settlements by laying waste the Indian country to the Genessee River, and destroying their fields and villages. Some of the tribes abandoned the country on his approach, and fled within command of the British forts in Canada, promiscuously settling there. They frequently invaded the frontier settlements, burning and murdering, and carrying off prisoners.

Great difficulties, meanwhile, had been growing out of the rapid depreciation of the Continental currency, or the bills of credit issued by Congress. A dollar in specie was frequently exchanged for forty, or even eighty, in bills. The common necessaries of life were enormously high; four month's pay of a soldier, it was said, would hardly procure his family a 1 ishel of wheat. The bill of a party of travellers in Pennsylvania, after six weeks' lodging, amounted to thirty-two thousand dollars in paper money. The daughter of Dr. Franklin wrote to him that she had to pay two hundred pounds for a winter cloak and hat, and gauze was fifty dollars a yard. The time came when her domestics were obliged to take two baskets to market—one empty to contain the provisions they purchased, the other full of continental money to pay for them. Yet in spite of the continued rise of prices, she says in January 1779, " there never was so much dressing and pleasure going on in the capital."

The Count D'Estaing returned with his fleet from the West Indies, and in concert with the troops of Gen. Lincoln, proceeded early in September to the siege of Savannah. Marion was at this siege, which continued a month. The celebrated Count Pulaski also was with the Americans. On one occasion, when the dragoons commanded by him were ordered to charge a party of British approaching the camp, that nobleman, who was a splendid horseman, was seen riding up and down the lines on his black charger, chapeau in hand, exclaiming now and then, in his imperfect English, "I am sorry for your country! I am sorry for your country!" He fell in the assault upon the city on the 9th of October. The Americans were driven back, and the enterprise was abandoned. The French fleet shortly after departed from the coast, and Gen. Lincoln retreated into South Carolina.

A cloud of despondency hung over the close of this year It was true that Great Britain was threatened by a combination of power, Spain having declared war against her; but her resources seemed to increase with the demand on them. In the United States the flattering hopes inspired by the alliance with France had not been realized. The continental army reduced in numbers and wretchedly clothed—the treasury empty—the paper currency rapidly diminishing in value—distress was brought on all classes, and the prospect seemed more than ever dark and discouraging. It needed all the prudence and the exertions of General Washington to keep the army from dissolution.

CHAPTER XV.

CAMPAIGN OF 1780—SURRENDER OF CHARLESTON—CONQUEST OF SOUTH CAROLINA—FIRST OUTBREAK OF RENEWED RESISTANCE.

THE successful defence of Fort Moultrie had secured for South Carolina a long exemption from the horrors of civil war; but she was now to become the most important theatre of operations. Sir Henry Clinton planned the campaign of 1780 on an extensive scale. In this transfer of the scene of action, military operations were nearly suspended at the North. Late in December, 1779, Gen. Clinton sailed with the bulk of his army from New York, arrived in about a month in Georgia, and on the 10th of February, quitted Savannah for the siege of Charleston, then defended by Gen. Lincoln.

The islands south of the city were captured, the fleet of Admiral Arbuthnot was anchored in the Charleston harbor, and on the 9th of April, the besiegers opened their batteries. The American militia, for the purpose of succoring the city, had assembled a force commanded br Gen. Huger, at Monk's Corner, on the upper part of Cooper river. Gen. Clinton sent a detachment, April 14th, which surprised and dispersed them—a number of the mounted militia escaping with the loss of their horses. The British overran the country, often venturing beyond their lines, when the inhabitants suffered much from their depredations. An anecdote is related of Mrs. Izard, who resided near Dorchester, within the range of their excursions. Her husband, who was aid to the commanding officer of the Light troops, was at home, when the alarm was suddenly given by the appearance of a party of British soldiers. He hastily concealed himself in a clothes-press, while his wife awaited the entrance of his enemies. A search proving unsuccessful, the soldiers threatened to fire the house; they robbed his wardrobe, and several of the marauders arrayed themselves in his best coats; valuable articles were seized in the presence of the lady, and an attempt was even made to force her rings from her fingers. Yet she betrayed no apprehension, knowing that her husband's safety depended on her self-possession. No sooner were the plunderers gone, than Mr. Izard made his escape, and quickly crossing the Ashley, gave notice to the Americans on the other side of the river of the proximity of the enemy. The British soldiers were intercepted by a body of cavalry that had pushed across Bacon's bridge, and so completely routed, that but a few of their number returned within their lines to relate the disaster.

Before this time, much difficulty having arisen from the want of ammunition, Gov. Rutledge had sent a supply from Charleston to the regiments throughout the State, to be in readiness for any disturbances that might arise. Many of these supplies were secured by the patriots in the back country, by secreting them in hollow trees and the like hiding-places. The wife of Col. Thomas, of Spartanburg district, preserved a portion stored in her house, by defending it, with the aid of two young men, against the assault of a party of tories. When the loyalists came to secure some in the charge of Mrs. Bratton, she was informed of their approach, and immediately laid a train of powder from the depôt to the spot where she stood. When the detachment came in sight, she set fire to the train and blew it up. The wife of Maj. Otterson, who lived on Tyger river, and chanced to know where a barrel of gunpowder was concealed in the woods, also prepared a train and blew it up, on hearing that a party of loyalists were coming for the treasure.

The whole country sympathized in the suffering and apprehension endured within the beleagured city. The son of Capt. Wade, who was at the time only five years old, was then with his grandmother, Mrs. Martin, in one of the western districts. He recollects walking in the piazza on a calm evening, when a light breeze blew from the east, and the sound of heavy cannon was distinctly heard in that direction. As report after report, which they knew must be from the city, reached their ears, the agitation of Mrs. Martin increased. She knew not what evils might be announced; she knew not but the sound might be the knell of her sons, three of whom were then in Charleston. Their wives were with her, and partook of the same heart-chilling fears. . They stood still for a few minutes, each wrapped in her own painful and silent reflections, till the mother at length, lifting up her hands and eyes, exclaimed fervently—" Thank Heaven, they are the children of the Republic!"

Charleston surrendered on the 12th of May, and Gen. Lincoln and the American army became prisoners of war This success seemed to insure the recovery of the southern section of the Union, and it was followed up by vigorous movements. The stronghold of Ninety-Six was taken, with Georgetown; and posts were established at different points throughout the State, which now lay at the mercy of the conqueror. Severe measures were adopted to overawe the inhabitants, and secure a return to their allegiance.

A body of four hundred militia, under the command of Col. Buford, retreating towards North Carolina, was pursued by Col. Tarleton, overtaken at the Waxhaws, and inhumanly cut to pieces, even while the men were entreating quarter This bloody slaughter was an earnest of what those who ventured resistance might expect. For some weeks all military opposition ceased; and it was the boast of Sir Henry Clinton that here, at least, the American Revolution was ended. A proclamation was issued, denouncing vengeance on all who should dare appear in arms, save under the royal authority, and offering pardon to those who would accept British protection by enrolling their names as loyal subjects of King George. The great body of the people, believing resistance unavailing, took the offered protection. Those in whose breasts the love of liberty was unconquerable, sought refuge in North Carolina. Sir Henry Clinton set sail early in June for New York, leaving Lord Cornwallis to command the army and re-establish the royal government.

But the spirit of a gallant people, brought for a season under subjection by the arm of power, was not extinct. A few resolute spirits, scattered over the country, were ready to seize the earliest opportunity of resistance. The first movement towards an outbreak occurred in Chester District. An aged patriot, named John Gaston, who resided on Fishing Creek, not far from Catawba River, had nine sons, whom he had brought up in the love of political freedom. He had been in the habit of sending one of them weekly to Camden, a distance of nearly fifty miles, for the only newspaper published in the State—" The South Carolina and American General Gazette." His sons and his nephews often met at his house to speak together of the aspect of affairs, and consult what steps were to be taken. While they were assembled one day, a messenger brought intelligence of the slaughter of Buford's men by Tarleton's cavalry. At this news, the young men rose with one accord, grasped each other by the hand, and voluntarily pledged themselves to suffer death rather than submit to the invader. This spontaneous vow was confirmed by a solemn oath, and thenceforward they continued in arms.

The wounded had been carried to Waxhaw Church as a hospital. The two daughters of Justice Gaston lost no time in repairing thither, and beheld a scene of misery. The floor was strewed with the wounded and dying American soldiers, suffering for want of aid; for men dared not come to minister to their wants. It was the part of woman to bring relief to the helpless and perishing. Day and night they were busied in aiding the surgeon to dress their wounds, and in preparing food for those who needed it; nor did they regard fatigue or exposure, going from place to place about the neighborhood to procure such articles as were desirable to alleviate the pain or add to the comfort of those to whom they ministered.

Rocky Mount had been selected by the British as a stronghold, and a body of the royal forces was there stationed. Handbills were then circulated, notifying the inhabitants of the country, that they were required to assemble at an old field, where Beckhamville now stands, to give in their names as loyal subjects, and receive protection. After this proclamation was issued, Col. Houseman, the commander of the post at Rocky Mount, was seen with an escort wending his way to the residence of Justice Gaston. He was met on the road by the old man, who civilly invited him into the house. The subject of his errand was presently introduced, and the Justice took the opportunity to animadvert, with all the warmth of his feelings, upon the recent horrible butchery, and the course pursued by the British government towards the American Colonies, which had driven them into the assertion of their independence. In despair of bringing to submission so strenuous an advocate of freedom, Col. Houseman at last left the house; but presently returning, he again urged the matter. He had learned, he said, from some of His Majesty's faithful subjects about Rocky Mount, that Gaston's influence would control the whole country; he observed that resistance was useless, and that true patriotism should induce the Justice to reconsider his determination, and by his example persuade his sons and numerous connections to submit to lawful authority, and join the assembly on the morrow at the old field. To these persuasions the old man gave only the stern reply—" Never!"

No sooner had Houseman departed, than the aged patriot took further steps. He immediately despatched runners to various places in the neighborhood, requiring the people to meet that night at his house. The summons was obeyed. Before midnight thirty-three men of active and powerful frames—men trained and used to the chase—were assembled. They had been collected by Capt. John McClure, and were under his command. Clad in their hunting-shirts and moccasins, with their wool hats and deer-skin caps, the otter-skin shot-bag and the butcher's knife by their sides, and armed with the rifle, they were ready for any enterprise in the cause of liberty. Early in the morning they paraded before the door of Justice Gaston. He came forth, and in compliance with the custom of that day, brought with him a large case bottle. Commencing with the officers, he gave each a hearty shake of the hand, and then presented the bottle. The men then took their course noiselessly along the old Indian trail down Fishing Creek, to the field, where many of the people were already gathered. Their sudden onset took by surprise the promiscuous assemblage, about two hundred in number, and the enemy was defeated.

Two more youths—William Stroud and Joseph Wade—who had enrolled their names with the British, at the beginning of the fight threw themselves on their faces upon the ground. But when McClure's party took possession, they rose from among the dead, and joined the ranks of their countrymen. Both were afterwards so unfortunate as to be captured by the royalists, who showed no mercy to those found in arms after having taken protection. Stroud was hung by the roadside, a placard forbidding his burial being fastened to the body, and Wade, it is said, received a thousand lashes.

This encounter was the first effort to breast the storm after the suspension of military opposition; the opening wedge to the recovery of South Carolina. Before the evening of that day, Justice Gaston was informed of the success of the enterprise, and judging wisely that his own safety depended on his immediate departure, his horse was presently at the door, with holster and pistols at the pommel of the saddle. The shot-bag at the old man's side was well supplied with ammunition, and his rifle, doubly charged, lay across the horse before him. Bestowing his parting blessing on his wife and grandchildren, he left home with his young son, Joseph, who was armed and mounted on another horse. On his way, he made a visit to Wazhaw church, where his daughters were still occupied with their labor of kindness, to carry the news of what " the boys," as he called them, had done. He then pursued his way till he could consider himself beyond the danger of pursuit.

Loud and long were the curses of Houseman levelled against him. The arch rebel, he declared, must be taken, dead or alive; and the King's loyal subjects were called upon to volunteer in the exploit of capturing and bringing to Rocky Mount a hoary headed-man, eighty years of age. Before the sun rose, about twenty redcoats were fording Rocky Creek, and wending their way towards Gaston's house. Mrs. Gaston and her little granddaughter, providentially advised of their approach, had quitted the house. Their place of concealment was so near, that they could distinctly hear the frightful oaths of the disappointed soldiers, and could see the redcoats passing to and fro through the yard. The aged matron, clasping her grandchild's little hands between her own, knelt upon the ground, and in that glen, sheltered by bushes, poured out her petition not only for her husband and children, but for the liberty of her country and its deliverance from evil and bloodthirsty men, who had not the fear of their Creator before their eyes. In the fervor of her supplication she prayed aloud. Her granddaughter, in describing the scene, said she might have been heard as far as the house, and it was fortunate that the soldiers did not discover her.

One of her grandsons, who was employed at work not far from the spot, heard the noise of the soldiers, and ascended a steep bluff within a short distance of the house, where he was concealed from view by the thick foliage. He heard the heavy strokes of their broadswords on the chair usually occupied by the Justice, with the wishes that he were in it to receive the cleaving blows. The house was plundered of everything and the stock carried off. The only article saved was the Family Bible, which Mrs. Gaston had taken with her in her flight. It is still kept in the family.

CHAPTER XVI.

A SCOTCH IRISH SETTLEMENT—RESULT OF MARTIN'S PREACHING—BATTLE AT MOBLEY'S MEETING-HOUSE.

It will be interesting to take a glimpse into what passed at this time in a quiet little settlement on Rocky Creek, another branch of the Catawba River. This settlement was composed of a congregation of recent emigrants from the North of Ireland—commonly called Scotch Irish. They had come to America about the year 1773, accompanied by their pastor the Rev. William Martin. Bounty lands had been bestowed by the government as inducements to emigration, and those who received such warrants, on their arrival took care to fix their location as near as possible to a central point, where it was their intention to build a meeting-house. Here, in the summer of 1773, the pious Covenanters might be seen from day to day, felling trees and clearing a space of ground, on which they reared a large log church, many of them living in tents at home, till a place was provided in which they could assemble for religious service.

A number of log cabins soon rose in the neighborhood, each with a patch of ground in which Indian corn was planted. The Irish emigrants were ignorant of the manner of cultivating this grain; but the first settlers, or "country-borns" were ready to offer assistance, and took pains to instruct them The wants of small families were supplied with small crops, for corn was then only used for making bread, the woods affording abundant supplies of grass, cane and wild pea vines to serve their horses and cattle for provender the year round. The streams abounded in shad and various other fish in their season, and the trusty rifle that hung on the rack over the door, was never brought back without having performed its duty in slaying the deer, or whatever small game might be sought in the forest. Often have the old men who lived at that day spoken of the abundance that prevailed; a good hunter, when he chose, making five dollars a day in deer skins and hams, while, if generous, he might give away the remainder of venison to the poor. The hams and skins were sent to Charleston and exchanged for powder, lead, and other necessary articles. The wealth of these primitive planters consisted in stock, their labors in tilling the earth, felling the woods and fencing their fields, while they were disturbed by none of the wants or cares created by a more advanced state of civilization. Such was the condition of the Covenanters who had left their native Ireland for the religious liberty found in the wilds. During seven years after their settlement in the woods, they enjoyed a life in which nothing of earthly comfort was wanting. Every Sabbath morning the parents, in their Sunday clothes, with their neatly-dressed and well-behaved little ones, might be seen at the log meeting-house; their pocket Bibles containing the old Psalms in their hands Turning over the leaves, they would follow the preacher in all the passages of Scripture cited by him, as he commented on his text. Their simple, trustful piety caused the wilderness to rejoice.

But this happiness could not be lasting. The rumor of war which had gone over the land, was heard even in this remote section, and these refugees who had found peace could not but sympathize with their oppressed brethren. Some, it is true, from the vicinity, had been out in what was called "the Snow Campaign,"—an expedition undertaken towards the close of 1775 against the fierce Cherokee Indians, and certain loyalists in the upper districts; some had been present at the attack on Sullivan's Island in 1776, and brought a report to those remaining at home. Yet, so far, this pleasant neighborhood had been spared; its families were unmolested, and the pure ordinances of the gospel were regularly administered, with none to make them afraid. This immunity was of short duration. Intelligence was brought of the surrender of Charleston. Still worse was the news from across the river —of the massacre at the Waxhaws. Directly after this appalling announcement, spread the rumor that a strong party of British was posted at Rocky Mount, that the people of Wateree were flocking to take protection as loyal subjects, and that the conquerors were sending forces in every direction to reduce the province to submission. Such was the aspect of affairs up to a certain Sabbath in June of this year.

On the morning of this memorable Sabbath, the different paths leading to the log meeting-house were unusually thronged. The old country folk were dressed with their usual neatness, especially the women, whose braw garments, brought

8*

from Ireland, were carefully preserved, not merely from thrift, but as a memorial of the green isle of their birth. Their dresses of silk, chintz, or Irish calico—and the fine broad-cloth coats, many colored hose, and silver knee-buckles worn by the men—gave the congregation assembled to worship in that rude sanctuary, a strange and motley appearance—European finery being contrasted with the homespun gowns, hunting-shirts and moccasins of the country people. It was always insisted on as a point of duty among the Covenanters, that children should be brought to church with their parents. The little ones sat between the elders, that they might be kept quiet during divine service, and be ready at the appointed hour for the catechism. The strict deportment and piety of this people had already done much to change the customs formerly prevalent; men and women who used to hunt or fish on the Sabbath now went regularly to meeting, and some notorious ones, whose misconduct had been a nuisance to the community, left the neighborhood.

On this particular day the whole neighborhood seemed to have turned out, and every face wore an expression of anxiety. Groups of men might be seen gathered together under shade-trees in every direction, talking in loud and earnest tones; some laying down plans for the assent of their friends; some pale with alarm, listening to others telling the news, and some transported with indignation, stamping the ground and gesticulating vehemently as they spoke. Everywhere the women mingled with the different groups, and appeared to take an active part in what was going on. At eleven o'clock the venerable form of Martin, the preacher, came in sight. He was about sixty years of age, and had a high reputation for learning and eloquence   He was a large and powerful man, with a voice which it is said might have been heard at a great distance. As he walked from the place where he had hitched his horse, towards the stand, it being customary, when the congregation was too large to be accommodated in the meeting-house, to have the service in the open air, the loud and angry voices ceased, and the congregation was soon seated in silence upon the logs around the stand.

When he arose to speak, every eye was fixed upon him. Those who had been most noisy expected a reproof for their desecration of the Sabbath; for their faithful pastor was never known to fail of rebuking those whose deportment was unsuited to the solemnity of the day. But at this time he too seemed absorbed with the subject that agitated every bosom. "My hearers," he said, in his broad Scotch Irish dialect— 'talk and angry words will do no good. *We must fight!* As your pastor—in preparing a discourse suited to this time of trial—I have sought for all light, examined the Scriptures and other helps in ancient and modern history, and have considered especially the controversy between the United Colonies and the mother country. Sorely have our countrymen been dealt with, till forced to the declaration of their independence. Our forefathers in Scotland made a similar one, and maintained that declaration with their lives; it is now our turn, brethren, to maintain this at all hazards."

After the prayer and singing of the Psalms—he calmly opened his discourse. He cited many passages from Scripture to show that a people may lawfully resist wicked rulers;

pointed to historical examples of princes trampling on the people's rights; painted in vivid colors the rise and progress of the Reformation, and finally applied the subject by fairly stating the merits of the Revolutionary controversy. Giving a brief sketch of the events of the war from the first shedding of blood at Lexington, and warming with the subject as he went on, his address became eloquent with the fiery energy of a Demosthenes. In a voice like thunder, frequently striking with his clenched fist the clapboard pulpit, he appealed to the excited concourse, exhorting them to fight valiantly in defence of their liberties. As he dwelt on the recent tragedy, his indignation reached its height. Stretching out his hand towards Waxhaw—" Go see," he cried—" the tender mercies of Great Britain! In that church you may find men, though still alive, hacked out of the very semblance of humanity; some deprived of their arms, some with one arm or leg, and some with both legs cut off. Is not this cruelty a parallel to the history of our Scottish fathers, driven from their conventicles, hunted like wild beasts, &c.?"

To this stirring sermon the whole assembly responded. Hands were clenched and teeth set in the intensity of feeling; every uplifted face expressed the same determination, and even the women were filled with the spirit that threatened vengeance on the invaders. During the interval of divine worship they went about professing their resolution to do their part in the approaching contest; to plough the fields and gather the crops in the absence of the men. In the afternoon the subject was resumed and discussed with renewed energy, while the appeals of the preacher were answered by even more energetic demonstrations of feeling. When the worship was concluded, and the congregation separating to return homeward, the manly form of Capt. Ben Land was seen walking among the people, shaking hands with every neighbor and whispering in his ear the summons to the next day's work.

On the way home from meeting, one of the Covenanters—William Anderson—was unusually silent, as if some weighty matter engaged all his thoughts. His wife spoke first, after she too had been reflecting. "I think, William, little Lizzy and I can finish the crop, and gather it in if need be, as well as take care of the stock."—"I am glad of that, Nancy," was the reply. "I was silent, for I did na ken how to let you know it, but to-morrow morning I leave home. The way is now clear; the word of God approves, and it shall ne'er be said that the Covenanters, the followers of the reformers of Scotland, would na lend a helpin' hand to the renewal of the Covenant in the land of America! Now, Nancy, Capt. Land will be out before day, giving notice that up at the cross road hard by, he will drill the men who are willing to fight; this was agreed upon as I left." Their conversation through the day was in the same strain. That Sunday evening wore away, and early on Monday morning the plough stood still in the furrow, and the best horse, saddled and bridled, was at the door. Mrs. Anderson had been up since a little after midnight, making hoe cakes on the hoe, and corn dodger in the oven, and while the cooking of meats was going on, busily plying the needle, running up sacks and bags to hold provision for man and horse on a long journey. As soon as he had taken his breakfast, William bade his wife farewell, mounted and rode off.

The effect of Martin's eloquence was speedily apparent. Early on that morning many of the Covenanters were seen drilling on the musterground, seven miles from Rocky Mount, under Capt. Land, while two miles above, at the house of a negro blacksmith, half a dozen more were getting their horses shod. Those at the musterground were charged upon by a party of British dragoons and dispersed, a traitor having carried news of them to the enemy. The Captain was overtaken and surrounded, and being attacked with their broadswords, defended himself bravely to the last. The party at the blacksmith's shop was also surprised, and one man killed. The dragoons then crossed Rocky Creek, and soon made their way to the rude stone hut which was the preacher's dwelling. They found the old divine in his study, preparing a sermon which was to be a second blast, made him their prisoner, and carried him like a felon to Rocky Mount. The country was daily scoured for the purpose of discovering and destroying the whigs, and the unoffending inhabitants were plundered. Meanwhile, the loyalists were collecting and strengthening the royal post.

The victory at the Old Field was followed by a battle at Mobley's Meeting-house, on the banks of Little River in Fairfield District. This attack was proposed by Col. Winn of Fairfield. A number of people from the vicinity had assembled in obedience to a summons from the commander at Rocky Mount, to take protection and enlist in the royal army; a suitable person being sent from headquarters with a force sufficient to sustain him in any necessary movement. This functionary after a while became wearied in the performance of his duties, and indulged himself in a nap; on awakening from which, some one accosted him with the question: "What if McClure should come upon us?" He replied—"I wish he would, for I am full of fight." This same redoubtable champion was found after the battle ensconced in the chimney corner.

In making his attack on this place, McClure surrounded three sides of the house, the fourth being guarded by a precipice down which it was supposed no one would venture to leap, though more British and loyalists perished in the attempt to escape this way than by the rifles of his sharp-shooters. The success of the Americans was as decided as it had been at Beckhamville.

CHAPTER XVII.

INCURSIONS OF HUCK—BATTLE AT WILLIAMSON'S—
" BLOODY BILL CUNNINGHAM."

THE " outlyers" in the middle country gathered under the command of Colonels Pickens and Williams, were not slow in doing their share of service. Many, too, of the patriots of York, Chester, and other border districts, who had fled to North Carolina, organized themselves in companies, and under brave leaders, began to collect on the frontier. McClure spread his men in small parties over the country. They harassed the enemy by sudden and desultory attacks. They depended on their own exertions for everything necessary to carry on the warfare; tabernacled in the woods and swamps, with beasts of the forest, and frequently wanted both for food and clothing.

The report of the disaster at Mobley's Meeting-house being carried to Rocky Mount, the commander of that post sent out a strong party under Capt. Christian Huyck or Huck, in pursuit of the whigs, who retreated across the Catawba, as far as Lincoln County in North Carolina. On this incursion of the royal troops, many outrages were committed on the helpless families where they passed. On Sunday morning, June 11th, the troops under Huck arrived at the house of the sister of John Gaston, near Fishing Creek Church. They immediately entered and plundered the house of everything, carrying away also the corn and wheat. Some of the grain being accidentally spilled in the yard, a tame pigeon flew down and picked it up. The brutal captain struck the bird, cutting off its head at a blow with his sword. Some of Huck's men then went to the barn, where Mrs. Strong's son had gone shortly before their arrival. He had taken his Bible with him, and was engaged in reading the sacred volume. They shot him dead upon the spot, and dragged him out of the barn. The officers then began to cut and hack the dead body with their broadswords, till the mother rushed from the house, and threw herself upon the bleeding and mangled corpse, resolving to perish by the cruel hands of her enemies, rather than see her child cut to pieces before her eyes.

On that Sabbath morning, the wife of the Rev. John Simpson, pastor of the church, while sitting at the breakfast table with her children, heard the report of the gun at her neighbor's. On the Friday previous, Mr. Simpson had shouldered his rifle and marched to the field under the command of Capt. McClure, who had been reared from infancy under his ministry. There the pastor, taking his place in the ranks with the brave men of York and Chester, encouraged and stimulated them by his counsel no less than his services. He had been marked out for vengeance, being supposed active in encouraging the enterprise at the Old

Field and Mobley's; and the enemy expected to find him on this occasion with his assembled congregation.

While the destroyers were at the church, some of the negroes overhearing them declare their intention to go to Mr. Simpson's house and "burn the rascal out," hastened to carry information to his wife, urging her to save herself and family by immediate flight. She looked out, and saw a body of men coming down the lane. Stopping only to gather up a set of silver tea-spoons, most valued as a gift from her mother, she took her four children and went out at the back door, concealing herself in the orchard in the rear. Here she was enabled to watch the movements of her enemies, without being herself discovered.

They rifled the house of everything valuable, took out four feather beds, and ripped them open in the yard; collected all the clothing, from which they selected such articles as they fancied for their own keeping, and having exhausted their invention in devising mischief, finally set fire to the house, which was soon burned to the ground. Just as they were going away, they noticed an outhouse, which contained a valuable library, and was usually occupied by Mr. Simpson as a study. This was soon also in flames. The men now left the premises, and as soon as they were out of sight, Mrs. Simpson hastened back to the house, rushed into the study and carried out two aprons' full of books. She could save no more, and in doing this, was much burned. The feathers in the yard had taken fire, but she succeeded in saving enough for one bed. She then went to the house of one of her neighbors, where she remained for four weeks, returning then to her own place, and taking up her residence in a small outhouse which had escaped the enemy's vengeance. Here she contrived to live with her five children and a young friend, receiving continual assistance from the people of her husband's charge, but not yet free from depredation and danger. At one time, when she had procured some cloth, out of which to make clothing for her children, she had cut out and was making up the garments, when a company of tories came along and plundered her also of these. She complained to the leader of the party, and he ordered his men to give them back. Some of the gang were dressed in Mr. Simpson's clothes, and strutting before her, tauntingly asked if they were not better looking men than her husband; telling her at the same time, that they would one day make her a present of his scalp! This marauding party took off her stock of cattle. Mrs. Simpson begged them to leave her one milch cow for her little children, but her request was refused. The property was restored, however, in an unexpected manner; after going two miles further on their way, the robbers put the cattle in a pen till morning; two large steers broke out during the night, opening a way for the rest, and the whole flock returned home.

About this time a force of volunteers and militia assembled under Gen. Rutherford, defeated a large party of loyalists under Col. Moore, at Ramsour's Mill. This battle, though it was much spoken of by aged men of Rowan and Mecklenburg, and deserves attention as the first American victory in North Carolina, has not been particularly noticed by any historian. Rutherford's cavalry, under the command of Col. Falt, was in advance, and charged with great impetuosity;

but was met with so much firmness by the enemy, that the column began to recoil. In the effort to restore order the colonel fell from his horse mortally wounded. Col. Locke was rapidly advancing meanwhile with his regiment to sustain the charge, but the confusion in the cavalry, with riderless horses dashing through the ranks, caused a panic among the infantry. An authoritative voice called out from the midst of the faltering ranks—" Retreat, men, and keep good order!" The tories pressed on vigorously, and would have won the day, but for the boldness of Capt. Dickey, who in a stentorian voice asked—" Who was the villain who ordered a retreat?" threatening to shoot him instantly through the heart. He then called on the men to follow him and charge through the tory lines, already somewhat disordered from their eager pursuit. The whigs rallied manfully, and rushed boldly to the charge, those who had no bayonets using their guns for clubs. Col. Fall, though near death, continued to cry out—" Fight on, my brave boys, I die for liberty!" The loyalists were completely routed, and many prisoners taken, the leader being captured afterwards by John Haynes, who was on guard at an outpost. He came with a white flag to request leave to visit his wounded, and was detained within the lines from fear that his men would renew the attack on learning how small a force had defeated them.

The whigs, gaining strength every day, and watchful for an opportunity favorable to their return, at length passed down the north side of the Catawba, and formed their camp near a stream called Clem's Branch, on the edge of Lancaster District. This district and that of Chester lay in front, be-

CHAPTER XVII. 189

tween them and the British posts at Rocky Mount and Camden. On one hand were the whigs of York, on the other those of Mecklenburg County, which lay on the east, the Catawba forming a defence on the west. No position could have been more judiciously selected than this in the heart of a whig population, and in time came encouraging reinforcements. It was here that Thomas Sumter, after his home had been burned and his family driven out shelterless, when he came forth to action, found the men who had been chased into North Carolina, resting upon the soil of South Carolina; the line of division probably passing through the camp.

During the weeks they occupied this encampment, the patriots were not idle. Sergeant Ben. Rowan, with a few men, went back into North Carolina nearly two hundred miles, for the purpose of procuring lead, and drove pack-horses before them laden each with about two hundred and fifty pounds' weight. Others were sent out after powder. The smiths were busy in every direction, manufacturing swords, and making and repairing those twisted rifles which did such destructive execution in the battles of the South. The active and enterprising John McClure, with his company of mounted riflemen, was constantly in the field, and others were out in different directions through the country, encouraging the desponding partizans, collecting recruits, and putting down the loyalists wherever they could. These movements annoyed and alarmed the British, who regarding the province as subdued, were not disposed to brook disrespect from a few stragglers Col. Floyd, a loyalist of York District, made grievous complaint at Rocky Mount, in consequence of which the commander again sent out Capt. Huck with an order to proceed to the frontier, and "push the rebels." With his band of redcoats and tories he scoured the country, punishing he obnoxious, enlisting loyalists, and plundering property; everywhere, it is said, cursing Presbyterians, and burning those Bibles which contained the old version of the psalms. In this second progress he visited the house of the mother of Capt. McClure. Her son James and a son-in-law had just returned from Sumter's camp. When the British drew near, both were busily employed in running bullets, having melted up for this purpose their mother's pewter dishes. So occupied were they, that the enemy had entered the lane before they were aware of their presence. To escape was out of the question, but James climbed the wall of a new house, and perched himself upon some plank lying on the windbeams. Here he was soon discovered and brought down, and with his brother-in-law, taken out into the yard and searched. Their pockets were full of pewter bullets, furnishing proof of their murderous designs against the King's men, and the sentence was pronounced that they were to be hanged at sunrise on the morning of the 12th of July. When the young men were secured, Huck stepped up to Mrs. McClure, and rudely asked where were her other sons. She bade him seek them in Sumter's camp. Huck then seized the Family Bible, and threw it into the fire. The matron sprang forward to recover it, and succeeded in dragging it from the flames, though one corner of it was badly burned. The captain struck her with the flat of his sword for her interference, and the soldiers set fire to the house;

but the women extinguished the flames. Others were busily engaged in destroying her property, carrying off whatever articles it suited their inclination to take. At length they departed, driving their prisoners before them.

As soon as the intruders were gone, Mrs. McClure despatched her daughter in all haste to Sumter's camp, to carry the news of the outrage she had suffered and the captivity of the young men. The young woman made her way to the camp, arriving late in the evening. The Americans had heard for several days previous of the march of Huck's party through the country, their progress being marked by cruelty and spoliation, and some from the vicinity had fled to the camp for safety. The news of the capture hastened their preparations for the expedition against him, and just after sunset the companies of John McClure and John Bratton—the York and Chester men—headed by their captains and under the command of Col. Neil, left Sumter's camp. The distance to be marched was thirty miles, and from the intelligence they had received, it was supposed that the enemy would be found at White's (now Crawford's) Mills, engaged in grinding the wheat and grain they had been for several days gathering throughout the country. The little band of patriots, only seventy-five in number, but resolved to peril their lives in avenging their neighbors' injuries, made directly for the mill—but did not find the enemy. The march was resumed, and a little before day they passed the house of old Mr. Adair. Observing the door ajar and light shining from the fire place, Bratton went up gently to the door and tapped. The old man was sitting up at the fire, two British officers having taken his bed From him they learned the disposition of the enemy at Williamson's.

Huck's party had stopped at Adair's house on their way to Williamson's. After they had robbed Mrs. Adair of her neckhandkerchief, rings and shoebuckles, and threatened to hang her husband, one of the officers commanded her to bring her sons into the King's service, promising to obtain for each a commission in the army. After they were gone, except the two officers who had quartered themselves there, Mr. and Mrs. Adair left the house quietly, and gained the shelter of a thicket, for they knew there would shortly be fighting at their neighbor's. These were the parents of Gov. Adair, of Kentucky, who acted so prominent a part at the battle of New Orleans, a third of a century afterwards.

On the preceding evening, Huck had stopped at Col. Bratton's house and endeavored to persuade Mrs. Bratton to influence her husband to join the royalists. On the matron's indignant refusal, the tradition is, that one of his officers seized a reaping hook that hung in the piazza, and brought it to her throat. Another interfered to protect her. She was then ordered to prepare supper for the men, after which they left her dwelling.

The troops of Huck lay encamped around Williamson's house. A fenced lane, along which sentinels were posted, passed the door. About daylight the party of Americans, having arranged their plan of attack, divided to enclose the enemy

McClure taking one division, went off to enter the lane at the further end, where the attack was to be commenced, Neil and Bratton entering at the near end, to take the enemy in rear McClure took a nigh cut, and came on the side of the lane, where he threw down the fence as he leaped over. It was now so light that his brother James, who was confined with other prisoners, in a corn crib, recognized him; but when the guard placed over them called out, "Who is there?" he replied, indifferently, "Oh, it is some of your tory friends." The drums and fifes of the enemy now began to play for morning parade. In an instant the sharp crack of McClure's rifle announced that his part of the game had commenced. Capt Huck instantly mounted, and several times rallied his men; but the determined spirit of the patriots carried all before them. The brief though bloody battle lasted about an hour. The rout was complete. Huck and Col. Ferguson fell, and their soldiers fled in all directions. Col. Bratton's house, around which the conflict raged, was open to the wounded of both parties, and Mrs. Bratton humanely attended the sufferers. Mrs. Adair also came to the battle ground, and going to a tent where the captain, who had spoken with her the night before, was lying, helped to dress his wounds, and reminded him that he had ordered her to bring in her rebel sons. "Here are two of them," she said, "and if the third had been within a day's ride, he would have been here also." The reply was—"It is a little too late."

McClure, mounted at the head of his men, pursued the flying enemy for nearly thirty miles. The bushes were the only places of safety between Williamson's and Rocky Mount; many prisoners were taken in the pursuit, and some were hid for weeks in the woods. The effect of this victory was of lasting advantage. From all the surrounding country men flocked to Sumter's camp. It was about this time that "the Bloody Scout," under the notorious Col. Cunningham, was committing unprecedented cruelties on the inhabitants of Union and Spartanburg Districts. This tory acted a prominent part also in the partisan warfare of Laurens, Newberry, and Edgefield Districts. He was commonly called "Bloody Bill Cunningham." Plundering and murder were his vocation, and his ruthless band was the terror of the country. A nephew of Judge Gaston was inhumanly butchered in his own yard, where he was occupied in shelling corn. His family fled back to Chester, while others, repairing to Sumter's camp with a supply of powder, brought intelligence of "Bloody Bill's" whereabouts. Another of John McClure's services was the driving of this notorious murderer from the vicinity. He was sent out by Sumter in pursuit of him, and having understood that he had crossed Broad River to the western side of York District, he soon struck his trail, and chased him across the district of Union. Cunningham fled some thirty miles towards Ninety-Six, and barely escaped, while four of his men were captured by McClure. The night he brought in these prisoners, Sumter broke up his camp at Clem's Branch, and marched down to Col. Davie's camp in the Waxhaws.

CHAPTER XVIII.

BATTLES OF ROCKY MOUNT AND HANGING ROCK—SURPRISE AT FISHING CREEK.

THE attention of Gen. Sumter was now directed to the royal post at Rocky Mount. On the 30th of July, the troops took up their line of march. Col. Davie, with his cavalry, took the road leading down the east side of the Catawba, to harass the British outposts at Hanging Rock, while Sumter took the road to Landsford, crossed the river at sunset, and marching all night, at sunrise next morning invested Rocky Mount.

The daughters of Justice Gaston, near whose house they marched, mounted early and gallopped towards the scene of action. While approaching, they met two or three fugitives, whom they stopped, and bade them return. When they wavered, one of the young women cried—" Give *us* your guns, then, and we will stand in your places !" The men wheeled about and returned. The females busied themselves during the action in rendering whatever services were required; helping to dress the wounds of the soldiers, and bringing water to allay their thirst. The action continued a great part of the day; the whigs firing from behind trees and rocks at every crevice of the log houses occupied by the enemy's garrison. Attempts were also made to set fire to the buildings by throwing faggots from the rocks, and by building brush-heaps from the rocks to the houses; but a heavy rain put out the fire, and late in the evening, as it was very dark, Sumter drew off his men. His want of success was compensated by a brilliant exploit of Davie on the other side of the river, who had charged upon a party of cavalry on their way to succor Rocky Mount, and captured sixty horse.

That night Sumter encamped on the very ground where he was surprised eighteen days afterwards. On the 6th of August he again crossed the river, marched all night, and a little after daylight commenced the battle of Hanging Rock. Hanging Rock is in Lancaster District, and remarkable not only for its association with that celebrated battle, but as a natural curiosity. On the east side of the creek many rocks are piled in an irregular group along the declivity of a steep hill. That called Hanging Rock is a single mass twenty feet in diameter, which on the side nearest the stream to which it gives its name, is scooped into a regular arch, under which several persons might be sheltered. Another boulder is poised on the edge of a larger rock, resembling a ship resting on the summit of a cliff, and looking as if a slight force would hurl it into the waters below. The battle ground is near this spot. Sumter's force, in three divisions, advanced on the camp of the tories under the command of Col. Morgan Bryan. His lines were posted on the brow of a steep hill beyond the creek, while the British camp lay nearly half a mile distant.

Sumter's centre line, led by the intrepid Capt. McClure,

CHAPTER XVIII.

came first within the enemy's view, and received the first fire. The contest then raged fearfully; bullets poured like hail; McClure was wounded in the thigh, but plugging the wound with wadding, dashed on in front of his men, his voice urging them forward heard above the din of battle and the shrieks of the wounded. After firing, they clubbed their guns, rushing into the camp and grappling with the foe. Where dead and wounded lay in heaps, McClure fell, pierced with several wounds, while at the same time his cousins, the four Gastons, lay bleeding around him. Some near him ran to his relief; but he ordered them back to the fight, and as he lay weltering in blood, his voice was still heard urging them on. As the tories fled towards the British camp, many of the whigs rushed pell-mell with them. One named Walker, hurrying along in their midst, was about to fire on those before him, when a tory close to him caught his arm, crying, "Those are on our side!" and then, as if struck with a sudden suspicion, asked "What is that green leaf in your hat for?" The whigs had taken the precaution to put each a leaf in their hats that morning before going into battle. The soldier pulled out the token, but the discovery was already made; one of the tories seized his gun, the other ran a bayonet through his hunting shirt. Letting the weapon go, he turned and fled back. "It appeared to me," he said, "that they fired fifty guns after me; every leap I gave, I heard something fall on the leaves which I took for blood, and thought I must be badly wounded, and would soon fall exhausted. I thought of the intolerable thirst I had witnessed in those bleeding to death, and my mouth began to feel parched. I had now reached the branch, and stooped to drink. On examination I found I was not hurt, but my powder horn was severely wounded, being pierced through with a rifle ball, and having lost the greater portion of its contents."

This battle was thought one of the most spirited and best fought actions by raw militia,—all volunteers—against British regulars, that took place during the war. It has not received due attention from American historians. The engagement lasted somewhat less than four hours, and was terminated by the British sounding a retreat, and sending in a flag with overtures for a truce, to bury the dead and succor the wounded. McClure's command sustained the largest share of the whole loss. He himself, thus stricken down in the bloom of life, was borne from the field to Waxhaw church, where the next day his mother came to nurse her gallant son. In a day or two the wounded were carried to Charlotte.

The news that a strong force, under the command of Gen. Gates, was approaching for the relief of the Southern provinces, gave a new impulse to the zeal of the patriots, and brought recruits to the standard of Gen. Sumter. Lord Rawdon concentrated his forces at Camden. By the 13th of August Gen. Gates rested at Clermont, thirteen miles from that town. He gave orders to Gen. Sumter to attack Carey Fort. On the 15th, Gates commenced his night march, and on the following day encountered the army of Lord Rawdon near Camden. He suffered a disastrous defeat, and immediately retreated into North Carolina.

The attack of Gen. Sumter on the convoy and Carey Fort was crowned with success, and with his three hundred prisoners and forty-four wagons loaded with munitions of war, he hastened to join Gen. Gates. On the way he received the news of his defeat, and also retreated, to place the stores he had captured in safety. His march was slow, for he was encumbered with prisoners and baggage-wagons—and a large part of his force was on foot. The march was kept up during the nights of the 16th and 17th; yet it was not more than forty miles above Camden that he pitched his camp on the ill-fated morning of the 18th of August. His encampment was in the stronghold of Fishing Creek, two miles from its junction with the Catawba, where a bend in stream and river leaves a ridge of elevated ground between them, from which both can be seen. In front and rear of this space deep ravines run from the river and the creek, leaving a narrow strip along which the road passes, while below, the road left the ridge and entered a valley with steep hills on either side. In this strong position, guarded by the Catawba on the east, and the creek on the west, the army feared no enemy's approach.

When the army halted and struck their tents, the guard, being mounted, repaired to their posts. The men in the camp who had no duty to do, and were not too hungry, were soon fast asleep in their tents, having had no rest for two nights. Some were engaged in slaughtering beeves, and every few moments the crack of a rifle might be heard, while some were cooking before the tents. The sentinels posted down the road towards the ford of the creek, were marching up and down the line appointed, while others of the guard made for the river, desirous of a bath, as the weather was oppressively warm, and intending to be back at the station in time to take their turn. The British, under Tarleton, meanwhile, came up the road from the stream unperceived, and found none to dispute their advance. Each dragoon had a foot soldier mounted behind him, and these dismounted near the camp. The first intimation given of their approach, was a general fire from Tarleton's dragoons, instantly followed by a bold charge into the midst of the camp.

In front, a short distance from the tents, Mrs. Peay, of Fairfield District, was seated upon a log feeding her two children. Her husband had gone into North Carolina after Gates' defeat, to join his force, and she, having to leave home because her neighbors were loyalists, thought it safest to travel with the army. She had with her a negro boy and two horses. As she sat upon the log, the British dragoons charged past her, and she would have been run over had not the log been large and furnished with branches, so that they were obliged to pass round it. With the assault, resistance and endeavors to escape, the wildest confusion ensued. She sat still, her eyes fixed on the terrible spectacle, and saw the defenceless or slumbering men shot down or cut to pieces, till she turned sickening from the scene of massacre. See saw a few of the regulars rallying behind the wagons, and returning the fire, and presently the bullets whistling near brought her to her recollection. Slipping down from the log, she pulled the children after her, and kept them close by her side till the firing ceased. When the British left the ground they took her servant and horses, and she was left with her children, alone with the dead and wounded. Next day she went with the little ones, who were crying for bread, to the house of a tory living in the neighborhood, to beg some food for them. He coolly told her there was the peach orchard, and she might take what she wanted; it was good enough for a rebel.

Gen. Sumter had stripped off his coat and boots, for he was in need of repose, and was lying fast asleep in his marquée. In the moment of alarm Capt. Steel's first thought was for him. Regardless of his own safety, he ran directly to the marquée, caught Sumter in his arms, and had carried him out through the back part of the tent before he was fully awake. He also seized the pormanteau in which, as he knew, valuable public papers were carried, and brought it with him. He bore the General to a horse ready saddled, and hastily assisted him to mount, bareheaded as he was. His rangers were already mounted and clustering round him, and under their protection he brought Sumter through a shower of bullets, while in all directions around them the soldiers were running, as many as could catch horses mounting and making off. Steel's party was hotly pursued; but whenever the British came too near, the rangers would wheel suddenly and fire upon them. As the foremost dragoons fell, their horses running loose were caught and mounted by the flying soldiers, and this proving a losing business, they soon abandoned the pursuit and returned to the disordered camp. One of Steel's company, a noble-looking youth of eighteen, rode up by the side of Sumter, took off his hat, and with a gesture of graceful courtesy, presented it to the General, tying a handkerchief round his own head.

At the time of the surprise, it is supposed that between one and two hundred young men were bathing in the river

The dragoons, pursuing those who fled, came in among them, and an indiscriminate slaughter ensued. One had his hair cut with a bullet, and was so stunned he would have been drowned, had not another dragged him upon a rock. Three were making for the opposite bank, when one of them called out that he was shot. His companions dragged him to a rock, and then hid themselves till the British had left the river. Many of the soldiers stood on the east bank of the river with no covering from the burning sun. Some of them went to the house of McMeans, whose wife gave them all her husband's clothes, and even exhausted her own wardrobe; so that more than one of the survivors of that disastrous day went home in petticoats!

Ben Rowan, "the boxer of the army," heard the firing of the sentinels in the direction of the creek, but supposed it to be the killing of beeves a little further from the camp. He was startled by the enemy's broadside, and seeing in an instant that all was lost, ran for safety to the place where the three hundred prisoners were under guard. They were shouting for joy and flinging up their hats, when with his Herculean strength he forced himself a pathway through and over them. Just as he got through them, he saw a loose horse grazing, and flung himself upon the animal without saddle or bridle, slapping first with one hand and then with the other to direct his course. The horse went off at a brisk pace through the woods, and Ben made good his escape, to be an actor in every subsequent battle of the South.

Joel McClemore, as he ran through the camp, picked up a rifle, not knowing if it were loaded or not; he was presently pursued by a dragoon, and after dodging from tree to tree for some time, got near the fence and succeeded in crossing it. It then occurred to him that the open field was not so safe as the woods in case of continued pursuit, and turning round, he said to the dragoon, in his Virginia vernacular, "I'll eat fire if you cross that fence but I'll shoot you!" The dragoon put spurs to his horse, and as he leaped Joel drew trigger at a venture. The gun went off, and the man fell, while the horse leaped the fence. Joel lost no time in mounting, and thus escaped with a fine horse, holster and pistols. A few regulars who contended for a time behind the wagons against overpowering numbers, were forced to yield. Everywhere up the river and creek the woods were full of men flying for their lives, while some who escaped butchery were driven back to the camp by the troopers.

The prisoners were placed under a strong guard, having to do without dinner as well as breakfast, with the prospect of the gibbet before many who had taken British protection, when they should reach Camden. Tarleton remained master of the field of slaughter, for it could not be called a battle. By his order the wagons for which they could not find horses were collected together and consumed, with such articles as could not conveniently be taken away. Long before sunset the British commenced their return march towards Camden, leaving the dead unburied, and the wounded who could not be removed, to perish. The march was continued several hours after dark. Some of the prisoners effected their escape by dropping off on the way and lying down till they were passed.

The scattered men of Sumter's army with one accord made

their way to Charlotte, as if that destination had been previously appointed. Those who went home stayed only long enough to procure such articles of clothing as they had lost, and went on. They might be seen the next day upon every road leading towards Charlotte. Sumter himself went on the same night.

Capt. Berry, who with some of his men had escaped after the defeat of Gen. Gates, on the night of the 17th wandered up the river as far as George Wade's house.* Wade, who came home in the night, gave him three hundred pounds of flour for his soldiers, and informed him that Gen. Sumter would be on the other side of the river the next morning. Berry crossed the next day with his command, and had not been an hour in camp before the surprise took place, in which he was captured; thus leaving one disastrous field to meet misfortune in another.

* A record of the military movements of this time is extant in a manuscript written by George Wade, then one of the wealthiest planters on the Catawba.

CHAPTER XIX.

SURPRISE OF STEEL—CONDITION OF THE COUNTRY.

While Gen. Sumter proceeded to Charlotte after the surprise, Capt. Steel returned by his order, with some fifteen men. His business was to collect recruits, and send them to join the General, who intended to rally his forces at Charlotte. On this mission he traversed the country day and night. Another object was to find the valise containing the public papers, which had been dropped by the man to whose care it was entrusted, shortly after they left the camp, and was supposed to be lost somewhere in the woods. Steel recovered it from a tory who had found and carried it to Wateree Creek. On his way back he chanced to meet the wife of one of his acquaintances, and stopped to bid her tell her husband that all patriots were summoned to meet their General at Charlotte, and that he must come and join him the next morning at Neely's on Fishing Creek, whence he could go on with his party. He was not aware that the man to whom he sent this message had turned loyalist. The woman, of course, immediately carried the news to her husband, who set out to collect tories for the purpose of intercepting Capt. Steel, travelling all night through the neighborhood, for the attack was to be at Neely's on the following morning.

Meanwhile the brave captain, suspecting no treachery, reached his home late that night, and once more embraced the excellent mother who had trained him to his present career of duty. Early the next morning he set off for Neely's, about four miles distant, Mrs. Steel accompanying him on horseback When they arrived, Mrs. Neely and her daughters immemediately busied themselves in preparing breakfast. The horses were hitched to trees in the yard, and two other daughters of the landlady went out into the cornfield to keep watch. All was silent for some time ; at length a man named Lockart left the premises, followed by a young lad, to get his horse from the pasture. While going through the field, he saw a body of tories, in two divisions, approaching through the standing corn. The leader, whom he recognized as one of his near neighbors and a noted loyalist, waved his hand at him in token that he should keep silence. Lockart paid no heed to the signal, but halloed with all his might to give the alarm at the house. Thereupon another of the advancing party snapped his gun at him ; Lockart then taking deliberate aim at the leader, fired and cut off his bridle reins, crippling one of his fingers, and stopping not to see the effect, turned and fled precipitately. In his flight he fell into a deep gully, which probably saved him, for the tories' shots passed over him as he lay still. The leader's horse in the meantime taking fright, ran away with him before he could recover his control of the bridle. This accident in all likelihood saved the party at the house.

Mrs. Steel was engaged at the time in combing the captain's hair. He boasted a remarkably fine head of hair; it was very long and of raven blackness, and was usually worn tied in a queue behind. John's important services to the whig cause, employing him both night and day, had of late left him little leisure for attention to his locks; they had been long uncombed, and probably showed very plainly the neglect they had experienced. The personal appearance of her son was a matter of pride to the matron, only less than her delight in his gallant conduct. While thus occupied, they heard the sharp crack of the rifle, followed immediately by Lockart's warning shouts, and the screams of the young girls who had been stationed in the field. In a moment after, several guns were fired in quick succession, and the girls were seen running towards the house, while the two divisions of the enemy, at no great distance behind them, could be perceived advancing through the standing corn. Not an instant was to be lost; yet such was the effect of sudden surprise on the brave men who, only two days before, had been taken unawares on Fishing Creek, that they seemed utterly at a loss what to do. Mrs. Steel alone retained perfect self-possession. Starting up, she called to them, "You must fight!" but directly, seeing the confusion that prevailed, she shouted an order for them to " clear themselves" as fast as possible. She urged her son to mount his horse at once, and save the public papers in his charge, while she pulled down the bars to let out him and his men. John was quick in all his movements, and it may easily be conceived that no time was wasted. First in the saddle, he spurred his noble horse towards the bars, which he cleared at a bound—his mother having had no time yet to let them down—and galloped off. He was followed by the greater number of his men, for whom Mrs. Steel removed the bars as fast as she could; some, however, were slower in getting off, and paid the penalty of their delay, being now exposed to the fire of the advancing tories.

About fifty guns were discharged at the bars, and two of the whigs fell dead from their horses, bearing Mrs. Steel under them to the ground. One who could not get his horse, in leaping had part of his foot shot off. Another's hunting-shirt filling with the wind as he rode, was riddled through and through with bullets that missed his body. Capt. Steel, determined to cut his way through the assailants, rode foremost up the lane at full speed, his long hair, unfastened, streaming in the wind, his rifle in one hand, held high above his head in defiance of the foe. He was closely followed by those of his company who had escaped. The tories, startled by the fury of their onset, gave way and scattered from the road, nor were they able to rally till the fugitives were beyond their reach. The whigs who were taken prisoners were carried to Camden; one or two died in the jail there, while others languished for seven months, suffering incredible cruelties.

Meanwhile the first thought of Mrs. Steel, as she struggled to release herself from the weight of the dead bodies, rising from the ground covered with their blood, her dress pierced in different places with bullet holes—was for "John and the papers." When she heard they were safe, she burst into an exclamation of thankfulness, and as she was fortunately unhurt, turned her attention to the relief of others. The

CHAPTER XIX.

tories, enraged at their disappointment, with one accord turned their course to Mrs. Steel's house. This they burned to the ground, and destroyed her property of every description, wherever they could find anything belonging to her.

The captain often related this adventure, and said that while flying along the lane with his hair streaming, he thought of Absalom, and vowed, if he escaped his fate while passing under the trees, to sacrifice the hair which had brought him into such peril. A youth in his company who also wore his hair in a queue, had it cut off by a rifle ball as he leaped the bars. The vow he then made was different from the captain's; for he resolved to wear it long while he lived, in defiance of British or tories, and religiously kept his resolution for more than half a century.

While the men flying from the disastrous field of Gen. Gates' defeat, were continually coming to Charlotte, and passing on, the gallant Capt. McClure was approaching the termination of his brief and brilliant career. The hero drew his last breath in Liberty Hall—the room in which the Mecklenburg Declaration was penned by Dr. Brevard—probably at the very hour when his compatriots under Sumter were routed fifty miles below. At the time there was a report that the British were coming, and everybody was leaving Charlotte. It was proposed to bury the corpse without a coffin. but his mother insisted on having him decently interred.

There were no men to render the last offices to the dead on the field of Sumpter's defeat, and it devolved upon the women to go down to the battle ground and see that they received sepulture. Mary Johnston, accom panied by Miss McClure, went the same night to Justice Gaston's, and found at home only the Justice, Mrs. Gaston and their granddaughter, Margaret McCreary. The house had been plundered of everything, and that night the aged couple slept upon cowhides, the two young women and Margaret occupying hides stretched on the floor. The next morning they prevailed on Margaret to accompany them to the field. As they drew near the spot of the disaster, with a natural reluctance to go alone where they must encounter so appalling a spectacle, they called at the house of a loyalist, and with some difficulty persuaded him to accompany them. Mrs. Johnston found the corpse of her father, hastily buried. Some of the bodies lay uncovered, and several were slightly covered with earth, which the hogs had partly rooted away.

Many of the women went to Charlotte to carry clothes and provisions to their friends. On their return, they were met by anxious inquiries from those who were uncertain as to the fate of their kindred. They also carried supplies to Camden, whither the unfortunate prisoners had been conveyed, driving pack-horses laden with the different articles. One Mary Gill, on a journey thither with a friend, chanced to stop for the night at a small cabin in the pine woods. She had suspicions of the place, which were confirmed when she saw a man go out at the back door as they asked admittance; but they were unable to go further, and concluded to avail themselves of the shelter. She determined, however, to keep watch, and tying her horse to the hasp of the door, she seated herself on the step, holding the reins in her hand. A tory within the cabin, not long afterwards, having parched some corn on the hearth, invited her with much importunity to come and take some. She left the horse for a moment to do so; but on returning to the door found the rope cut and the horse gone She charged the tory with having a hand in this piece of villany, and being of masculine strength, threatened to punish him; but he protested his innocence, and her companion interceded for him. On her arrival at Camden, Miss Gill complained to a British officer, who promised to attend to the matter; but the horse was never recovered.

One striking instance of devotion and heroism should be mentioned. Thomas McCalla, a soldier in Capt. Steel's company, had been taken a prisoner to Camden. For a month his wife could obtain no tidings of him. In the midst of her distress, her children fell ill with the small-pox—that dreadful scourge of the whole country—and after their recovery she determined to go to Camden to seek her husband. Having set her house in order, she was in the saddle long before day, taking the road leading down on the west side of the Catawba. The mountain gap on Wateree Creek was passed ere the sun rose, and by two o'clock she had crossed the river, passing the guard there stationed, and entered Camden. Desiring to be conducted to the presence of Lord Rawdon, she was escorted by Major Doyle to the head-quarters of that commander, who then occupied a large ancient-looking house on the east side of the main street.

Her impression at first sight was favorable; he was a fine-looking young man, with a countenance not unprepossessing. Being desired to explain the object of her visit, she pleaded her cause with the eloquence of nature and feeling; making known the distressed situation of her family at home, the anxiety of mind she had suffered on account of the absence of her husband and her ignorance of his fate, and her urgent need of his care and protection. From Major Doyle she had at length learned that he was held a prisoner by his lordship's orders. She had come, therefore, to entreat mercy for him; to pray that he might be released and permitted to go home with her.

Lord Rawdon heard her to the end. His reply was—"I would rather hang such rebels than eat my breakfast." This insulting speech was addressed to his suppliant while her eyes were fixed on him in the agony of her entreaty, and the tears were streaming down her cheeks. His words dried up the fountain at once, the spirit of an American matron was roused, and she turned on him a look of the deepest scorn. A moment after, with a struggle to control her feelings, she said, " I crave of your lordship permission to see my husband." Doyle now interposed, and requested his lordship to step with him into another apartment. When they returned, Rawdon said to his visitor, with a stately coldness—"Major Doyle, madam, has my permission to let you go into the prison. You may continue in the prison *ten minutes only*. Major, you have my orders." So saying, he bowed politely both to her and the officer, as intimating that the business was ended, and they were dismissed. They accordingly quitted the room.

Thus ended the interview from which she had hoped so much. What had been granted seemed a mockery rather than an alleviation of her sorrow. But even this indulgence, the Major informed her, had been reluctantly granted at his earnest intercession; and he took occasion to blame her own exhibition of spirit. "It was with great difficulty," he observed, "that I got this permission for you. His lordship said, 'She can cry, and I believe she can fight, too! did you see what a look she gave me? Major, such a woman might do harm; she must not be permitted to pass and repass, unless some one of the officers is with her. She must stay only ten minutes, and it must be in your presence.'"

The sight of the prison-pen almost overcame the fortitude of the resolute wife. An inclosure like that constructed for animals, guarded by soldiers, was the habitation of the unfortunate prisoners, who sat within on the bare earth, many of them suffering with the prevalent distemper, and stretched on the ground, with no shelter from the burning sun of September. "Is it possible," cried she, turning to Doyle, "that you shut up men in this manner, as you would a parcel of hogs!" She was then admitted into the jail, and welcome indeed was the sight of her familiar face to McCalla. When the ten minutes had expired, she again shook hands with him, assuring him she would shortly return with clothes for his use, and what provisions she could bring; then turning, she walked away with a firm step, stopping to shake hands with young John Adair and the other captives with whom she was acquainted. The word of encouragement was not wanting, and as she bade the prisoners adieu, she said, "Have no fear; the women are doing their part of the service." "I admire your spirit, madam," Doyle observed to her, "but must request you to be a little more cautious."

Mrs. McCalla was furnished by the Major with a pass,

which she showed to the officer on duty as she passed the guard on her return, and to the officer at the ferry. She rode with all speed, and was at home before midnight; having had less than twenty-four hours for the accomplishment of her whole enterprise; in that time riding one hundred miles, crossing the river twice, and passing the guard four times It is proper to say that she met with kind treatment from other British officers at this time, for they were favorably impressed by her courage and strength of affection. Even the soldiers, as she passed them, paid her marks of respect. The tories alone showed no sympathy nor pity for her trials; it being constantly observed that there was deeper hostility towards the whigs on the part of their countrymen of different politics, than those of English birth.

Mrs. McCalla began her work immediately after her arrival at home; making new clothes, altering and mending others, and preparing the provisions. Her preparations being completed, she again set out for Camden. This time she had the company of one of her neighbors, Mrs. Nixon, whose brother, John Adair, has been mentioned as among the prisoners. Each of the women drove before her a pack-horse, laden with the articles provided for the use of their suffering friends. From this time she made her journeys about once a month, carrying clean clothes and provisions; being often accompanied by other women bound on similar errands, and conveying articles of food and clothing to their captive fathers, husbands and brothers.

One of the patriotic efforts of the women of Fishing Creek neighborhood is worth remembrance. The rich lands were well adapted for the growth of wheat, which was extensively cultivated by the 'Pennsylvania Irish' settlers. The harvest was in June; but all the men able to bear arms having taken the field, none remained to secure the crop, on which the support of their families depended. The young women, with spirit equal to that of their gallant brothers, formed a company of reapers for cutting and garnering the grain They went day after day from one farm to another, and reaped the crop with the assistance of the matrons and a few old men. The only question they asked was, "Is the owner out with the fighting men?" and an affirmative answer was sufficient to engage them at once in the labor. It was no small undertaking, five or six weeks of unceasing toil being necessary to gather in the harvest through the country. It seemed that Providence smiled on the generous enterprise; there were no storms during that period to ravage the fields, and it was related for years afterwards as very remarkable, that some of the crops of 1780 were secured several weeks after the grain was fully ripe. Scarcely was the work accomplished, before British and tories were plundering every where and laying waste the country, determined to vanquish the spirit of resistance by distressing rebel families.

During the summer, families through the country, near the scene of warfare, lived chiefly on roasted corn, without bread, meat, or salt. Hickory ashes were used, with a small quantity of salt, for preserving beef when it could be had. Leather shoes were replaced by woollen rags sewed round the feet, and of beds and bedding nothing was left. The beds were generally ripped open by the depredators, the feathers scattered and the ticking used for tent cloths. The looms were robbed of the cloth found in them; and hence the females of the country resorted to various expedients to manufacture clothing, and preserve it for their own and their friends' use. A family living on Pacolet River built a loom between four trees in the forest, and wove in fair weather, covering the loom and web with cow-hides when it rained. On one occasion, when the whigs had obtained a quantity of salt by taking a fort, it was sent up by wagons to York District, to be distributed by pecks among the widows of those who had fallen in battle. The women went on horseback for their pecks. At another time, one rode eighty miles for a bushel, concealing the guinea appropriated for the purchase, in the hair braided on the top of her head.

Not only did the labors of the field devolve on the women during this period, but they frequently had to devise means of assisting or sheltering the hunted whigs. Their friends could not venture on a visit home without watching their opportunity. North of Fishing Creek settlement lay the black-jack region, at that time an open prairie, on which persons could be seen at a great distance. The patriots coming to visit their families, always endeavored to pass over this plain by night, though to do so, they were often under the necessity of lying by all day. As they approached their homes, they usually discovered some signal hung out by the women, by which they understood whether or not they could enter their houses with safety.

The whigs concealed as much of their property as they could; sometimes depositing grain for the use of their families in the barns of kind-hearted loyalists. A cave, still to be seen in a deep ravine on Rocky Creek, was a place of deposit for many articles, hidden from the cruel marauders who took advantage of the state of confusion to plunder helpless families. Gangs of robbers went about through the country, and it might truly be said that spoliation and murder were the order of the day. Well ran the old song--

> " Carolina, South and North,
> Was filled with pain and woe:
> The tories took their neighbors' worth,
> And away a whig must go."

CHAPTER XX.

THE WARNING AT GREEN SPRING—BATTLE OF KING'S
MOUNTAIN—BLACKSTOCKS—STATE OF CHARLESTON
AND THE COUNTRY

The late succession of disasters had completely prostrated the country's rising hopes. But the dark hour was the harbinger of brighter prospects; far up among the mountains were gathered bands of patriots, ere long to descend like the mountain torrent from their heights. It is said that more than three thousand were collected at Gilberttown, Rutherford, North Carolina. In September, Lord Cornwallis despatched Col. Ferguson to the frontier, to sweep the country, and encourage the loyalists to take up arms. A number of abandoned outlaws hung around his camp, committing depredations and cruelties wherever they passed; robbing whigs of their negroes, horses, cattle, and every valuable article of property The militia of the country assembled to interrupt their march, and several skirmishes took place between the straggling parties.

One battle of considerable importance was fought in Spartanburg District, at the "Green Spring." About two hundred men, commanded by Col. Clarke, of the Georgia volunteers, having received intelligence that a larger body of tory militia was recruiting for the horse service, under the command of Ferguson, determined to attempt to rout them. The Americans stopped for refreshment at the house of Capt. Dillard, who was with them as a volunteer, and were entertained with milk and potatoes. They marched on, hearing that a scouting party was in advance of Ferguson's station, and encamped for the night at Green Spring. The same evening Ferguson, with a party, arrived at Dillard's, and made inquiries respecting Clarke and his men. Mrs. Dillard replied that they had been gone a long time, and at the bidding of the officers prepared supper. Going to and from the kitchen, she overheard much of their conversation, and ascertained that they knew where Clarke was encamped, and were to pursue him, with a view to a surprise, as soon as they had taken their meal. No time was to be lost. She hurried the supper, and as soon as the officers had sat down, slipped out by a back way. Late and dark as it was, her determination was to go herself and apprise Clarke of his danger, in the hope of being in time for him to make a safe retreat; for she believed that the enemy were too numerous to justify a battle.

She went to the stable, bridled a young horse, and without saddle, mounted and rode with all possible speed to the place described. It was about half an hour before day when she came in full gallop to one of the videttes, by whom she was immediately conducted to Col. Clarke. She called to the colonel, breathless with eagerness and haste, "Be in readiness either to fight or run; the enemy will be upon you immediately, and they are strong!"

In an instant every man was up, and no moments were lost in preparing for action. The intelligence came just in time to put the whigs in readiness. Ferguson had detached Dunlap, with two hundred picked mounted men, to engage Clarke and keep him employed till his arrival. These rushed in full charge into the American camp; but the surprise was on their part. They were met hand to hand, with a firmness they had not anticipated. Their confusion was increased by the darkness, which rendered it hard to distinguish friend from foe. The battle was warm for fifteen or twenty minutes, when the tories gave way.

Col. Ferguson hastened to secure himself an advantageous position for contending with the mountaineers collected to oppose him. He left one of his men concealed in the cellar of a house on the road side, whose business it was to ascertain the number and character of those who were pressing on his rear. This spy making himself rather conspicuous, was taken by the pursuing whigs, and forced to give the information they desired. The practice among their riflemen of picking off the officers in an engagement, had produced much confusion in the British ranks, and it being known to the leaders, some had adopted the expedient of disguising themselves before going into action. This prisoner was asked if Ferguson went to battle in disguise, and said, "He has a large check shirt which he wears over his uniform." This information being spread among the soldiers, it is easy to account for the fact that Col. Ferguson was shot through the arm at the commencement of the battle of King's Mountain; his fine white horse being seen not long after, dashing down the hill without a rider.

While the "liberty men," of the frontier districts had fled to the mountains, the women, busily occupied in the labors of the house and field, were harassed by visits from marauding loyalists. A notorious robber, one Edmund Russell, was known to have his retreat at Sandy River. After the battle of King's Mountain, a party of twenty whigs, headed by William White, went in quest of him. White had ventured home to see how matters were going on, and finding his wife and sisters in the field with a basket of wheat which they were beginning to sow, he alighted from his horse to show them "the cast of the hand," as he called it,—not venturing more, for he knew his movements were watched. The enemy heard, indeed that he "was at home sowing wheat," and sent men to capture him after he had gone after Russell.

The robber, afraid to live above ground, had made himself a den in the earth some distance from his house, where he had provisions brought to him. This den was in the woods, and so covered as to be undistinguishable from the ground above it. When the whigs were approaching his house they met two children carrying a bottle of milk, but could obtain from them no information as to his whereabouts. One of the party suddenly exclaimed—"Here is smoke issuing from the ground;" and presently Russell sprang out and ran away. Fear lent him wings, but it was of no avail, seventeen guns being fired at him in rapid succession.

The battle of King's Mountain was soon followed by the retreat of Lord Cornwallis from Charlotte to Winnsboro

The militia of the country *took toll* as the British army passed at every suitable thicket; a single whig sometimes riding up, picking off his object, and making good his escape. Col. Tarleton for a short time halted his legion at White's Mills on Fishing Creek, midway between Charlotte and Winnsboro, on a lookout for the mountain men on their return from the scene of the battle. Cornwallis encamped on the plantation of John Service, a shrewd fellow, who succeeded in making the British commander believe him an idiot. On being told his lordship's name, he asked "if he was related to John Wallis the shoemaker up the road." Lord Cornwallis gave orders that nothing of the simpleton's should be molested.

On the 12th of November, Col. Wemyss, who attacked Sumter's band of volunteers, was defeated and taken prisoner. After this action, Gen. Sumter, aware that Tarleton had been despatched in pursuit of him, with a view to another surprise like that on Fishing Creek—made a hasty retreat, and took up his position at Blackstock's, near Tyger River. On the retreat he sent Col. Taylor, with a detachment of fifty men, to fetch flour from a mill in the vicinity. Taylor expected the General to remain where he was till his return; but shortly after his departure information was brought of the near approach of Tarleton's cavalry, and Sumter moved off to secure his position. Taylor knew nothing of Tarleton's approach, and was not a little displeased when he returned with the flour and did not find the General. His men were hungry, and he allowed two or three hogs to be cleaned and cooked, and some of the flour made into bread. While the soldiers were baking the bread, in the fashion of Johnnycake, on pieces of pine bark, two officers who had been sent back by Sumter to watch the enemy's movements, dashed up in fiery haste to bring the news that Tarleton was just at hand. The hogs and the dough were thrown into the wagon uncooked, and the men drove the wagon into camp at a full gallop. As they turned the corner of a little stable the firing commenced. In this action Sumter received a severe wound, and was carried on a litter the same night into North Carolina. Capt. Steel returned home in November, and by the aid of his rangers, reduced his neighborhood to order, organizing the militia, bringing some of the tories to trial and execution for murder, driving others of the worst from the country, and pardoning less culpable offenders who promised reformation. The condition of the times demanded such summary measures; a fatal disease threatened destruction to the body of the state, and it needed a sharp weapon and an unshrinking hand to eradicate it.

The deplorable sufferings of the unfortunate prisoners in Charleston had moved the sympathy of the people of Western Carolina; for news came that many were perishing of want and disease. The men could not go thither; but the women gathered clothing, medicines, and provisions, and travelled long journeys, encountering danger as well as hardship, to minister to them. The mother of Andrew Jackson, returning to the Waxhaws, after a journey to Charleston to carry clothing and other necessaries to some friends on board the prison ship, was seized with the prison fever, and died in a tent, in the midst of the wide, sandy wilderness of pines. She and her children had quitted their home after the slaughter of Buford's regiment, when the women and children fled from the ravages of the merciless enemy, and had found a place of refuge in Sugar Creek congregation, where they remained during part of the summer.

In Charleston many cruelties were exercised, not only on the imprisoned soldiers, but on the unoffending inhabitants— women and children. The patriotic ladies refused to join in the amusements of the city while in the hands of the British; but gave their energies to the relief of their friends, being the more active when military efforts were suspended. Many and ingenious were the contrivances they adopted, to carry supplies to the defenders of their country. Sometimes cloth for a coat, fashioned into an appendage to female attire, would be borne away, unsuspected by the vigilant guards, and afterwards converted into regimental shape. Boots, "a world too wide" for the delicate wearer, were often transferred to the partisan who could not procure them for himself. A horseman's helmet has been concealed under a well-arranged headdress; and epaulettes delivered from the folds of a matron's simple cap. Other articles in demand for military use, as feathers and cockades, more easily conveyed, were regularly brought by some stratagem or other.

Mr. Simms says, "The women would often procure passes to go to their farms or plantations in the country. They seized these occasions for carrying forth supplies of cloth, linen, and even gunpowder and shot, to their countrymen in the brigade of Marion. These commodities were concealed beneath their garments; and, in preparation for their departure, the dimensions of the good women were observed sensibly to increase. At length it was noticed by the officers on guard, that the lady, who when she left the city was of enormous bulk, would return reduced to a shadow. Strange suspicions naturally ran in their heads as to the causes of a change so surprising; at length a jury of spinsters was provided, and the fat ladies were taken into custody. The discovery was amazing; bales of blue broadcloth were unrolled from about the slenderest waists; and swan and duck shot, and gunpowder and ball, rolls of duck, cotton flannels, &c., appeared from beneath the ample petticoats. This put a stop to their growth, as well as their peregrinations."

One lady who visited the city relates in her letters that she went on board the prison ship, and drank coffee with the prisoners awaiting an exchange. Another was accustomed to wear a bonnet decorated with *thirteen* small plumes, as a token of her attachment to republican principles. Some would not attend church, as they had been accustomed, in the city, while prayers were offered there for the success of the British arms. It might have been said of many female patriots who evinced zeal in support of the cause which then appeared the worse, that they appeared to consecrate every thought to the interests of America. They received under their hospitable roof the sick and wounded, gave them their personal attention and sympathy; and divided of their substance among those who needed aid. The prisoners were visited at regular intervals and favors were solicited in their behalf from the British officers, which were sometimes granted to female intercession. Their sufferings appealed to female benevolence also among the loyalists Some of those most attached to the royal cause were indefatigable in their attentions to the sufferers, whom many feared to visit in consequence of the prevalence of a contagious fever in the hospitals. The English were well supplied with necessary stores; the Americans were destitute, and therefore experienced their kindness and bounty. Their servants were continually employed in carrying them nourishment and articles needed; and in some cases they paid the hire of nurses, where personal services were indispensable. They soothed the death-bed of many with the consolations of religion, prayed with those who were in danger, and joined with the convalescent in returning thanks.

When the British took possession of Charleston, the house in which Mrs. Motte resided, was selected as the head-quarters of Colonels Tarleton and Balfour. From this abode she determined not to be driven; and presided daily at the head of her own table, with a company of thirty British officers. The duties forced upon her were discharged with dignity and grace, while she always replied with becoming spirit to the discourteous taunts frequently uttered in her presence against her "rebel countrymen."

A beautiful country-seat, called Accabee, seven miles from Charleston, was noted during the war as a place of refuge; being unmolested because Mrs. Elliott, its owner, had no male relative to be obnoxious to the British. The mansion was of brick, solidly built; with a piazza in front, and a garden and lawn extending to the Ashley River. The grounds were covered with grass, on which sheep might be seen lying under the magnificent live oaks decorated with the floating silvery moss so beautiful in the low country. The graceful

CHAPTER XX. 227

fringe tree and magnolia grandiflora, with other ornamental trees, grew in clumps in front and on either side. In the rear, a portico looked on an avenue of flowering locusts, nearly a mile in length. At one time, when Col. Lewis Morris was on a visit here to the daughter of Mrs. Elliott, whom he afterwards married, the attention of the family was drawn to the windows by an unusual noise, and they perceived that the house was surrounded by the Black Dragoons, in search of the young officer, who had no time to escape. Miss Elliott went to one of the windows, opened it, and presenting herself to the view of the dragoons, demanded what they wanted "We want the rebel!" was the reply. "Go and look for him in the American army!" answered the young girl. "How dare you disturb a family under the protection of both armies?" Her firmness and resolution conquered; and the enemy departed without further molestation.

The daring exploits of Marion have not been noticed, because they are not so intimately connected with prominent movements of the war as those of Sumter. After the fall of Charleston, when all seemed lost, and parties of British were laying waste the country in every direction, he collected a little band of bold and active troopers at Lynch's Creek, and drilled them regularly for service. He now held a general's commission from Gov. Rutledge. With this band, called "Marion's brigade," he commenced his forest warfare, taking refuge in swamps and fastnesses known only to themselves, and harassing the enemy from his impenetrable retreat, till the very name of the brigade became a terror throughout the country to British and loyalists. No vigilance could guard against his attacks; no effort could force him to open conflict. The enemy was astonished at his feats, and the success of his gallant deeds greatly aided the cause.

Marion's favorite retreat on Snow's Island, at the confluence of Lynch's Creek and the Pedee, was wild and solitary enough for a scene of romance. Deep swamps formed the border of the island, enclosed with running water; there were canebrakes in which game was to be found, and the central elevated ground was covered with tall forest trees. Marion and his men lived here on the plainest fare. It is related that towards the close of 1780, a British officer from Georgetown came to his camp to negotiate for an exchange of prisoners. Marion invited him to dinner, which consisted of roasted potatoes, served on pieces of bark. The Briton asked if their ordinary fare was no better, and was told it was not; if they drew good pay; not a cent. On his return to his friends, he observed that he had little hope of conquering a country whose defenders could thus submit to toil and privation simply for the love of liberty.

CHAPTER XXI.

STATE OF THE COUNTRY IN OTHER DISTRICTS.

Many incidents might be mentioned to show the condition of the country, and the state of popular feeling, while the British were making efforts to establish an undisputed control over the State. But space permits only one or two examples. It should be borne in mind that the experience of an individual is always described as illustrative of many others in similar circumstances. The wife of Col. Thomas, who was a prisoner at Ninety-Six, went to visit him and her two sons, his companions in rigorous captivity. By chance she heard a tory woman say to some others: " To-morrow night the loyalists intend to surprise the rebels at Cedar Spring." She was thrilled at alarm with this intelligence; the Cedar Spring was within a few miles of her house; the whigs were posted there, and among them were some of her own children. Her resolution was taken at once; she determined to apprise them of the enemy's intention, before the blow could be struck. Bidding a hasty adieu to her husband and sons, she was upon the road as quickly as possible; rode the intervening distance of nearly sixty miles the next day, and arrived in time to bring information to her sons and friends of the impending danger. The moment they knew what was to be expected, a brief consultation was held; and measures were immediately taken for defence. The soldiers withdrew a short distance from their camp fires, which were prepared to burn as brightly as possible. The men selected suitable positions in the surrounding woods.

Their preparations were just completed, when they heard in the distance, amid the silence of night, the cautious advance of the foe. Slowly and warily they advanced, till they were already within the glare of the blazing fires; they supposed the intended victims wrapped in heavy slumber; they heard but the crackling of the flames, and the hoarse murmur of the wind as it swept through the pine trees. Giving the signal for the onset, they rushed towards the fires, eager for slaughter; but suddenly the flashes and shrill reports of rifles revealed the hidden patriots. To their consternation, they found themselves assailed in the rear by the party they had expected to strike unawares. Thrown into confusion by this unexpected reception, overwhelming defeat was the consequence to the loyalists.

The wife of Captain Richardson, who lived in Sumter District, sustained more than her share of the trials which fell to woman's lot in the midst of the storm and struggle. Her husband had been taken prisoner at the fall of Charleston, and sent to a military station on John's Island, where he nearly fell a victim to the small-pox. The British having failed to observe the conditions on which he had surrendered, as soon as he recovered sufficiently to move about, he made his escape, and returned to his home, where he concealed himself in the Santee Swamp. This extensive swamp-land borders the river for many miles, presenting to the view a vast plain of dense woods which seem absolutely impervious. The recesses of those dark thickets, where the trees grow close together, and are interlaced by a luxuriant growth of giant creepers, often afforded hiding-places for the hunted Americans. At this time the British troops having overrun the State, Col. Tarleton had made the house of Capt. Richardson, with some others, a station for his regiment of cavalry. They lived luxuriously on the abundance of his richly-stocked and well-cultivated plantation; while Mrs. Richardson and her children, it is said, were furnished with but a scanty share of provisions. Yet every day she sent food from her small allowance by an old and faithful negro, to her husband in the swamp. She had expected the seizure of her horses and cattle, and had sent Richardson's favorite riding horse into the swamp for concealment, with a few cattle which she wished to save for future need. The horse was shut up in a covered pen in the woods, which had once been used for holding corn. Sometimes also, Mrs. Richardson ventured to visit her husband, taking with her their little daughter. These stolen meetings were full of consolation to the fugitive. The spot he had chosen for his retreat was a small knoll or elevation in the heart of the swamp, called "John's Island," by way of distinction from another in the neighborhood, occupied by other whigs, which bore the name of "Beech Island."

It was not long before the British had information of his escape. They naturally concluded that he was somewhere in the vicinity of his family and relatives. A diligent search was instituted, and they watched to surprise him, or find some clue to his retreat. Not unfrequently did the men boast in the presence of the wife, of what they would do when they should capture him. On one occasion some of them displayed in her sight their swords reeking with blood—probably that of her cattle—and told her it was the blood of Capt. Richardson, whom they had killed. At another time they brought intelligence that he had been taken and hanged. In this state of cruel suspense she sometimes remained for several successive days, not knowing whether to believe or distrust the horrible tales brought to her ears.

One day, when the troops were absent on some expedition, Capt. Richardson ventured home on a visit. Before he thought of returning to his refuge in the forest, a patrolling party of the enemy appeared unexpectedly at the gate. Mrs. Richardson, with great presence of mind, seeing the British soldiers about to come in, pretended to be intently busy about something in the front door, and stood in the way, retarding their entrance, till her husband had time to retire through the back door, into the swamp near at hand. The captain was not idle in his seclusion; but collecting around him the whigs of his acquaintance, he trained them daily in cavalry exercise. When Tarleton ravaged the plantation and burnt the dwelling of his deceased father, Gen. Richardson he passed so near the ruins as to see the extent of the desolation.

Several times did he peril his life to visit his amiable family At one time, after he had joined the forces of Marion, he and some of his friends had scarcely reached his house when a party of British and tories was seen advancing rapidly down the avenue. To remount in all haste their wearied steeds, and ride down the bank at the rear of the house, seeking concealment in the swamp, offered the only chance for escape. In this they all succeeded, except a young man with whom Mrs. Richardson was well acquainted. In vain did she intercede for him with the officers, and with streaming eyes implore them to spare his life. They hanged him on a walnut tree only a few paces from her door. When she complained with tears of this cruelty to herself, and barbarity towards one who had risked his life in defence of her husband, they jeeringly told her they "would soon have him also, and then she should see him kick like that fellow." To such atrocities could the passions of brutalized men lead them, even in an age and nation that boasted itself the most enlightened on earth!

The portion of the State comprising Spartanburg and Union Districts witnessed many deeds of violence and blood, and many bold achievements of the hardy partisans. So prevalent was loyalism in the darkest of those days, so bitter was the animosity felt towards the whigs, and so eager the determination to root them from the soil, that the very recklessness of hate gave frequent opportunities for the betrayal of the plans of their enemies. Often were the boastings of those who plotted some midnight surprise, or some enterprise that promised rare pillage—uttered in the hearing of weak and despised women—unexpectedly turned into wonder at the secret agency that had disconcerted them. The tradition of the country teems with accounts of enterprise in this kind of service.

One young girl, Miss Langston, residing in Laurens District, having heard by accident that the "Bloody Scout" were about to visit the "Elder settlement" where her brother and some friends were living, determined at all hazards to give them warning. She was obliged to leave her home alone, by stealth, and at the dead hour of night. Many miles were to be traversed, and the road lay through woods, and crossed marshes and creeks where the conveniences of bridges and foot-logs were wanting. She walked rapidly on, heedless of slight difficulties; but her heart almost failed her when she came to the banks of the Tyger—a deep and rapid stream, rendered more dangerous by the rains that had lately fallen. But the thought of personal danger weighed not with her; she resolved to accomplish her purpose, or perish in the attempt. She entered the water; but when in the middle of the ford, became bewildered, and knew not which direction to take. The hoarse rush of the waters, which were up to her neck—the blackness of the night—the utter solitude around her—the uncertainty lest the next step should ingulph her past help, confused her, and she wandered some time in the channel without knowing whither to turn her steps. But the energy of a resolute will, under the care of Providence, sustained her.

Having with difficulty reached the other side, she lost no time in hastening to her brother, informed him and his friends of the preparations made to surprise and destroy them, and urged him to send his men instantly in different directions to arouse and warn the neighborhood. The soldiers had just returned from a fatiguing excursion, and complained that they were faint from want of food. The noble girl, not satisfied with what she had done, was ready to help them still further by providing refreshment immediately. Though wearied, wet and shivering with cold, she at once set about her preparations. A few boards were taken from the roof of the house, a fire was kindled with them, and in a few minutes a hoe-cake, partly baked, was broken into pieces, and thrust into the shot-pouches of the men. Thus provisioned, the little company hastened to give the alarm to their neighbors, and did so in time for all to make their escape.

At a later period, the father of Miss Langston incurred the displeasure of the loyalists in consequence of the active services of his sons in their country's cause. A party came to his house with the desperate design of putting to death all the men of the family. The sons were absent, but the feeble old man was in their power. One of the company drew a pistol and deliberately levelled it at his breast. Suddenly a shriek was heard, and his young daughter sprang between her aged parent and the fatal weapon. The brutal soldier roughly ordered her to get out of the way, or the contents of the pistol would be instantly lodged in her own heart. She heeded not the threat, but clasping her arms tightly around the old man's neck, declared that her own body should first receive the ball aimed at his heart! There are few human beings, even of the most depraved, entirely insensible to all generous impulses. On this occasion the conduct of the daughter, so determined to shield her father's life by the sacrifice of her own, touched the heart even of a member of the "Bloody Scout," and Langston was spared.

The state of a half savage region of country near the frontier in Georgia, may be illustrated by the following anecdote, well remembered in that State. In a portion of Wilkes—now Elbert County—called by tories, "The Hornet's Nest," on account of the number of whigs among the inhabitants, a stream named "War-woman's Creek," joined Broad River. It was so called on account of a zealous tory-hating heroine who lived on its banks. On the occasion of an excursion from the British camp at Augusta, into the interior for the purpose of pillage and murder, five loyalists separated from their party, and crossed the river to examine the neighborhood and pay a visit to their old acquaintance, Nancy Hart. When they arrived at her cabin, they unceremoniously entered it, and informed her they had come to learn the truth of a story, that she had secreted a noted rebel from a party of "king's men," who, but for her interference, would have caught and hung him. Nancy undauntedly avowed her agency in the fugitive's escape. She had heard at first, she said, the tramp of a horse, and then saw a man on horseback approaching her cabin. As soon as she knew him to be a whig flying from pursuit, she let down the bars in front of her cabin, and motioned him to pass through both doors and take to the swamp. She then put up the bars, entered the cabin, and closed the doors. Presently some tories rode up to the bars, calling vociferously for her. She muffled up her head and face, and opening the door, inquired why they disturbed a sick, lone woman. They said they had traced a man they wanted to catch near to her house, and asked if any one on horseback had passed that way. She answered no, but that she saw some one on a sorrel horse turn out of the path into the woods, two or three hundred yards back. "That must be the fellow!" said the tories; and asking her direction as to the way he took, they turned about and went off, "well fooled," concluded Nancy, " in an opposite course to that of my whig boy, when, if they had not been so lofty minded, but had looked on the ground inside the bars, they would have seen his horse's tracks up to that door, as plain as you can see the tracks on this floor, and out of t'other door down the path to the swamp."

This bold story did not much please the tory party, but they contented themselves with ordering her to prepare them someting to eat. She replied that she never fed traitors and king's men if she could help it—the villains having put it out of her power to feed even her own family and friends, by stealing and killing all her poultry and pigs, "except that one old gobbler you see in the yard." " And *that* you shall cook for us," said one who appeared to be a leader; and raising his musket he shot down the turkey, which another brought in and handed to Mrs. Hart to be cleaned and cooked without delay. She stormed awhile, but seeming at last disposed to make a merit of necessity, began with alacrity the arrangements for cooking, assisted by her daughter, a little girl ten or twelve years old.

The spring—of which every settlement had one near—was just at the edge of the swamp; and a short distance within the swamp was hid among the trees a high snag-topped stump, on which was placed a conch-shell. This rude trumpet was used by the family to convey information, by variations in its notes, to Hart or his neighbors, who might be at work in a field or "clearing" at hand—to let them know that the "Britishers" or tories were about—that the master was wanted at the cabin—or that he was to keep close, or "make tracks" for another swamp. While cooking the turkey, Nancy sent her daughter to the spring for water, with directions to blow the conch in such a way as should inform her father there were tories in the cabin; and that he was to keep close with his three neighbors until he should again hear the signal.

While the men, who had become merry over their jug of liquor, were feasting upon the slaughtered gobbler, Nancy waited on the table, and occasionally passed between them and their muskets. She had contrived that there should be no water in the cabin; and when it was called for, despatched Sukey a second time to the spring, with instructions to blow such a signal on the conch as should call up Hart and his neighbors immediately. Meanwhile she had managed by slipping out one of the pieces of pine which form a "chinking" between the logs of a cabin, to open a space through which she was able to pass to the outside two of the five guns. She was detected in the act of putting out the third. The men sprang to their feet; when, quick as thought, Nancy brought the piece she held, to her shoulder, declaring she would kill the first man who approached her. The men arriving from the field, the tories were taken prisoners, and, sad to relate! received no more mercy than had some of the whigs at the hands of their enemies.

CHAPTER XXII.

INCURSION INTO NEW JERSEY—INDIAN RAVAGES IN THE VALLEY OF THE MOHAWK.

Some events that occurred at the North during the summer of 1780, demand our attention. One of these is an incursion into New Jersey. On the 7th of June some British troops left Staten Island, under the command of the Hessian General Knyphausen, and landed at Elizabethtown before daylight. Their design was to strike terror into the country, and their march into the interior was marked by pillage and devastation. Several houses were fired and the inhabitants left destitute of provisions or shelter. As they approached the village of Connecticut Farms, four miles from Elizabethtown, many families fled to Springfield, driving their cattle before them.

In a predatory incursion of British and tories, in January of this year, they had burned the church at Elizabethtown, then used as a hospital for the sick and wounded of the American army. The weary soldiers were accustomed to sleep upon its floor, and eat their hurried and scanty meals from the seats of the pews; so that worshippers on the Sabbath were not unfrequently compelled to stand through the service. The pastor, James Caldwell, was extremely obnox ious to the British and loyalists, on account of his zeal and activity in the cause of his country, and his great popularity in the community. No effort was spared to do him injury; a price was set upon his head, and it is said that while preaching the gospel of peace to his people, he was often forced to lay his loaded pistols by his side in the pulpit. At this time his temporary residence was at Connecticut Farms.

When informed of the enemy's approach, Mr. Caldwell put his elder children into a baggage waggon in his possession as commissary, and sent them to some of his friends for protection. Three of the younger ones, one an infant, remained with their mother in the house. Mr. Caldwell had no fears for the safety of his wife and young family; for he believed it impossible that resentment could be extended to a mother watching over her little ones. He had that morning taken an early breakfast, intending to join the force collecting to oppose the enemy. Having in vain endeavored to persuade his wife to go with him, he returned to make a last effort to induce her to change her determination; but she remained firm. She handed him a cup of coffee, which he drank as he sat on horseback. Seeing the gleam of British arms at a distance, he put spurs to his horse, and in a few minutes was out of sight.

Mrs. Caldwell herself felt no alarm. She had hid several articles of value in a bucket and let it down into the well, and had filled her pockets with silver and jewelry. She saw that the house was put in order, and then dressed herself with care, that, should the enemy enter her dwelling, she might, to use her own expression—"receive them as a lady." She took the infant in her arms, retired to her chamber, the window of which commanded a view of the road, and seated herself upon the bed. The alarm was given that the soldiers were at hand. But she felt confidence that no one could have the heart to do injury to the helpless inmates of her house. She had just nursed the infant and given it to the nurse, who was in the room. A soldier left the road, and crossing a space of ground to reach the house, came to the window of the room, put his gun close to it, and fired. Two balls entered the breast of Mrs. Caldwell; she fell back on the bed, and in a moment expired. After the murder, her dress was cut open, and her pockets were rifled by the soldiers. Her remains were conveyed to a house on the other side of the road; the dwelling was then fired and reduced to ashes with all the furniture. The ruthless soldiers went on in their work of destruction, pillaging and setting fire to the houses, piling beds and clothing in the street and destroying them, till the village was laid waste.

This deliberate and barbarous murder had a great effect on public feeling, exciting a universal sentiment of horror, and filling all with one desire to drive the invaders from their soil. "The Caldwell tragedy," says one of the journals of the day, "has raised the resolution of the country to the highest pitch." The advance of a body of troops from Morristown compelled the invaders to retire; and a second advance met with repulse at Springfield.

The history of the Scoharie settlements and the valley of the Mohawk is full of interest, but would occupy an entire volume by itself. The Mohawk Valley was one of the richest agricultural districts in the country, and one of the most populous at the period of the Revolution. It presented an inviting aspect to the plundering savages and the refugees who shared a precarious subsistence among them and in the wilds of Canada. Scarcely any other section was so frequently invaded and overrun by the enemy. Month after month during seven years its villages and settlements were attacked or destroyed, its farms laid waste, and the inhabitants driven from their homes, or killed and captured. The settlers in each neighborhood were obliged to band together for their mutual defence, forming parties to serve as scouts through the country, for the traveller from place to place was liable to attack in the lonely forest, or to a bullet or arrow aimed from the covert of rocks or bushes.

During the summer of 1778, the Indians and tories being sufficiently employed in the destruction of Wyoming and Cherry Valley, the Mohawk Valley remained unmolested, with the exception of a descent upon the German Flats. In the spring of 1779, Gen. Clinton moved up the Mohawk and encamped at Canajoharie, and in this summer also little mischief was done. But in the spring of 1780 the Indians again appeared, infuriated at the destruction of their villages by Gen. Sullivan, and eager to wreak vengeance on the unoffending inhabitants. In August, Brant, with an army of Indians and loyalists, burst upon the defenceless settlements, plundering, burning, and desolating the country; while in the autumn Sir John Johnson ravaged the north side of the river. Thus ne destruction of the Mohawk settlements was almost complete, and if here and there a small one escaped, it afforded but a temporary shelter, being likely to be destroyed by the next storm that should sweep over the land.

By way of showing what numbers suffered, we will trace a few incidents in the experience of a single family—that of Martin Van Alstine, then living in the neighborhood of Canajoharie. While the enemy, stationed at Johnstown, were laying waste the country, parties continually going about to murder the inhabitants and burn their dwellings, this neighborhood remained in comparative quiet, though the settlers trembled as each sun arose, lest his setting beams should fall on their ruined homes. Most of the men were absent, and when at length intelligence came that the destroyers were approaching, the people were almost distracted with terror. Mrs. Van Alstine called her neighbors together, endeavored to calm their fears, and advised them to make immediate arrangements for removing to an island belonging to her husband near the opposite side of the river. She knew that the spoilers would be in too great haste to make any attempt to cross, and thought if some articles were removed, they might be induced to suppose the inhabitants gone to a greater distance.

The seven families in the neighborhood were in a few hours upon the island, having taken with them many things necessary to their comfort during a short stay. Scarcely had they secreted themselves before they heard the dreaded warhoop, and descried the Indians in the distance. It was not long before one and another saw the homes they loved in flames. When the savages came to Van Alstine's house, they were about to fire that also, but the chief, interfering, informed them that Sir John would not be pleased if that house were burned—the owner having extended civilities to the baronet before the commencement of hostilities. Mrs. Van Alstine was thus enabled to give shelter to the houseless families who had fled with her. The fugitives, however, did not deem it prudent to leave their place of concealment for several days, the smoke seen in different directions too plainly indicating that the work of devastation was going on.

Later in the following autumn an incident occurred productive of trouble. Three men from the neighborhood of Canajoharie, who had deserted the whig cause and joined the British, came back from Canada as spies, and were apprehended and executed. Their prolonged absence causing uneasiness to their friends in Canada, some Indians were sent to reconnoitre and learn something of them. They returned immediately, and a party was dispatched to revenge the death of the spies upon the inhabitants. In their progress they came to the house of Van Alstine, where no preparations had been made for defence, the family not expecting an attack. Mrs. Van Alstine was personally acquainted with Brant, and it may have been owing to this circumstance that the members of the family were not killed or carried away as prisoners. The Indians came upon them by surprise, entered the house without ceremony, and plundered and destroyed everything in their way. The most valued articles, brought from Holland, were broken one after another, till the house was strewed with fragments. As they passed a large mirror without demolishng it, the family hoped it might be saved; but presently two of the savages led in a colt from the stable, and the glass being laid in the hall, compelled the animal to walk over it

The beds which they could not carry away they ripped open, shaking out the feathers and taking the ticks with them. They also took all the clothing. One young Indian, attracted by the brilliancy of a pair of inlaid buckles on the shoes of the aged grandmother seated in the corner, rudely snatched them from her feet, tore off the buckles, and flung the shoes in her face. Another took her shawl from her neck, threatening to kill her if resistance were offered. They then broke the window glass throughout the house, and unsatisfied with the plunder they had collected, bribed a man servant to show them where some articles had been hastily secreted. He treacherously disclosed the hiding-place, and the winter clothing of the family was soon added to the rest of the booty.

The provisions having been carried away, the family subsisted on corn, which they pounded and made into cakes. They felt much the want of clothing, and the mother gathered the silk of milk-weed, of which, mixed with flax, she spun and wove garments. The inclement season was now approaching, and they suffered severely from the want of window glass, as well as their bedding, woollen clothes, and the various articles, including cooking utensils, taken from them. The most arduous labors could do little towards providing for so many destitute persons; their neighbors were in no condition to help them, the roads were almost impassable, besides being infested by Indians, and their finest horses had been taken. In this deplorable situation, Mrs. Van Alstine proposed to her husband to join with others who had been robbed in like manner, and make an attempt to recover their property from the Indian castle, eighteen or twenty miles distant, where it had been carried. But the idea of such an enterprise against an enemy superior in numbers and well prepared for defence, was soon abandoned.

As the cold became more intolerable and the necessity for doing something more urgent, unable longer to witness the sufferings of those dependent on her, she resolved to venture herself on the expedition. Her husband and children endeavored to dissuade her, but firm for their sake, she left home, accompanied by her son, about sixteen years of age. The snow was deep and the roads in a wretched condition, yet she persevered through all difficulties, and by good fortune arrived at the castle at a time when the Indians were all absent on a hunting excursion, the women and children only being left at home. She went to the principal house, where she supposed the most valuable articles must have been deposited, and on entering was met by the old squaw who had the superintendence, who demanded what she wanted. She asked for food; the squaw hesitated; but on her visitor saying she had never turned an Indian away hungry, sullenly commenced preparations for a meal. The matron saw her bright copper teakettle, with other cooking utensils, brought forth for use. While the squaw was gone for water, she began a search for her property, and finding several articles gave them to her son to put into the sleigh. When the squaw, returning, asked by whose order she was taking those things, Mrs. Van Alstine replied, that they belonged to her; and seeing that the woman was not disposed to give them up peaceably, took from her pocket-book a paper, and handed it to the squaw, who she knew could not read. She asked whose name

was affixed to the supposed order, and being told it was that of
"Yankee Peter"—a man who had great influence among the
savages, dared not refuse submission. By this stratagem Mrs.
Van Alstine secured, without opposition, all the articles she
could find belonging to her. She then asked where the horses
were kept. The squaw refused to show her, but she went to
the stable, and there found those belonging to her husband
in fine order—for the savages were careful of their best
horses. She bade her son cut the halters, and finding themselves at liberty they bounded off and went homeward at full
speed.

The mother and son now drove back as fast as possible.
They reached home late in the evening, and passed a sleepless night, dreading instant pursuit and a night attack from
the irritated savages. Soon after daylight the alarm was
given that the Indians were within view, and coming towards
the house. Van Alstine saw no course to escape their vengeance, but to give up whatever they wished to take back;
but his intrepid wife was determined on an effort, at least, to
retain her property. As they came near she begged her husband not to show himself—for she knew they would immediately fall upon him—but to leave the matter in her hands.
The intruders took their course first to the stable, and bidding all the rest remain within doors, the matron went out
alone, followed to the door by her family, weeping and entreat
ing her not to expose herself. Going to the stable, she in
quired in the Indian language what the men wanted. The
reply was "our horses." She said boldly—"They are ours
you came and took them without right; they are ours, and we

mean to keep them." The chief now came forward threateningly, and approached the door. Mrs. Van Alstine placed herself against it, telling him she would not give up the animals they had raised. He succeeded in pulling her from the door, and drew out the plug that fastened it, which she snatched from his hand, pushing him away. He then stepped back and presented his rifle, threatening to shoot her if she did not move ; but she kept her position, opening her neckhandkerchief and bidding him shoot if he dared. It might be that the Indian feared punishment from his allies for any such act of violence, or that he was moved with admiration of her intrepidity ; he hesitated, looked at her for a moment, and then slowly dropped his gun, uttering in his native language expressions implying his conviction that the evil one must help her, and saying to his companions that she was a brave woman and they would not molest her. Giving a shout, by way of expressing their approbation, they departed from the premises. On their way they called at the house of Col. Frey, and related their adventure, saying that the white woman's courage had saved her and her property, and were there fifty such brave women as the wife of " Big Tree," the Indians would never have troubled the inhabitants of the Mohawk Valley.

CHAPTER XXIII.

TREASON OF ARNOLD—CONTRIBUTIONS IN PHILADELPHIA—
REVOLT OF PENNSYLVANIA TROOPS—GREENE AT THE
SOUTH—BATTLE OF THE COWPENS.

One of the most remarkable incidents of the war occurred in September of 1780. Benedict Arnold, who held the rank of Major-General in the American army, and had served with high distinction, had been appointed commandant of Philadelphia after its evacuation by the British. His extravagance had impaired his fortune, and being destitute of moral principle, he did not scruple to supply himself with the means of maintaining his ostentatious style of living by fraud and dishonest use of the public funds. For this he was tried by a court martial, found guilty, and sentenced to receive a reprimand from the Commander-in-Chief. This painful duty was discharged by Washington with all possible delicacy, but Arnold's pride was deeply wounded, and he formed a secret purpose of revenge.

While residing in Philadelphia, his accomplishments and the splendor of his equipments, with perhaps his insolent opposition to the local authorities, had won favor for him in what might be called the exclusive and aristocratic circle of loyal ists. The daughter of one of the most prominent families in this circle—Margaret Shippen—became his wife. She was young, beautiful and gay, and had been greatly admired by the British officers. It is likely that her taste for luxury and display encouraged her husband's propensity to extravagance, but not at all probable that she was the instigator of his crime against his country. Nor can it be supposed that he even confided to her the perilous scheme he was pondering; for it was neither necessary nor safe to do so. She was made the instrument, however—in all probability an unconscious one— of the intercourse carried on while the iniquitous plan was maturing. A letter from Maj. André to her, offering to procure supplies from New York of certain millinery articles for her use, is supposed to cover a meaning understood by Arnold alone. He and André had kept up a correspondence under feigned names from the spring of 1779.

The American post at West Point was a formidable barrier to British incursions northward from New York. The command of this important position was given by Washington to Arnold at his earnest solicitation. He occupied as his headquarters the house of Beverley Robinson, a loyalist— situated on the east side of the Hudson, a little below West Point. Maj. André, aid-de-camp to Sir Henry Clinton, and Adjutant-General of the British army, was instructed to negotiate with him for the surrender of this fortress. Their communications were carried on through an American named Joshua Smith. An interview at length took place between the two officers—André coming on shore and accompanying Arnold to Robinson's house. The agreement was then finally concluded. Arnold promised to deliver the post into the hands of the British, having stipulated for a large sum of money and a high rank in the royal army.

When Maj. André wished to return to New York he found himself unable to get on board the Vulture, whence he had landed. He therefore set out by land, accompanied by Smith, and bearing a passport signed by Gen. Arnold, which served for his protection in passing the American posts, representing him as a person employed by the General on important business. On the borders of the neutral ground—a region of country between the two hostile lines—Smith bade his companion farewell. André, now feeling almost secure, pressed on towards New York. He was stopped near Tarrytown by three men belonging to the whig militia, John Paulding, David Williams, and Isaac Van Wart. Their suspicions were awakened by some inconsistency in his answers; they arrested and searched him, and found the treasonable dispatches of Arnold in his boots.

By this providential discovery the country was saved from a train of disasters. The captors took their prisoner to Col. Jameson, the commander of he American outposts. He had implicit confidence in Gen. Arnold, and wrote to inform him of the arrest of a person called Anderson, travelling under his passport. This was an indiscreet procedure; for it enabled the traitor to save himself by timely flight to the enemy.

General Washington, on his way from Hartford, stopped with his officers at West Point. His aids-de-camp—among them La Fayette—were at breakfast with Gen. Arnold when the letter arrived which bore to the traitor the first intelligence of André's capture. He left the room immediately, went to his chamber, sent for his wife, and briefly informed her of the necessity of his instant flight to the British. The news overwhelmed her, and she fell in a swoon on the floor, while her guilty husband made his escape on board the Vulture, then lying in the river.

The utmost horror and indignation was felt through the whole country and in Europe at this heinous treason. John Jay, writing from Madrid to Miss Livingston, says—"All the world here are cursing Arnold, and pitying his wife." The unfortunate André was tried by a court martial, and condemned to death as a spy. The bravery and excellent character of this amiable young officer appealed to general sympathy, and his sad fate was much commisserated. But the public safety required the rigid execution of the penalty imposed by the usages of war, and the sentence was executed. Arnold escaped the vengeance of his indignant countrymen; but he was regarded with contempt even by those who had expected to profit by his crime, and his name descended to after ages under a load of infamy.

The American people, in their generous sympathy for André, have almost forgotten the daring and self-devotion of one of Connecticut's noblest sons—Capt. Nathan Hale. In September, 1776, when Washington, after his retreat from Long Island, was encamped on Harlæm Heights, it became important for him to know the situation of the British army, and the indications of its future movements. Hale offered to devote himself to the perilous enterprise. He crossed the Sound from Norwalk to Huntington in the disguise of a schoolmaster, and travelling westward at length entered New York. Having gained the desired information, he set out on his return, passing through the Island to a spot previously designated, where a boat was to receive him. As he approached the shore he mistook a British craft for the one he expected. Discovering his error, he attempted to retrace his steps; but it was too late; several muskets were levelled at him, and he was obliged to surrender. Being searched, it was ascertained that he was a spy. He was taken immediately to New York, and the next morning hung upon a tree. His execution was attended with circumstances of aggravated cruelty; the consolations of religion were denied him; he was refused a Bible and the attendance of a clergyman. The letters he had written to his friends were destroyed. Yet the zeal of the patriot was strong in death. His last words, as he stood friendless and alone beneath the tree, were: "I only regret that I have but one life to give for my country."

It should not be forgotten that in the autumn of this year the ladies of Philadelphia united in their memorable contribution for the relief of the suffering American soldiers. The diminished resources of the country scarcely allowed the scantiest supply of clothing and provisions, and the ability if not the benevolence of the citizens seemed almost exhausted by repeated applications. An association was formed and a lady president appointed, with a committee to collect the contributions. The work was charity in its genuine form, and from its purest source—the voluntary outpouring of the heart. They solicited money and other gifts from house to house, and sacrificed their trinkets and jewelry to swell the fund. The result was remarkable. The aggregate amount of contributions in the city and county of Philadelphia was not less than seven thousand five hundred dollars in specie; much of it, too, paid in hard money at a time of the greatest appreciation. "All ranks of society seem to have joined in the liberal effort, from Phillis, the colored woman, with her humble seven shillings and sixpence, to the Marchioness de La Fayette, who contributed one hundred guineas in specie, and the Countess de Luzerne, who gave six thousand dollars in continental paper." La Fayette sent the offering in his wife's name, with a graceful letter to the president of the association.

The Marquis de Chastellux, describing a visit paid to Mrs. Bache, at whose house many of the shirts provided for the soldiers were cut out, says: "She conducted us into a room filled with work lately finished by the ladies of Philadelphia. This work consisted neither of embroidered tambour waistcoats, nor of network edging, nor of gold and silver brocade. It was a quantity of shirts for the soldiers of Pennsylvania. The ladies bought linen from their private purses, and took a pleasure in cutting them out and sewing them. On each shirt was the name of the married or unmarried lady who made it, and they amounted to twenty-two hundred."

This seasonable aid did more than simply remove the pressure of want; it had a moral effect in stimulating the soldiers to perseverance, and inspiring them with confidence. Gen. Washington, in his letter of acknowledgment to the committee of ladies, says: "The army ought not to regret its sacrifices or its sufferings, when they meet with so flattering a reward as in the sympathy of your sex." Nor was such generosity or zeal limited to a single city or State. Among examples too numerous to mention, is one of a lady of New Jersey, whose gates on the public road bore the inscription—" Hospitality within to all American officers, and refreshment for their soldiers ;" an invitation not likely to prove a mere form of words on the regular route between the northern and southern posts of the army. Instances, too, occurred in which respectable strangers, who had taken quarters at the public house, were invited to the comforts of a private table and fireside. A gentleman taken ill at the tavern was brought by Mrs. Wilson's domestics to her dwelling, the best medical aid and nursing secured for him, and hospitality extended to the friends who came to visit him during a long illness.

The same lady was visited by General and Mrs. Washington, a short time after the execution of Maj. André. Their approach, with the General's staff, and the escort of a troop of horse, was announced to her in time to have dinner in readiness for a party of thirty or forty. Before these distinguished guests took their departure, a concourse of people from the adjacent country and the towns in the vicinity had crowded round the house to catch a glimpse of the idolized Chief. A few members of the legislature, and the prominent gentlemen of the neighborhood were admitted and formally introduced. As it was impossible for the multitude to obtain entrance, a little stratagem was devised by one of the gentlemen, by which those without could be gratified without subjecting the General to the annoyance of a mere exhibition of himself. Knowing his admiration of a fine horse, he ordered an animal remarkable for its beauty to be brought into the street, and then invited him out to inspect it. Thus an opportunity was afforded to the whole assemblage to gaze upon and salute him with their cheers.

At the commencement of 1781 the balance of success—notwithstanding the immense expenditure of blood and toil—seemed as likely to turn in favor of.Great Britain as America. The former power, it was true, was involved by the Revolution in a war with three European nations—Holland having also become her enemy. Yet the army of Sir Henry Clinton was abundantly supplied, not only with men but with munitions; while that of Washington still suffered terribly from the want of pay, clothes, and provisions. The necessity became so pressing as to cause discontent among the soldiers, which on the 1st of January, 1781, broke out in a revolt of the Pennsylvania troops. The mutineers abandoned their camp, and determined to present themselves before Congress to demand redress of their grievances. They were met at Princeton by emissaries of the British Commander-in-chief—Sir Henry Clinton—who sought to entice them by alluring promises into the service of His Majesty. The men, however, had not lost their love of country, although driven to sedition by distress; they indignantly seized the British agents and delivered them as prisoners to Gen. Wayne. The difficulties of which they complained were adjusted by prudent concessions, their most pressing wants being relieved, and they then returned to their duty.

The suffering condition of the troops in general calling loudly for relief, Congress found it necessary to adopt ener getic measures. At this crisis, Robert Morris, a wealthy merchant of Philadelphia, was appointed superintendent of the treasury, and established the bank of North America. It was chiefly the beneficial influence of his financial operations that saved the army from disbanding, and enabled Congress to prosecute the war with renewed vigor.

In January the traitor Arnold, in command of the British forces, made a descent on Virginia, ravaging the coasts, and destroying public and private property. Gen. La Fayette was ordered with troops into that State for the purpose of intercepting and capturing him, and the French fleet stationed at Rhode Island sailed to take part in the expedition. The British Admiral Arbuthnot prevented its success by sailing from New York, attacking the French fleet, and driving it back to Rhode Island. Arnold thus escaped from the danger that had threatened him, and his countrymen were disappointed in the hope of making an example of a traitor. In March he was joined by Gen. Phillips of the British army, and their work of devastation was continued.

When Arnold left New York, Colonels Dundas and Simcoe —officers who possessed the entire confidence of Sir Henry Clinton—were sent with him. He could adopt no measure of importance without consulting them. It has been said that the English General gave them a " dormant commission," authorizing them to supersede and arrest him, should they suspect him of sinister intent. It is evident that he was not implicitly trusted by the commander

The breezes of fortune which had fanned into life the expiring embers of opposition to English tyranny at the South, had been so variable that the hopes of the people, raised at times by success, were often trembling on the verge of extinction. On the other hand, the reverses that had befallen the British arms had exasperated the loyalists, and embittered the enmity felt towards the stubborn people who refused to be conquered. The whigs were hunted like deer, and chased from one place of shelter to another. Such was the condition of things, when the destiny of the South was committed to the hands of a soldier of consummate genius, in whom all had implicit confidence. The following verse of a popular Revolutionary song was appropriate:

> " General Greene, Rhode Island's son,
> Commissioned from on high,
> In that distressed hour did come,
> And away our fears did fly."

After his defeat near Camden, Gen Gates was removed from the command of the army at the South, and Gen. Greene, of Rhode Island, appointed in his place. When he took the command he established his encampment on the banks of the Pedee, opposite Cheraw. From the first outbreak in June, the whigs had endeavored to hold the upper part of the State —returning continually when driven back. Greene extended his posts across the country; Gen. Morgan resting at the "Big Springs," and further west Col. Lacy at Fort Lacy, on Turkey Creek. The first movement of Greene was to send Morgan across the Catawba westward that he might check the devastations of the British and loyalists. Lord Cornwallis had for a long time projected an expedition into North Carolina; but the first attempt had been baffled by the fall of Col. Ferguson at King's Mountain. He now determined a second time upon advancing against that State, and being unwilling to leave Morgan in his rear, despatched Tarleton to encounter him. Morgan at first retreated, and was closely pursued by Tarleton. Just before their encounter, a party of loyalists came to the house of a widow who lived near Grindal Shoal, a little south of Pacolet River, and committed some depredations. They burned the straw covering from a rude hut in which the family lodged, while a relative ill of the small-pox occupied the house. Mrs. Potter and her children had built this lodge of rails, for their temporary accommodation. The soldiers attempted to take off her wedding-ring, which, as it had been worn for years, became imbedded under the skin in the effort to force it from her finger. They swore it should be cut off, but finally desisted from the attempt. On the same march, Tarleton encamped at the house of John Beckham, whose wife saw for the first time this renowned officer while standing in her yard, and ordering his men to catch her poultry for supper. She spoke civilly to him, and hastened to prepare supper for him and his suite, as if they had been honored guests. When about to leave in the morning, he ordered the house to be burned, after being given up to pillage, but on her remonstrance recalled the order. All her bedding was taken, except one quilt, which soon shared the same fate.

Near the Catawba, a woman, supposed to be a tory, was taken and brought for examination to Gen. Morgan. It proved to be our old acquaintance, Mrs. McCalla, on her way home from Charlotte. Lord Cornwallis had expressed a willingness to release her husband on his parole, provided Sumter would be security that the parole should be kept. The wife, accordingly, had made her way to the American general, and was now returning with the paper which she fancied would secure the captive's freedom. She was much amused at being taken for a loyalist, and after producing the paper in Sumter's handwriting to remove suspicion, gave Gen. Morgan an account of her visit to the headquarters of Cornwallis at Winnsboro' on New Year's day, and her sight of the review of the troops.

Gen. Morgan halted his force at the Cowpens, near the line of division between North and South Carolina. Here, on the evening of the 16th of January, it is said that he called a council of war, summoning all his commissioned officers, and stating the circumstances in which they were placed, asked if they would burn their hard-earned bacon and flour, and fly across the mountains, or would stand by and defend it. Col. Washington replied—" No burning—no flying—but face about and give battle to the enemy, and acquit ourselves like men!" The tradition is also that when Col. Tarleton took leave of Lord Cornwallis, he desired him to put off dinner on the third day till after three o'clock, and Gen. Morgan should be his guest at table; for he expected to take him and his men prisoners without difficulty.

The battle of the Cowpens—one of the most celebrated in the Revolution, was fought on the 17th of January, and resulted in the total defeat of the British. Col. Pickens, who like Marion and Sumter, had kept up a guerilla warfare by night and day, commanded the militia, and had a large share in winning the victory. He obtained from Congress the appointment of Brigadier-General.

One incident has been frequently mentioned. Col. Tarleton, flying at full speed, for he feared that his retreat would be cut off, was closely pursued by Col. Washington. Coming up with his foe, Washington struck him, and wounded two of his fingers—his sword passing through the guard of Tarleton's. This gave occasion for a severe repartee by a Carolinian lady. In reply to a sarcastic observation of the British Colonel, that he should like to have an opportunity of seeing this favorite hero, Col. Washington, Mrs. Ashe, of Halifax, said, "if you had looked behind you, Col. Tarleton, at the battle of the Cowpens, you would have had that pleasure."

This event revived the spirits of patriots throughout the country. Everywhere, as the news spread, men who had before been discouraged flew to arms. On the 22d of January six wagons were loaded with corn at Wade's Island, sixty miles down the Catawba, for the use of Gen. Davidson's division. The whig country of Chester, York, and Lancaster, may be said to have risen in mass, and was rallying to arms. Mecklenburg, North Carolina, was again the scene of warlike preparation; for the whigs hoped to give the enemy another defeat at Cowans or Batisford on the Catawba. On the 24th of January Gen. Sumter crossed this river at Landsford, and received a supply of corn from Wade's Island. His object was to cross the districts to the west, in the rear of the advancing British army, to arouse the country and gather forces as he went, threaten the English posts at Ninety-Six and Granby, and go on to recover the State.

While Cornwallis marched from his encampment on Service's plantation, the whigs of Chester were hovering near, watching the movements of the hostile army as keenly as the eagle watches his intended prey. One of their bold exploits brought about the liberation of the unhappy prisoners of Chester District, who had languished in jail at Camden so many months. Eleven of them were given in exchange for two British officers. Thus McCalla and Adair were released. They were waited for by the faithful women—the wife and sister—and as they marched with the companions of their long imprisonment through the streets of Camden, passing the British guard, they sang at the top of their voices the songs of the liberty men.

GENERAL GREENE.

Page 263.

CHAPTER XXIV.

RETREAT OF GREENE—RETURN—BATTLES OF GUILFORD
AND HOBKIRK'S HILL—FORT MOTTE.

AFTER the battle of the Cowpens, Gen. Morgan hurried on with his prisoners towards Cowan's Ford on the Catawba, followed by the British, who hoped to prevent his crossing the river. At this juncture Gen. Greene arrived, having left the main body of his army at his camp near Cheraw, and took the command of Morgan's division. The retreat was continued, while Cornwallis eagerly pursued him. On the issue of that memorable retreat hung the fate of the South. The British general well knew that the destruction of that army would secure his conquests. While Cornwallis was crossing the Catawba, Greene was approaching the village of Salisbury, North Carolina. The prisoners taken at the Cowpens were conveyed with the army—the intention being to take them to Virginia. Greene waited till midnight for the arrival of a body of militia under Gen. Davidson, who had been stationed at the ford to dispute the passage of the river. The news reached him at length of their defeat and dispersion by the British troops, and the death of Davidson.

His aids having been despatched to different parts of the

retreating army, he rode on with a heavy heart to Salisbury. It had been raining during the day, and his soaked and soiled garments and appearance of exhaustion, as he wearily dismounted from his jaded horse at the door of the principal hotel, showed that he had suffered much from exposure to the storm, fatigue, and harassing anxiety. Dr. Reed, who had charge of the sick and wounded prisoners, was engaged in writing paroles for such of the officers as could not go on. From his apartment overlooking the main street, he saw his friend, unaccompanied by his aids, ride up and alight; and hastened to receive him as he entered the house. Startled by his dispirited looks—he could not refrain from noticing them with anxious inquiries; to which the wearied soldier replied: "Yes—fatigued—hungry—alone, and penniless!"

The melancholy reply was heard by one determined to prove, by the generous assistance proffered in time of need, that no reverse could dim the flame of disinterested patriotism. Gen. Greene had hardly taken his seat at the well-spread table, when Mrs. Steele, the landlady of the hotel, entered the room, and carefully closed the door behind her. Approaching her distinguished guest, she reminded him of the despondent words he had uttered, implying, as she thought, a distrust of the devotion of his friends, through every calamity, to the cause. Money, too, she declared he should have, and drew from under her apron two small bags full of specie, probably the earnings of years. "Take these," said she, "for you will want them, and I can do without them."

The General resumed his journey, continuing the retreat. The evening after the battle at Cowan's Ford, the British troops passed by the farm of James Haynes, which the soldiers pillaged, plundered his house, and made the owner, sixty years of age, and in feeble health, a prisoner. They boasted to him and his family that they had killed his son-in-law, Capt. Scott, and intimated that his sons, who were with the republican army, were either killed or prisoners. They emptied the bedticks, filled them with all the meal found in the house, and carried them off. Having stripped the old man of his coat, over-coat, and silver buckles, they drove him before them. Mrs. Haynes sent for a friend, who, having been driven from home with her children, was living in one of the outhouses on her plantation, to come and stay with her. The afflicted matron, conducting family worship that night, prayed fervently for the deliverance and freedom of her country, and the interposition of a protecting Providence for the rescue of her husband. " God prosper the right !" was frequently repeated by her in the prayer. The next morning, as nothing in the way of provisons remained on the premises, Mrs. Brown went into the meal-room and swept up the meal scattered on the floor, from which she prepared a little hasty pudding for the children. The family tradition is, that the daughter of Haynes made her way forty miles through the country, infested with marauders, to inform her brothers of their father's capture, and that the sons pursued and found him, nearly exhausted, by the roadside, and bore him to his home.

Both armies hurried on to the Yadkin River, but Cornwallis was there again disappointed in the hope of overtaking his enemy; the sudden rise of the waters, as in the Catawba, preventing his immediate passage. The superstitious deemed these remarkable occurrences a special interposition of Providence in favor of the American cause. So near were the adverse parties, that a race for life within speaking distance was not an uncommon occurrence. John Haynes, sent out as a scout with three others, was pursued through a lane a mile long by Tarleton's dragoons, who had suddenly emerged from a clump of trees near them. In this pursuit the royalists destroyed the property of the widow Brevard, the mother of the Brevard who had drawn up the Mecklenburg Declaration of Independence. "She has seven sons in the rebel army," was the reason given by the officer for permitting her house to be burned and her farm plundered.

Gen. Greene, now joined by the rest of his army, retreated yet further towards Virginia. On the 15th of February Cornwallis, still in vigorous pursuit, a third time reached the bank of a river (the Dan) just as the rear guard of the American army had crossed. Mortified at his repeated disapointments, he then gave up the pursuit, and turned his course slowly southward.

For some days his army was encamped within the bounds of the congregations under the pastoral care of the Rev. David Caldwell—the oldest and largest Presbyterian congregations in the county of Guilford. This eminent scholar and divine, like his namesake of New Jersey, had become obnoxious to the royalists on account of his efforts and influence in the cause of national independence. He had been repeatedly harassed by the British and tories; a price had been set on his head, and a reward offered for his apprehension. On the 11th of March, while he, like most of the men of the neighborhood, was with Greene's army, the British marched to his plantation and encamped there—the officers taking possession of his house. Mrs. Caldwell was at home with her children when they arrived. They at first announced themselves as Americans, and asked to see the landlady; but a female domestic who had ascertained, by standing on the fence and seeing redcoats at a distance, that they belonged to the army of Cornwallis, quickly communicated her discovery to her mistress. Excusing herself by saying that she must attend to her child, Mrs. Caldwell retired within the house, and immediately gave warning to two of her neighbors who happened to be there, that they might escape through the other door and conceal themselves. She then returned to the gate. The party in front, when charged with being British soldiers, avowed themselves such, and said they must have the use of the dwelling for a day or two. They immediately established themselves in their quarters, turning out Mrs. Caldwell, who with her children retired to the smoke house, and there passed a day with no other food than a few dried peaches and apples, till a physician interposed, and procured for her a bed, some provisions, and a few cooking utensils. The family remained in the smoke house two days and nights—their distress being frequently insulted by profane and brutal language. To a young officer who came to the door for the purpose of taunting the helpless mother, by ridiculing her countrymen, whom he termed rebels and cowards, Mrs. Caldwell replied, "Wait and see what the Lord will do for us." "If he intends to do anything," pertly rejoined the military fop, " 'tis time he had begun." In reply to Mrs. Caldwell's application to one of the soldiers for protection, she was told she could expect no favors, for that the women were as great rebels as the men.

After remaining two days, the army took their departure from the ravaged plantation, on which they had destroyed everything; but before leaving Dr. Caldwell's house, the officer in command gave orders that his library and papers should be burned. A fire was kindled in the large oven in the yard, and books which could not at that time be replaced, and valuable manuscripts which had cost the study and labor of years, were carried out by the soldiers, armful after armful, and ruthlessly committed to the flames. Not even the family Bible was spared, and the house, as well as plantation, was left pillaged and desolate.

Gen. Greene having received reinforcements in Virginia, now recrossed the Dan into North Carolina. Gen. Pickens and Col. Lee at this time encountered a body of loyalists on their way to join Tarleton, who mistaking his soldiers for Britons, were captured while waving their caps and shouting "God save the King." Greene's army being still further augmented, he no longer avoided an engagement with the enemy, but advanced to Guilford Court House, and there awaited the arrival of Cornwallis.

On the 15th of March was heard the roar of that battle which was to compel the retreat of the invaders, and achieve the deliverance of North Carolina. Two collections of women, belonging to Dr. Caldwell's congregations in Buffalo and Alamance, assembled, and while the conflict was raging fiercely between man and man, engaged in earnest prayer for their defenders, their families, and their country. Many others sought the divine aid in solitary places. One pious woman sent her son frequently, during the afternoon, to the summit of a little hill near which she spent much time in prayer, to listen and bring her word which way the firing came—from the southward or the northward. When he returned and said it was going northward—" Then," exclaimed she, " all is lost! Greene is defeated." But all was not lost; the God who hears prayer remembered his people.

After the cold, wet night which succeeded the action, the women wandered over the field of battle to search for their friends, administer the last sad rites to the dead, and bear away the wounded and expiring. One officer who had lain thirty hours undiscovered, was found in the woods by an old lady, and carried to his house, where he survived long enough to relate how a loyalist of his acquaintance had passed him the day after the battle, had recognized him, and bestowed a blow and an execration, instead of the water he craved to quench his consuming thirst. Conscience, however, sometimes avenged the insulted rights of nature; the man who had refused the dying request of a fellow creature, was found after the officer's death, suspended on a tree before his own door.

The British, who were left in possession of the field, claimed the victory in this battle, and an order was issued in Charleston for a general illumination in honor of it. It is related of a Mrs. Heyward that she refused to permit lights to be placed in her windows, and when an officer called to demand the reason of this mark of disrespect, replied that her husband was a prisoner at St. Augustine, and she would not join in celebrating a victory gained by his enemies, even if the consequence must be the destruction of her dwelling. Yet although the loss of the Americans was great, the result was unfavorable to Lord Cornwallis. He retired soon afterwards to Wilmington. After remaining there nearly three weeks, while Greene advanced to the encounter with Lord Rawdon, he set out on his march from Wilmington, bent on his cherished purpose of achieving the conquest of Virginia.

On his march towards Halifax, he encamped for several days on the river Neuse, in what is now called Wayne County, North Carolina. His headquarters were at Springbank, while Col. Tarleton, with his renowned legion, encamped on the plantation of Lieutenant Slocumb. These level and extensive fields presented an inviting view of fresh verdure from the mansion house. Lord Cornwallis himself gave it the name of "Pleasant Green." The owner of this fine estate— already mentioned as figuring in the action at Moore's Creek —was in command of a company of light horse raised in his neighborhood, whose general duty it was to act as rangers, scouring the country for many miles round, watching the movements of the enemy, and punishing the loyalists when detected in pillage and murder. At the present time Slocumb having returned to the vicinity, had been sent with twelve or fifteen recruits to act as scouts in the neighborhood of the British general. He reconnoitred the army of Cornwallis, and then with his party pursued his way slowly along the bank of the river towards his own house, little dreaming that his beautiful and peaceful home was then in the possession of the terrible Tarleton.

CHAPTER XXIV. 271

Col. Tarleton, when he selected this spot for his encampment, rode up to the front piazza accompanied by two aids, and followed by a guard of some twenty troopers. Mrs. Slocumb was sitting there with her child and a relative, and a few house servants. To the British officer's announcemen that the service of His Majesty required the temporary occupation of her property, she replied that the family—consisting only of herself, her sister and her child, with a few negroes —were his prisoners. Tarleton then ordered one of his aids to pitch the tents and form the encampment in the orchard and field on their right; desiring the other aid to detach a quarter guard and station piquets on each road. The piazza commanded a view of the ground on which the camp was arranged. An avenue half a mile in length, stretched to the road. On one side of this avenue was a fence and a thick hedge-row of forest trees; on the other the common rail fence seven or eight feet high. The encampment was completely screened by the fences and hedge-row from the view of any one approaching from down the country.

While orders were given to different officers who came up at intervals to make their reports, a tory captain was directed to take his troop and patrol the country for two or three miles around. This order, given in Mrs. Slocumb's hearing, greatly alarmed her; for she expected her husband that day. By way of precaution, she sent for an old negro, and gave him directions to take a bag of corn to a mill about four miles distant, on the road her husband must travel, and warn him of the danger of approaching his home. With the indolence and curiosity natural to his race, however, the black remained loitering about the premises, lurking under the hedgerow to admire the red coats, dashing plumes, and shining helmets of the British troopers.

Meanwhile dinner was prepared and set before the royal officers. The dessert was suddenly interrupted by the rapid discharge of fire-arms, appearing to proceed from a wood a short distance eastward. Tarleton ordered a captain to take his troop in the direction of the firing, and walked out into the piazza, followed by the anxious ladies. From Mrs. Slocumb's answers to his questions, he became apprehensive that the skirmish in the woods was only the prelude to a concerted attack on his camp by some of the forces of Col. Washington. He hastened to mount his horse, and giving a loud order to form the troops on the right, dashed down the avenue to a breach in the hedge-row, leaped the fence, and in a moment was at the head of his regiment.

The firing in the wood was from the party of Slocumb, who had encountered and routed the tory captain sent to reconnoitre the country. Some of the tories were presently seen in the open grounds east of the plantation, closely pursued by four of the Americans, while a running fight was kept up with different weapons, in which four or five broadswords gleamed conspicuous. The pursuers were too busy to see anything else, and entered the avenue at the same moment with the party pursued. With what horror and consternation did Mrs. Slocumb recognize her husband, her brother, and two of her neighbors, in chase, already half-way down the avenue, and unconscious that they were rushing into the enemy's midst!

CHAPTER XXIV. 273

About the middle of the avenue one of the tories fell; and the course of the young officers was suddenly arrested by the negro, who sprang directly in front of their horses, crying, "Hold on, massa! Look yon!" A glance to the left showed the young men their danger: they were within pistol shot of a thousand men drawn up in order of battle. Wheeling their horses, they discovered a troop already leaping the fence in the avenue in their rear. Quick as thought they again wheeled their horses, and dashed down the avenue directly towards the house, where stood the quarter-guard to receive them. On reaching the garden fence, they leaped that and the next, amid a shower of balls from the guard, cleared the canal at one tremendous leap, and scouring across the open field to the northwest, were in the shelter of the wood before their pursuers could clear the fences of the enclosure.

A platoon had commenced the pursuit; but the trumpets sounded the recall before the flying Americans had crossed the canal. This forbearance was caused by the belief that the men who so fearlessly dashed into the camp, were supported by a formidable force at hand. Had the truth been known, the fugitives must have been captured and secured. This little incident may afford some idea of scenes that were of frequent occurrence during the continuance of warfare at the South.

Slocumb and his companions passed rapidly round the plantation, and returned to the ground where the encounter had taken place, collecting on the way the stragglers of his troop. Near their bivouac he saw the tory captain's brother, who had

12*

been captured by the Americans, hanging by a bridle rein from the top of a sapling bent down for the purpose, and struggling in the agonies of death. Hastening to the spot he severed the rein with a stroke of his sword, and with much difficulty restored him to life.

The dignified and liberal courtesy of Mrs. Slocumb towards her unbidden guests, was acknowledged by strict orders that no depredations should be committed, though not even military authority could save the farm-yard poultry and stock from a hungry soldiery. Her plate and other valuables, on the news of the army's approach, had been buried at the edge of a marsh near at hand; the soldiers suspected the place of deposit, and plunged their pike staffs into the ground about the spot till they discovered the treasure; but they were compelled to restore it. When the army broke up their encampment, ample remuneration was offered by Col. Tarleton for the trouble given, and a sergeant with a guard was ordered to remain till the last soldier had departed, to insure protection to a lady whose noble bearing had inspired them all with profound respect.

In the meantime Gen. Greene, who had been bold enough to return to South Carolina, after several changes of position, entrenched his army at Hobkirk's Hill, a mile from the British post at Camden. On the 25th of April, Lord Rawdon attacked him. The British had the advantage in the battle which ensued; yet as before, its consequences were favorable to the Americans. Soon afterwards Rawdon evacuated Camden, and anxious to maintain his posts, directed his first effort to relieve Fort Motte, at that time invested by Marion and Lee.

This fort, which commanded the river, was the principal dépôt of the convoys from Charleston to Camden and the upper districts. It was occupied by a garrison, under the command of Capt. M'Pherson, of one hundred and sixty-five men, having been increased by a small detachment of dragoons from Charleston, a few hours before the appearance of the Americans. The large new mansion-house belonging to Mrs. Motte, which had been selected for the establishment of the post, was surrounded by a deep trench, along the interior margin of which was raised a strong and lofty parapet. Opposite, and northward, upon another hill, was an old farm-house, to which Mrs. Motte had removed when dismissed from her mansion. On this height Lieut. Col. Lee had taken position with his force; while Marion occupied the eastern declivity of the ridge on which the fort stood; the valley running between the two hills permitting the Americans to approach it within four hundred yards.

M'Pherson was unprovided with artillery, but hoped to be relieved by the arrival of Lord Rawdon to dislodge the assailants before they could push their preparations to maturity. He therefore replied to the summons to surrender, which came on the 20th of May, that he should hold out to the last moment in his power. In the night a courier arrived from Gen. Greene to advise the besiegers of Rawdon's retreat from Camden, and urge redoubled activity; and Marion persevered through the hours of darkness in pressing the completion of their works. The following night Lord Rawdon encamped on the highest ground in the country opposite Fort Motte; and the despairing garrison saw with joy the illumination of his fires; while the Americans were convinced that no time was to be lost.

The large house in the centre of the encircling trench, left but a few yards of ground within the British works uncovered; burning the mansion, therefore, must compel the surrender of the garrison. This expedient was reluctantly resolved upon by Marion and Lee, who found himself compelled to inform Mrs. Motte of the unavoidable necessity of the destruction of her property. Mrs. Motte not only assented, but declared that she was "gratified with the opportunity of contributing to the good of her country, and should view the approaching scene with delight." Shortly after she sent for Lee, and presenting him with a bow and arrows, which had been imported from India, requested that they might be used to convey combustible matter to the house.

Everything was now prepared for the concluding scene. The lines were manned, and an additional force stationed at the battery, to meet a desperate assault, if such should be made. The American entrenchments being within arrow shot, M'Pherson was once more summoned, and again more confidently asserted his determination to resist to the last.

The scorching rays of the noonday sun had prepared the shingle roof for the conflagration. The return of the flag was immediately followed by the shooting of the arrows, to which balls of blazing rosin and brimstone were attached. They struck, and set fire in different quarters of the roof. M'Pherson immediately ordered men to repair to the loft of the house, and check the flames by knocking off the shingles, but they were soon driven down by the fire of the six pounder; and no other effort to stop the burning being practicable, the commandant hung out the white flag, and surrendered the garrison at discretion.

If ever a situation in real life afforded a fit subject for poetry, by filling the mind with a sense of moral grandeur— it was that of Mrs. Motte contemplating the spectacle of her home in flames, and rejoicing in the triumph secured to her countrymen—the benefit to her native land,—by her surrender of her own interest to the public service. After the captors had taken possession, M'Pherson and his officers accompanied them to her dwelling, where they sat down to a sumptuous dinner.

The ladies of Charleston showed their good wishes for the success of the American general, by dressing in *green*, and wearing green feathers and ribbons; thus retaliating the provocations of their invaders. It had previously been the custom of the whig ladies to wear deep mourning. One of them passing the house of Gov. Rutledge in company with an English officer, took a piece of crape that had been accidentally torn from the flounce of her dress, and tied it to the front railing, expressing at the same time her sorrow for the Governor's absence, and her opinion that his house, as well as his friends, ought to wear mourning.

CHAPTER XXV.

ATTACK ON NINETY-SIX—BATTLE OF EUTAW—MARCH OF CORNWALLIS INTO VIRGINIA—SIEGE OF YORKTOWN—BURNING OF NEW LONDON—SURRENDER OF CORNWALLIS.

EARLY in June, the successes of the Americans had been such that the posts of Eutaw Springs, Ninety-Six, and Charleston, were the only ones held by the British. Gen. Greene proceeded against the strongly fortified one at Ninety-Six. After a siege of nearly four weeks the approach of Lord Rawdon rendered it necessary to attempt carrying the place by storm. When he had determined on this, Greene, with characteristic humanity and delicacy, gave notice of his intention to Mrs. Cruger, the wife of the commander of the garrison, with whom he was acquainted. He also dispached a sergeant and guard of eight men to protect the house in which she resided from dangers that might be apprehended in the heat of the assault. When the cannonading commenced, she was engaged in sewing up guineas in a girdle; an occupation which she continued in spite of the alarm occasioned by the successive reports. The assault was made on the 18th of June, but the assailants were driven back, and the army retreated before the British commander had arrived.

SURRENDER OF CORNWALLIS.

Page 278.

Miss Moore, a young lady who had lodged in the house with Mrs. Cruger, returned to her home on Saluda River the day before Lord Rawdon's troops passed along the road, not far from the dwelling of her parents. A sanguinary skirmish took place here between Rawdon's men and a body of Col. Washington's cavalry, sent to impede their progress. Soon after, one of the royal officers came to the house, where there were none but women, and advised the family to take care of their property. The caution was not unnecessary, for they were presently intruded upon by several British soldiers. In their search for plunder, they rolled down from above stairs some apples that had been gathered and stored for the use of the family. The soldiers below began picking them up as they fell on the floor; Miss Moore commanded them to desist, and gathering some of the fruit in her apron, offered it to a non-commissioned officer who stood by. Struck with the cool courage and determination of so young a girl, he made some remark expressive of his admiration, and ordered the soldiers instantly to desist from their rude trespass. He then informed her that the men were killing her father's sheep in the lot. Miss Moore hastened thither, followed by him. Two men were in the act of slaughtering one of the sheep; but at the officer's bidding, with the threat of reporting them to the commander, they were compelled to let them go.

After Greene had thus fallen back, some of the whig families near Saluda River, fearing to remain, fled to his camp for protection. Among these was the family of Gen. Pickens, who was then with Greene's army. Instead of providing for their safety, Pickens immediately sent them back to share the common sufferings of the country, thereby to show that the spirit of resistance was undying.

The enthusiasm which prevailed among the people and prompted to so many acts of personal risk and sacrifice, was fostered by Gen. Greene. A daring exploit of two young women in this district has been often mentioned among the traditions of South Carolina. It is said that the wives of two officers, absent with the army, having heard that a British courier conveying despatches was to pass along the road that night, disguised themselves in their husbands' clothes, provided themselves with arms, and took their station among the bushes by the roadside. When the courier appeared, guarded by two officers, they leaped from their covert, presented their pistols at the officers' breasts, and demanded the instant surrender of the party. Then men, taken by surprise, yielded immediately, and were put on their parole. The women, having secured the papers, hastened home by a short cut through the woods, and sent the documents by a trusty messenger to Gen. Greene.

Another traditional anecdote of female agency is characteristic. After Greene had passed Broad River he was desirous of sending an order to Gen. Sumter, then on the Wateree, to join him, that they might attack Lord Rawdon, who had divided his force. The country to be passed through was full of blood-thirsty loyalists, and it was difficult to find a man willing to undertake a mission so dangerous; but a young girl—Emily Geiger—offered to act as messenger. Greene gave her the letter, at the same time informing her of the contents, to be communicated to Sumter verbally in case of

CHAPTER XXV.

accident. On the second day of her journey she was intercepted by one of Rawdon's scouts. Coming from the direction of Greene's army, and blushing a good deal as she attempted to give an account of herself, she was suspected and placed in confinement, while the officer sent for a tory matron to search her. As soon as the door was closed, Emily ate up the letter, piece by piece. After the search, nothing of a suspicious nature being found about the prisoner, she was permitted to depart whither she said she was bound. She took a route somewhat circuitous to avoid detection, arrived at Sumter's camp, and delivered her message.

It was now Lord Rawdon's turn to retreat, and he retired to Orangeburg. Not venturing to attack him here, Greene withdrew with his main army, for the unhealthy season, to the hills that border on the Santee. It was not long before Lord Rawdon took his departure for England, leaving Col. Stewart in command of his forces. At this time was enacted the melancholy tragedy of the execution of Col. Isaac Hayne, in Charleston. He was a patriot who had submitted to British rule to avoid being thrown into prison, but afterwards had taken up arms against the invaders. Being captured, he was condemned to death by Col. Balfour, the commandant of Charleston. Many petitions were sent for mercy in his behalf, and his children, with tears, besought his life; but in vain.

In September, Gen Greene proceeded against the British forces, pursued them to Eutaw Springs, and on the 8th, engaged them in that bloody battle. This action may be said to have closed the war in the Carolinas, the British being forced to retire to Charleston, which city and Savannah, were all they retained of their conquests in South Carolina and Georgia. The happy issue of the campaign, and the deliverance of the South, after a long and bloody contest, are to be ascribed to the energy and genius of General Greene.

The celebrated Col. Washington was wounded and taken prisoner at the battle of Eutaw Springs, and sent to Charleston. In the hospital there he first saw Jane Elliott, a young and beautiful girl, who, not content with giving a large portion of her property to establish hospitals and aid the wounded American soldiers, herself visited the sufferers in certain wards. His gratitude, and her sympathy for his misfortunes, laid the foundation for a lasting regard between them; they pledged their faith to each other, and were married in the spring of 1782.

In the meantime Lord Cornwallis marched on to Halifax. While in this neighborhood, it is said, the influence of one of his officers—Col. Hamilton—who had resided there before the war, did much to mitigate the evils usually attendant upon the march of a hostile force. He showed a regard to his old acquaintances, by inducing the commander to forbid the molestation of the persons or property of non-combatants. One of the most cruel tragedies enacted this summer was the murder of Dr. Alexander Gaston at Newbern. He was one of the most zealous patriots in North Carolina—being a member of the committee of safety for the district where he resided, and serving in the army at various periods of the war; and his devotion to the cause of freedom, while it secured the confidence of the whigs, gained him the implacable enmity of the opposite party. On the 20th of August, a body of tories entered Newbern, some miles in advance of the regular troops, who had, marched with a view of taking possession of the town. The Americans, taken by surprise, were forced to give way after an ineffectual resistance. Gaston, unwilling to surrender, hurried his wife and children from their home, hoping to escape across the river, and thus retire to a plantation eight or ten miles distant. He reached the wharf, and seized a light scow for the purpose of crossing the river. But before they stepped on board, the tories came galloping in pursuit. There was no resource but for him to push off from the shore where his wife and little ones stood—she alarmed only for him. Throwing herself in agony at the feet of their enemies, she implored his life, but in vain. They sacrificed him in the midst of her cries for mercy—and the musket which found his heart was levelled over her shoulder! Even then the indulgence of grief was denied her; for she was compelled to exert herself to protect his remains. In her lonely dwelling she kept watch beside the beloved and lifeless form, till it was deposited in the earth.

Proceeding northward, Cornwallis was met at Petersburg by Arnold with the troops of Gen. Phillips, who had died a few days before. Gen. La Fayette was employed in the defence of Virginia, but from want of sufficient force could do nothing to check the enemy's progress. Cornwallis moved into the interior and harassed the country, destroying much property. Col. Tarleton, with his corps of cavalry, made a secret expedition to Charlottesville, intending to capture the Virginia Legislature, and the Governor, Thomas Jefferson. His success was prevented by a patriotic stratagem. At the time of his march, it chanced that some of the members were at the house of Col. Walker, twelve miles from the town. This was directly on the route, and the first intimation the family had of the enemy's approach, was the appearance of Tarleton's legion at their doors. Having secured a few of the legislators the British Colonel ordered breakfast. Mrs. Walker delayed the preparations for the meal, for the purpose of enabling the members who had escaped to reach the town, give the alarm, and remove such portions of the stores as could be saved. Tarleton, thus baffled in the object of his expedition, returned to join the main army.

In the midst of these movements towards the subjugation of the State, Lord Cornwallis was suddenly called to the seacoast by Sir Henry Clinton. The Commander-in-Chief expected that the combined French and American forces would attack New York, and wished Cornwallis to remain near the coast, that if necessary he might come speedily to his assistance. Cornwallis proceeded accordingly to Portsmouth, and thence to Yorktown, on the south side of York River. This place he proceeded to fortify.

It was true that General Washington had designed to attack New York; but he changed the plan in August, and after deceiving Clinton with the belief that New York was threatened, till it was too late to arrest his movements, marched southward with the allied army, and on the 30th of September completely invested Yorktown A French fleet, commanded by the Count de Grasse, had before this entered Chesapeake Bay, and blocked up the mouths of James and

York Rivers; thus cutting off all communication between Yorktown and New York. La Fayette, joined by a large French force, was ready to prevent a retreat southward by land. Cornwallis was thus enclosed without prospect of relief. An attempt to send him succor from New York was defeated.

Sir Henry Clinton made a vain effort to check the advance of Washington in the beginning of his march, by sending Arnold, who had returned from Virginia, to ravage Connecticut. On the 6th of September, New London was burned, and a large amount of property was destroyed. A detachment was directed to attack Fort Griswold at Groton, on the opposite side of the river. When it was taken by assault, no mercy was shown by the conquerors. Col. Leydard, who commanded the fort, was slain in the act of surrender, with the sword he had placed in the hand of the commander of the assailants—and after an indiscriminate butchery, such of the prisoners as showed signs of life, were thrown into a cart, which, heaped with mangled bodies, was started down a steep and rugged hill towards the river. Its course being interrupted by stones and logs, the victims were not precipitated into the water; and, after the enemy had been driven off by the roused inhabitants of the country, friends came to the aid of the wounded, and several lives were preserved. But their sufferings, before relief could be obtained, were indescribable. Thirty-five men, covered with wounds and blood, trembling with cold and parched with thirst, lay all night upon the bare floor, almost hopeless of succor, and looking to death as a deliverance from intolerable anguish.

One instance of compassion is worthy of remembrance The morning after the massacre, a young woman left her home, three miles distant, and came in search of her uncle, who had joined the volunteers on the first alarm of invasion, and was known to have been engaged in the disastrous conflict. He was among those wounded unto death. His niece found him in a house near the scene of slaughter, where he had shared the attention bestowed on the rest. His wounds had been dressed, but it was evident that he could bear no further removal, and that life was fast departing. Still perfect consciousness remained, and with dying energy he entreated that he might once more behold his wife and child. Such a request was sacred, and the sympathizing girl lost no time in hastening home, where she caught and saddled the horse used by the family, placed upon the animal the delicate wife, whose strength could not have accomplished so long a walk, and taking the child herself, bore it in her arms the whole distance, and presented it to receive the blessing of its expiring father.

The progress of the siege of Yorktown has been fully described in other works. An attempt to retreat on the part of the besieged was frustrated, and on the 19th of October the posts of Yorktown and Gloucester, with more than seven thousand soldiers, were surrendered to Washington, the shipping being delivered into the hands of De Grasse. Five days afterwards, Sir Henry Clinton arrived with an armament of seven thousand at the mouth of the Chesapeake, but being informed of the surrender, returned to New York. The allied forces then separated. The Count De Grasse sailed for the

West Indies; the French army, under Rochambeau, was cantoned during the winter in Virginia, and the main body of the American army returned to its late position on the Hudson. A strong detachment, under Gen. St. Clair, was sent to the South to strengthen the forces of Gen. Greene.

Thus the year 1781, which had commenced with disasters in different parts of the country, ended in decisive success. The victory of Yorktown in effect recovered the whole country. British power was now reduced to merely defensive measures, and limited to the posts of New York, Charleston, and Savannah. The people manifested the greatest joy at this deliverance. The auspicious event was celebrated in various places throughout the country. In acknowledgment of the Divine Power that had protected America, the members of Congress went in procession to the principal church in Philadelphia to return thanks, and the 13th of December was appointed a day of public thanksgiving and prayer.

In the midst of exultation, however, courtesy to the vanquished was not forgotten. After the capture of Yorktown, the superior officers of the American army, with their allies, vied with each other in acts of civility and attention to the captive Britons. Entertainments were given to them by nearly all the Major-Generals, and the other officers freely aided by contributing such means as they possessed. In allusion, probably, to expenditures of this kind, Col. Stewart, of New Jersey, said to his daughter on his return home—"Well, Martha, my dear, I come to you a thousand dollars out of pocket by the surrender of Yorktown. But I care not The struggle is over, and my country is free!"

The meeting of Gen. Washington with his venerable mother, after the victory which decided the fortune of America, is thus described by Mr. Custis: "After an absence of nearly seven years, it was at length, on the return of the combined armies from Yorktown, permitted to the mother again to see and embrace her illustrious son. So soon as he had dismounted, in the midst of a numerous and brilliant suite, he sent to apprise her of his arrival, and to know when it would be her pleasure to receive him. She was alone—her aged hands employed in works of domestic industry, when the good news was announced; and it was further told that the victorious chief was in waiting at the threshold. She welcomed him with a warm embrace, and by the well-remembered and endearing names of his childhood. Inquiring as to his health, she remarked the lines which mighty cares and many trials had made on his manly countenance—spoke much of old times, and old friends; but of his glory, *not one word!*

"Meantime, in the village of Fredericksburg, all was joy and revelry. The town was crowded with officers of the French and American armies, and with gentlemen from all the country around, who hastened to welcome the conquerors of Cornwallis. The citizens made arrangements for a splendid ball, to which the mother of Washington was specially invited. She observed, that although her dancing days were *pretty well over*, she should feel happy in contributing to the general festivity, and consented to attend.

"The foreign officers were anxious to see the mother of their chief. They had heard indistinct rumors respecting her remarkable life and character; but forming their judgment from European examples, they were prepared to expect in her that glare and show which would have been attached to the parents of the great in the old world. How were they surprised when the matron, leaning on the arm of her son, entered the room! She was arrayed in the very plain, yet becoming garb worn by the Virginia lady of the olden time. Her address, always dignified and imposing, was courteous, though reserved. She received the complimentary attentions which were profusely paid her, without evincing the slightest elevation; and at an early hour, wishing the company much enjoyment of their pleasures, and observing that it was time for old people to be at home, retired, leaning as before on the arm of her son."

Many of the French troops marched to Boston before they embarked, in December, for their own country. Count Segur thus mentions their entrance and reception: " Before we entered Boston, our troops changed their dress in the open air, and in a short time appeared so well attired, it seemed incredible that this army, marching from Yorktown, could have travelled over such an extent of country, and have been exposed to all the inclemency of a rainy autumn, and a premature winter. No review or parade ever displayed troops in better order, presenting a more imposing and brilliant appearance. A large part of the population of the town came out to meet us. The ladies stood at their windows and welcomed us with the most spirited applause. Our stay was enlivened by continual rejoicings, fêtes and balls succeeding each other day after day. The attentions paid us showed with equal sincerity sentiments of joy at the triumph of

13   z

the allied armies, and of sorrow at our approaching departure."

He says of Boston : " It may there be seen that refinement and republicanism are not incompatible; for in no part of the country is a more agreeable society to be found. Europe nowhere offers to our admiration women adorned with greater beauty or elegance, with superior education, or more brilliant accomplishments, than the ladies of this place, such as Mesdames Jarvis, Tudor, and Morton. Mrs. Tudor, who was afterwards seen and admired in France, has become celebrated for her writings, so full of talent and wit. One of these, written in French, and remarkable for its elegance of style, was addressed to the Queen of France, Marie Antoinette, and was brought over and presented to that princess by the Marquis de Chastellux."

CHAPTER XXVI.

EARLY SETTLEMENTS AT THE WEST—KENTUCKY—
TENNESSEE.

THE Western and North-western territory of the United States was an almost pathless wilderness at the commencement of the Revolution. A few hardy adventurers had explored its forests; they were followed by a few woodsmen, who shouldered their rifles and plunged into the wilderness, and then came a wagon or two, slowly breaking its rough way, bearing families whom the hardships of frontier life had emboldened to seek a new home. These enterprising pioneers, whose adventures shed a coloring of romance over the early history of the whole region, braved perils we nowadays shudder even to hear of; for they were forced to dispute the grounds they occupied with fierce tribes of Indians. The Shawanees, Delawares and Wyandots of the North, and the Cherokees, Creeks, and Catawbas of the South, who often waged bloody wars against each other, were alike disposed to meet with ferocious hostility the white men who dared invade the country they claimed.

Kentucky was first explored about the middle of the eighteenth century. It was the red man's favorite hunting ground; the stronghold of fierce and warlike tribes. Daniel Boone, who penetrated the country in 1769, may be regarded as the earliest pioneer. The reports spread by his party through Virginia and North Carolina, of the fertility of the soil and other advantages excited much attention, and in 1772 and 1773 permanent settlements began to be made west of the Alleghanies. In the summer of 1774, Harrod built a log cabin on the spot where Harrodsburg now stands—the foundation of the earliest station. Boonsborough was founded in the following spring, and within two months the wife and daughters of the pioneer—the first white women who ever stood upon the banks of the Kentucky River—came to take up their residence in the fort. This station, with Harrodsburg, became the nucleus of emigration and settlement, and the central object of Indian hostilities.

Other families came in the same year to join the little colony—and other cabins and forts were erected. The dangers to which the new settlers were exposed in the "dark and bloody ground," as the name "Kentucky" was interpreted—soon became apparent. In July, 1776, three young women were surprised by a party of Indians, carried captive, and recovered at a distance of forty miles. This was but the beginning of troubles. An invasion of the savages, shortly after Kentucky had been erected into a county by the legislature of Virginia drove the hunters and surveyors from the woods to take refuge in the forts. These withstood their assaults; and "after sweeping through Kentucky like a torrent for several weeks, the angry tide slowly rolled back to the north." But these perils did not prevent the continual arrival of reinforcements

DANIEL BOONE

of settlers from North Carolina and Virginia. Even among the women, fear was less strong than the love of adventure. The wife of Whitley, one of the most distinguished of the early pioneers, to his observation that he had heard a fine report of Kentucky, and thought they could live there with less hard work—answered; " Then, Billy, I would go and see!" In two days he was on his way with axe and plough, and gun and kettle. Thus the stream of settlement flowed year after year.

The pioneers were chiefly men who had encountered the difficulties experienced in settling the frontiers of the colonies, and who were accustomed to deal with the Indians. Their primitive condition was scarcely less simple than that of the savages. The men built cabins, blockhouses, and forts; hunted, cleared land and planted grain; while the women milked, cooked the meat, pounded the corn or ground it in hand mills, and occasionally run bullets. Deer skins were used for garments. The hunting shirt, worn universally by the men, was made sometimes of this material, dressed, but generally of linsey or coarse linen. A wallet was stitched in the bosom, to carry bread or ammunition, and the belt or girdle held the bullet bag, and the tomahawk, or scalping-knife, worn by each hunter, who carried his long rifle in his hand. The leggins and moccasins were made of deer skin, and the common shirt and jacket, and caps of native fur, completed the ordinary attire.

Buffalo and bear skins served for beds. There being no shops or stores, almost every article in use was of home manufacture. The table furniture consisted of wooden vessels and utensils, made or turned in the rudest manner. Iron forks or tin cups were extremely rare. The slab that served for a table was made of a flat piece of timber, split and roughly hewn, and rude benches formed the seats. If one desired his bed elevated above the floor or the ground, the bedstead was made by laying slabs across long poles, supported by forked poles driven into the ground; or pieces of hewn timber were let into the sides of the cabin. The cradle was a small rolling trough like those used in collecting sap for maple sugar. Yet notwithstanding this simplicity in furniture, their food was the choicest of game, and the richest of milk and butter, partaken with a relish health and labor alone can give. The luxuriant pastures of the woods, where the pea vine and the wild cane abounded, supplied the cattle with provender, and game was so abundant that buffaloes were frequently shot merely for the tongues. But for this bountiful provision of nature the country could not have been maintained against the Indians, whose frequent depredations destroyed the fields. Hospitality, too, that virtue of a primitive society, was always cheerfully exercised.

The West, thus filling with a hardy population, became year after year more interesting to the parties contending during the Revolutionary war. The different expeditions into that country soon aroused British jealousy; for the government dreaded the influence of the pioneer leaders on the minds of their savage allies. The English commandant at Detroit sought to bring all the savage tribes under his control, and to incite them against the Americans. He urged them to hostile inroads by every incentive, and paid a price for the scalps brought; while an expedition of Indians and Canadians was prepared against the forts and stations. The fierce spirit of the barbarians of the forest thus stimulated by abundant supplies of ammunition and liquors, furnished from north-western military posts of the British—the terrors of their incursion were increased tenfold. The men, women, and children were driven from their homes to take shelter in the forts, and these were kept in a continual state of alarm. The narrative of the perils and trials of the inhabitants, and of frequent scenes of bloody strife, embraces incidents of personal adventure more surprising than any romance.

The name of George Rogers Clark, called by Randolph "the Hannibal of the West," is conspicuous in the history of the conquest and settlement of the whole country. The brilliant expedition planned by him was undertaken in the beginning of 1778, and conducted successfully by his heroism and perseverance. His party marched through trackless forests, over the region that now forms the State of Illinois, to the ancient French village of Kaskaskias, and took the town, with the British commandant. The French inhabitants submitted to the new power—transferring their allegiance to the government of the United States. The governor of the British force in the north-west, furious at this invasion, collected an army of savages, and made preparations to advance upon his adventurous enemy; but before his project was ripe for execution, Col. Clark marched boldly through the wilderness to his citadel at Vincennes, and captured the governor and his garrison. The whole country was then subjected, and the conquest achieved, which has been said to be the true basis of the claim of the United States to a northern boundary on the Lakes.

In 1779, many families removed to Kentucky from Virginia and the neighboring States; the hunters of the elk and buffalo being succeeded by more eager hunters for land. Their pursuits were carried on in the midst of Indian hostilities. The tide of emigration flowed yet more copiously in the two following years, notwithstanding that every portion of the country was continually kept in alarm by Indian ambushes, and their fields were often laid waste. The hostilities of the savages were not checked by the approach of peace. In August, 1782, a large army of warriors traversed the northern part of Kentucky, and appeared unexpectedly before Bryant's Station, near Lexington. An incident of this siege strikingly displayed the intrepidity of the western women.

The garrison was supplied with water from a spring at some distance from the fort, near which a considerable body of the Indians had been placed in ambush. Another party in full view was ordered to open a fire at a given time, with the hope of enticing the besieged to an engagement without the walls, when the force at the spring could seize the opportunity of storming one of the gates. The more experienced of the garrison felt satisfied that Indians were concealed near the spring, but conjectured that they would not show themselves until the firing on the opposite side of the fort should induce them to believe that the men had come out, and were engaged with the other party. The need of water was urgent, and yielding to the necessity of the case, they summoned all the women. Explaining to them the circumstances in which they were placed, and the improbability that any injury would be offered them, until the firing had been returned from the opposite side of the fort, they urged them to go in a body to the spring, and bring up each a bucket full of water. They had been in the habit of bringing water every morning, and should the men go at this time, it was feared that the Indians would suspect that their ambuscade was discovered, and would instantly rush upon them or shoot them at the spring.

The boldest of the women at once declared their readiness to brave the danger, and the more timid rallying in their rear, they all marched down to the spring, within shot of hundreds of the enemy! The steadiness and composure of their movements completely deceived the savages; not a shot was fired, and having filled their buckets, they brought them into the fort in safety.

Ohio was in part settled by pioneers from New England. An anecdote of a young widow, afterwards the wife of one of the early adventurers in the valley of the Ohio River, may serve for a picture of the common experience of those days. She was living in the spring of 1774 with her brothers on Grave Creek, and kept house alone while they were absent on their hunting excursions. Having been on a visit to her sister who resided at a distance of fifty miles upon the banks of the Ohio, opposite Yellow Creek, she returned home, as she had gone, in a canoe by herself. Setting out in the afternoon she paddled till dark; then, knowing when the moon would rise, she landed, fastened her boat to the willows, and lay in a clump of bushes near the shore, till the moon had cleared the tree tops. As she waded a few paces in the water to reach the canoe, she trod on the dead body of an Indian, not long killed, whom she had not before seen. She did not scream, knowing it might be dangerous; but stepping quietly into the boat, went on, and reached the mouth of Grave Creek early the next morning.

Not long afterwards, while on her knees blowing the fire one morning, she heard steps, and looking round saw a tall Indian standing by her. He motioned her to be silent, and shook his tomahawk at her; then looked around the cabin for plunder, and seeing her brother's rifle hanging on hooks over the fire place, seized it and departed. The young woman showed no fear while he was there, but as soon as he was gone left the cabin and hid herself in the corn till her brother's return. This Rebecca Williams was afterwards famous among the borderers of the Ohio River for her medical and surgical skill.

The history of the trials and sufferings of the early settlers of Tennessee, in their years of border warfare with the Delawares, Shawnees, Creeks and Cherokees, exists only in the memory of a few of their descendants. Yet in the midst of these were enacted deeds of heroism and chivalry which might well challenge a comparison with those of Kentucky. About the year 1772, a few adventurous spirits in Virginia and North Carolina, allured by the tales told by hunters and trappers of beautiful valleys and meandering streams beyond the Alleghany mountains, sought new homes in the lovely valley of the Watauga, now the Holston River, in what is now Sullivan County, East Tennessee.

Among the earliest of these hardy pioneers were the Bled-

CHAPTER XXVI.

soes and the Shelbys, who settled twelve miles above the Island Flats. These first settlers were harassed continually by the hostile inroads of their savage neighbors; scenes of bloody strife were common, and almost every dwelling was a fort; yet the population of their settlements rapidly increased. In June, 1776, more than seven hundred Indian warriors advanced on the settlements upon the Holston, and a battle, called the battle of Long Island, was fought near the Island Flats, in which the militia, commanded by Col. Bledsoe, routed the savages after a severe conflict. A constant succession of Indian troubles marked the years succeeding. In 1779, Bledsoe and others crossed the Cumberland mountains, and explored the valley of the Cumberland River. Their alluring report of the country on their return induced many of the inhabitants of East Tennessee to make preparation for striking out still further into the wilderness, to establish a new colony west of the mountains.

Gen. James Robertson, of North Carolina, in concert with Col. Donaldson, started from Watauga about the middle of December. Robertson led a land expedition, the object of which was to cross the mountains, proceed to a place then known as the Big Salt Lick, now Nashville, establish a fort, build houses and open fields. Donaldson conducted a flotilla of rudely constructed flat-boats, which, bearing the old men, women, and children, and the baggage of the pioneers, descended the Holston, for the purpose of following Tennessee River to some point beyond its pass through the mountains. The land party was to join the flotilla somewhere on the great bend of the Tennessee, and conduct them to their new home in the valley of the Cumberland. It was a dark and fearful voyage, that descent of the Watauga and Tennessee, through the hunting grounds of the warlike Cherokees and Creeks. To daily attacks from the Indians, who from the shores of the narrow river fired on the voyagers as they descended the rapid current in their frail open boats, now and then boldly pushing out in their canoes to assault them, were added the dangers of the rapid and meandering stream, where sunken rocks and dangerous rapids threatened to engulf the frail barks in its boiling eddies. To aggravate these horrors, when the voyagers, their numbers reduced by disease and the murderous savages, reached the head of the Muscle Shoals, no sign could be discovered of Gen. Robertson Col. Donaldson and his party found themselves environed by dangers which might have unnerved the stoutest heart. An unexplored wilderness on either side, seven hundred miles of up-stream navigation behind them, with thousands of armed warriors ready to fall upon them, while in advance was heard the roar of the turbid waters as they dashed amongst the projecting rocks of the Muscle Shoals. It was a fearful alternative, but death was certain in the rear or on either flank, and after weighing well all the dangers of his situation, Col. Donaldson determined to descend the Tennessee to its mouth and attempt to reach the Big Salt Spring by the ascent of the Cumberland.

On the 24th of April, 1780, four months and two days after leaving Watauga, those who survived of this adventurous party of pioneer voyagers reached the spot where Nashville now stands. Here they met their friends, who had succeeded in reaching the same place some weeks before Interesting indeed was the re-union, but not without its sorrows; for many a father, mother, brother, sister, looked in vain for those they had hoped to meet. These parties of wayworn travellers, and two smaller ones, constituted the entire colony of Cumberland Valley, numbering less than five hundred souls, of whom one hundred and fifty were all that were able to bear arms. From their arrival, for fifteen years, a bloody war was waged against them by the Creeks, Cherokees, and Shawnees. Thus driven at once into a state of war, every man became an armed occupant, who held his life and his fort or blockhouse only by the strength of his arm.

The settlers lived in forts, each containing half a dozen or more families, and were compelled to work their small fields with guns by their sides. Books, schools, churches, academies, they had none. Toil and danger were their only schoolmasters, and stern necessity their only pastor and lawgiver Capt. Ridley had established a small fort near Nashville, in which military rule was necessarily preserved, while various persons, pursuing the bent of their own interest, established others, in which they rallied their friends and retainers to repel the assaults of Indian marauders. In the space of thirty miles around Nashville were a dozen such forts, and in and around these were all the inhabitants of the valley. Of necessity, social intercourse was kept up by occasional visits from one to another; but the road being often rendered dangerous by Indian ambuscades, it required more than a common share of bravery for small parties, especially of females, to venture, though the distance between the forts was only two or three miles.

2 A

No brief notice like the preceding can convey an adequate idea of the difficulties and dangers encountered by these early settlers; but it may awaken curiosity to examine other records. When hostilities ceased between Great Britain and the United States, other emigrants of exhausted fortunes, or who had spent their prime in fighting the battles of their country, sought homes in the west, in the expectation of peace and security. But the Indians at intervals continued their incursions. The settlements, notwithstanding, advanced in strength and prosperity, increasing every year, till they were able to claim admission as States into the Union

CHAPTER XXVII.

CONCLUSION.

WHEN the news reached England of the event that had finished the work of wresting America from British possession, it was met by a general expression throughout the whole nation of desire for peace. In May, 1782, Sir Guy Carleton, appointed to succeed Sir Henry Clinton as Commander-in-Chief, arrived in New York, with instructions to terminate the war by amicable negotiation. Active hostilities between the two armies were suspended during this year; though some skirmishes, and many robberies, took place. Congress appointed John Adams, Benjamin Franklin, John Jay, and Henry Laurens Commissioners for the United States, to negotiate a treaty of peace. Preliminary articles were signed at Paris on the 30th of November, 1782. After the adjustment of affairs between Britain and France, the definitive treaty was signed on the third of September, 1783. By the terms of this treaty, the Independence of the United States was fully acknowledged, and the extent of territory conceded was equal to their most enlarged expectations.

On the 19th of April, 1783, eight years from the battle of Lexington, a formal proclamation of the cessation of hostilities was made to the American army. The news of peace was everywhere received with joy. The army was disbanded by order of Congress on the 3d of November following. The arrears due the officers and soldiers, and the wretched condition of the finances, had caused difficulties which it was feared would inflame the discontent of the army into insurrection. But the prudence and firmness of General Washington averted the danger; the soldiers were persuaded to oppose all illegal proceedings for obtaining redress, and satisfactory arrangements were finally made by Congress. The soldiers returned peaceably to their homes, to enjoy the blessings the toils of war had purchased.

Savannah was evacuated by the British in July, 1782, and Charleston the 14th of December of the same year. It was expected that New York, the last city occupied—where the British Commander-in-Chief had his head-quarters—would be evacuated by Sir Guy Carleton in August, 1783. But the loyalists, remembering the cruelties they had exercised towards their countrymen—especially those whom the fortune of war had placed among them as prisoners—feared retribution after the departure of the British troops. Threats of retaliation, and denunciatory resolutions passed at whig meetings held in various parts of the country, alarmed them to such a degree, that they flocked in great numbers to New York, and claimed the protection of the British General.. To transport so vast a body of exiles, with their families and effects, to Nova Scotia, the Bahamas, or Britain, required more shipping than lay in port. A delay ensued in consequence, while Carleton sent to the West Indies, and even to England for additional transports ; and it was not till the 25th of November that the last remnant of a foreign soldiery set foot on board their vessels

Early on the morning of this day, the American troops, under the command of General Knox, marched from Hærlem to the Bowery Lane, where they took up their position. The citizens began to throng the thoroughfares, eager to participate in the joyous excitement of the occasion. About ten o'clock an American guard relieved the British guard at the city prison, and the latter joined a detachment of British troops then on parade in Broadway, which wheeled into platoons and marched down to the Battery. There they embarked in boats to go on board their shipping. At one o'clock, the British soldiers having abandoned their various posts, the American troops moved down the Bowery to take possession of Fort George at the Battery. General Knox, with a number of officers and citizens on horseback, then rode up to the Bowery to receive General Washington and Governor George Clinton, who, with their suites, made their public entry into the city on horseback, followed by the Lieutenant-Governor and Senators. The cavalcade proceeded to the Battery, whither orders had been sent to hoist the American flag at the Fort, and fire an appropriate salute. Some British underlings, however, had unreeved the halyards, knocked the cleats off the flag staff, and slushed it, so that it might be impossible for the Americans to hoist their banner before the British shipping should be out of sight.

The Americans on the other hand, were anxious that their late enemies should see the colors of the United States wave over the city. Several persons made ineffectual efforts to climb the staff; at length a sailor was furnished with a number of cleats hastily prepared, with which he filled his pockets, and winding the halyards round his waist, and taking a hammer and nails in his hands, commenced his ascent, nailing the cleats on either side as he clambered up. Having reached the top, he reeved the halyards and descended, while amidst the loud huzzas of congregated thousands, and the thunder of artillery, in full view of the departing English, the stars and stripes were hoisted, and floated proudly on the breeze; the band at the same time striking up the national air of "Yankee Doodle." The intrepid sailor was not only welcomed with acclamations, but received a more substantial token of approbation in a contribution for his benefit among those present. This interesting scene over, the Commander-in-Chief and other general officers sat down to a public dinner given by the Governor at Francis' Tavern, at the corner of Wall and Nassau streets. On the following Tuesday, a brilliant display of fireworks was exhibited at the Bowling Green.

On the 23d of December, a scene of lofty moral grandeur was presented, by the appearance of Washington in the Hall of Congress at Annapolis, to resign his commission as Commander-in-Chief. In the presence of a large concourse of spectators, he delivered his simple and affectionate farewell address, commending the interests of his country to the protection of Heaven, and taking his leave of the employments of public life. He then retired as a private citizen to his country-seat at Mount Vernon, followed by the heartfelt gratitude and affection of the whole nation.

Thus was American Independence established. From this fortunate termination the most beneficial results were anticipated, not only for the United States, but for the whole civilized world. The nation newly founded was expected to cultivate republican virtues which other nations might emulate. It was to exhibit the advantages of universal intelligence and progress. It was to illustrate the great principles which lie at the foundation of a people's true prosperity, and thus to overthrow the ancient systems of error and tyranny.

In reviewing the events briefly sketched, it will be seen at how vast an expense of blood and suffering, of toil and treasure, was purchased the national freedom which, with its countless blessings, is our inheritance. The price was paid with a full reliance on the Divine protection for a righteous cause. Guizot says truly—" While they rebelled against the authority of the King and Parliament of Britain, they were submissive to the will of God and the precepts of the Gospel; while struggling for independence, they were governed by the same faith which had brought their ancestors to this land." It will be seen, moreover, that the men and women of America during the Revolution, acted with one heart and one mind. In their entire devotion to the cause—whether at the East, in the Middle States, or at the South—one spirit is seen to govern them. They thought not of sectional distinctions; they felt and acted like brethren. It is this sanction of right, and this union of feeling and interests, which throw a halo of moral sublimity around the perilous adventures and daring deeds so thickly sown in the history of those times. Let all Americans who love their country ponder on the lesson conveyed

Let them cherish the UNION of these States, as they honor the memory of those noble men who did and suffered so much to cement it. Let them never part with that precious legacy bought with their fathers' blood, and transmitted to them to be kept inviolate for their own children. For the security of this inestimable possession, let them sacredly preserve the spirit of disinterestedness, of patriotism, of RELIGION—the seed of all that is good and elevated in the social life of the Republic.

THE END.

www.ingramcontent.com/pod-product-compliance
Lightning Source LLC
Chambersburg PA
CBHW030753230426
43667CB00007B/951